Exploring Social Issues
Using SPSS® for Windows™

Exploring Social Issues

Using SPSS® for Windows™

Joseph F. Healey
Christopher Newport University

Earl R. Babbie
Chapman University

Fred Halley
SUNY-Brockport

Pine Forge Press

Thousand Oaks, California • London • New Delhi

For information, address:

 Pine Forge Press
A Sage Publications Company
2455 Teller Road
Thousand Oaks, California 91320
(805) 499-4224
E-mail: sales@pfp.sagepub.com

Sage Publications Ltd.
6 Bonhill Street
London EC2A 4PU
United Kingdom

Sage Publications India Pvt. Ltd.
M-32 Market
Greater Kailash I
New Delhi 110 048 India

Production: Mary Douglas/Myrna Engler-Forkner, Rogue Valley Publications
Copy Editor: Lura Harrison
Interior Designer: Lisa Mirski Devenish
Cover Designer: Paula Shuhert and Graham Metcalfe
Production Manager: Anne Draus, Scratchgravel Publishing Services
Print Buyer: Anna Chin

Printed in the United States of America
97 98 99 00 01 10 9 8 7 6 5 4 3 2 1

ISBN 0-7619-8526-3

SPSS, SPSS^X, SPSS/PC+, Studentware, and Studentware Plus are registered trademarks of SPSS, Inc., Chicago, Illinois. Microsoft is a registered trademark and Microsoft Windows is a trademark of Microsoft Corporation. All other product names are trademarks or registered trademarks of their respective companies.

The authors and publisher have taken care in the preparation of this book but make no expressed or implied warranty of any kind and assume no responsibility for errors or omissions. No liability is assumed for incidental or consequential damages in connection with or arising out of the use of the information or programs contained herein.

ABOUT THE AUTHORS

Joseph F. Healey is Professor of Sociology at Christopher Newport University in Virginia. He received his Ph.D. in Sociology and Anthropology from the University of Virginia. He has written a statistics textbook, two texts on minority groups in the United States, and articles on minority groups, the sociology of sports, social movements, and violence.

Earl Babbie, Chapman University, is best known for his many texts in research methods as well as introductory sociology that have been widely adopted throughout the United States and the world.

Fred Halley, State University of New York College at Brockport, has been developing computer-based tools for teaching social science since 1970. He has served as a collegewide social science computer consultant, directed Brockport's Institute for Social Research, and now directs the college's Data Analysis Laboratory.

ABOUT THE PUBLISHER

Pine Forge Press is a new educational publisher, dedicated to publishing innovative books and software throughout the social sciences. On this and any other of our publications, we welcome your comments. Please call or write us at:

Pine Forge Press
A Sage Publications Company
2455 Teller Road
Thousand Oaks, CA 91320
(805) 499-4224
E-mail: sales@pfp.sagepub.com

Visit our new World Wide Web site, your direct link to a multitude of on-line resources:

http://www.sagepub.com.pineforge

Brief Contents

Detailed Contents

Chapter 6   Socialization: What Kinds of Children Do Americans Want? / 121

Chapter 7   Crime, Fear, and Punishment / 143

Chapter 9   Inequality and Gender / 205

Chapter 10   Inequality and Race / 239

Preface

This workbook is a "hands-on" introduction to the craft of social research. It is intended for use in introductory sociology courses or courses on social problems and may be combined with most of the standard textbooks in the field. Students are involved in the process of social research from the first chapter: indeed, the student *is* the principal researcher. Most exercises are open ended and the student is required to frame hypotheses, choose variables, and interpret results. The text provides abundant explanations, examples, and hints, but ultimately this is a "self-writing" textbook, and no two students will complete it in exactly the same way. Students take an active role and test their own ideas about topics such as divorce, abortion, crime, inequality, prejudice, and television violence.

Links to the sociological literature are established in two ways. First, students are always urged to use their textbook and other course materials to develop hypotheses and interpret results. Second, about half the chapters include exercises drawn from sociological research, giving students the opportunity to test or expand on ideas and theories from the literature.

This text uses SPSS for Windows Student Version to analyze the 1994 General Social Survey (GSS). It includes an overview of the research process, an introduction to SPSS for Windows, and a description of the 1994 GSS. The package is self-contained (no additional documentation is needed), and students are guided step-by-step through all exercises. No previous experience with computers, Windows, SPSS, statistics, or social research is required to use this text successfully.

Chapters are arranged in an order that roughly parallels the organization of most introductory sociology texts. Following the first chapter, we cover the research process, culture, socialization, deviance, inequality, and social institutions. Issues and problems that are of interest to students are stressed throughout.

Each chapter includes explanations of basic research principles and techniques, exercises, research reports, and end-of-chapter independent projects. The exercises are basically demonstrations, and students are expected to "follow along" with their own computers. In the research reports, students apply what they learned in the explanatory sections and exercises. The research reports follow a standardized, fill-in-the-blank format for presenting and analyzing results, but space is always left for students to summarize their results in their own words. This format is designed to ease the often burdensome chore of deciding "what to say" about the results (and will also ease the instructor's burden of checking the reports).

End-of-chapter projects are of two types. Independent Projects afford an opportunity to further pursue projects begun in the chapter. Comparative Analyses provide historical depth and analyze trends over time by comparing 1994 results and patterns with data from the 1972 General Social Survey.

Data analysis begins with univariate frequency distributions and percentages and builds through descriptive statistics, charts and graphs, bivariate tables, tests of significance and measures of association, scatterplots, and Pearson's r. Students are introduced to multivariate analysis in the form of controlling for a third variable in bivariate tabular analysis. Statistical presentations stress the simpler techniques and more "intuitive" (vs. mathematical) understandings, as is appropriate at the introductory level. Most chapters rely on bivariate tables for statistical analysis, an approach that is consistent with the type of data contained in the General Social Surveys. Each of the first ten chapters introduces a new technique, SPSS procedure, or statistic. The last two chapters apply these techniques to new material and may be covered in any order. To provide maximum flexibility, there is considerable choice of topics within each chapter and in the end-of-chapter exercises.

Acknowledgments

We acknowledge a number of people who have been instrumental in making this book a reality. First and foremost, Steve Rutter and Jean Skeels of Pine Forge Press have been full partners from start to finish. They are able to bring enthusiasm, commitment, and ingenuity to every book they work on. Our thanks go to Rogue Valley Publications and Scratchgravel Publishing Services for their work in producing this book. A special thanks to Matt Archibald, University of Washington, for his careful review of the SPSS commands. We would also like to thank the many reviewers who helped us along the way: Marybeth Ayella, St. Joseph's University; Ray Daville, Stephen F. Austin University; David Karp, University of Washington; Peter Lehman, University of Southern Maine; Joe Lengermann, University of Maryland, College Park; Brad Lyman, Baltimore City Community College; Edgar (Ted) Mills, University of Connecticut; Elizabeth Nelson, California State University, Fresno; and Assata Zerai, Syracuse University.

Exploring Social Issues
Using SPSS® for Windows™

Chapter 1   Getting Started: Social Research, Data Sets, and Frequency Distributions

You are about to begin a research project that explores important issues and concerns in the United States today. You will be actively involved in the project—in fact, you will *be* the principal investigator and actually *do* the research. You will analyze religious values, attitudes toward abortion, racial prejudice, fear of crime, inequality, and many other topics. You'll be addressing real problems, real opinions, and real people: There is nothing fictitious or artificial about the exercises in this text. You will be given plenty of guidance and examples, but the major responsibility for posing research questions, seeking answers, and coming to conclusions will fall on you.

To conduct the investigation, you will learn to use a powerful tool for research, called *SPSS for Windows, Student Version* (or SPSS for short). With this package of computer programs, you can analyze data with relative ease, using the same routines and procedures as professional researchers who have years of experience. You will use SPSS to analyze the **General Social Survey** (or **GSS**), a "public opinion poll," which questions Americans about many different issues and problems. The GSS has been administered almost every year since 1972 and has been the basis of thousands of research projects, dissertations, and journal articles. Social scientists have used the GSS to analyze everything from opinions about AIDS to participation in sports and church attendance. The projects in this text concentrate on the 1994 General Social Survey but the 1972 version is also included so that you can explore changes in U.S. society over time.

With the help of this text, you will use SPSS and the GSS to probe a variety of topics. The ultimate goal of this text, however, is not just to introduce you to computers and surveys but to get you involved in the craft of social research and the endless challenges of analyzing society. This book is largely blank, as befits a research project that has not yet begun. The pages will be filled in by you, the principal investigator. At this point, we cannot know exactly where the research will lead, what conclusions will be drawn, or even what questions might be asked. The exact course of a scientific investigation becomes clear only as we *do* the research, so let's get started. After a brief orientation to the GSS and to SPSS for Windows, Student Version, you will begin the research process by producing some background information about the 1994 GSS sample.

Data Sets

The subjects for the research projects included in this text are approximately 1500 adult U.S. citizens who were questioned about issues ranging from racial prejudice to their television-watching habits. To complete the research projects, you will make conclusions about U.S. society as a whole (the **population**) based on the information supplied by these 1500 subjects (the **sample**). What can be learned about the 250 million residents of the United States from such a small sample?

Actually, quite a lot. It is common to use samples of about 1500 respondents to make generalizations to "all Americans." These generalizations are possible because respondents are selected by a complex and rigorous process that ensures that the sample will be **representative** of the population. This means that the sample will reproduce the characteristics of the population from which it was selected. In other words, if the population of all U.S. citizens is 40% Republican or 25% Catholic, the sample will also be about 40% Republican and 25% Catholic. You can think of the sample as a smaller version, or miniature snapshot, of the United States at a specific point in time. Anything you learn about the GSS sample will also be true (with certain limitations and qualifications) for the U.S. population.

Three data sets are included with this text: one for the 1972 GSS and two for the 1994 GSS. (The differences between the two 1994 data sets are explained in Chapter 3.) For both years, respondents were selected by *random sampling*. The researchers began by randomly selecting cities and counties across the country. They next randomly selected city blocks (or the rural equivalent) in each chosen city or county, and they then chose households at random for each block. Finally, a professional interviewer called on each household and asked the survey questions face to face.

You can be very confident that the GSS samples accurately reflect the characteristics, attitudes, and behaviors of all adult Americans. However, because they are random samples, they are unlikely to be *exactly* the same as the population. We need to anticipate some degree of **sampling error**, or some differences between the GSS samples and the U.S. population. For example, suppose you learn that about 42% of the 1994 GSS respondents considered themselves to be strongly religious. If the sample is representative, close to 42% *of the population* will also consider themselves to be strongly religious. Because of sampling error, however, it would not be surprising if there was a slight difference between sample and population percentages. For example, the actual population percentage might be 40% or 45%, rather than exactly 42%. It is extremely unlikely, however, that the percentage of strongly religious people in the population is actually 8% or 90%. As a rule of thumb, you can assume that percentages computed from the GSS samples will be within plus or minus 3 points of the population percentages (for example, if 42% of the sample is strongly religious, it is very safe to conclude that between 39% and 45% of the population is strongly religious).

Some final points about the 1994 GSS data sets supplied with this text need to be made. First, because of the limitations of our software, we cannot use the complete 1994 GSS sample. The full 1994 sample consists of almost 3000 respondents, but the Student Version of SPSS for Windows is limited to just 1500 cases. To accommodate this limitation, we used a random procedure to draw a smaller sample of about 1500 cases from the full 1994 GSS sample. What this means is that you will conduct your research on a random sample of a random sample. In turn, this means that the size of our sampling error will increase. Still, you can assume that the patterns you find in the samples will approximate the actual characteristics of the U.S. population.

Second, as you will soon notice, the database does not include scores for every case on every variable. Sometimes, this is because respondents refused to answer the question (this is noted as "NA" or "No Answer" in the database) or didn't have the requested information ("DK" or "Don't Know"). For most variables, these non-responses are not a major problem and will decrease sample size only slightly.

Some variables, however, have scores for only two-thirds or one-half of the sample. This pattern of missing data results from the fact that not all respondents were asked to answer the more than 600 items on the full 1994 survey. The designers of the GSS want to maximize the amount of information they get on the U.S. population every year, but they also want to keep the length of the interview to less than an hour. To do this, they give slightly different versions of the survey to different groups of people. For example, some respondents will be questioned about their attitudes toward abortion, whereas other respondents will be given a version of the interview that asks about crime instead.

As you will see, situations in which many respondents are "missing" can cause problems, especially given that we are able to use only half of the sample. We will deal with these problems as they arise, but, for now, you should realize that variables not having complete information on the full sample are not unusual or a particular cause for alarm.

EXERCISE 1.1   **An Introduction to SPSS for Windows, Student Version**

The statistical package used in this text (the Student Version of SPSS for Windows) includes a large array of procedures, options, and subprocedures. This makes SPSS a powerful and useful tool, but also means that we need to specify exactly what we want the program to do. Generally, we give directions to SPSS by selecting commands from lists or *menus*, which appear on various screens. You can move through the menus or from one menu to another in various ways, but you usually use the mouse attached to your computer. Your mouse has several buttons in front, and you issue commands to SPSS by pushing (or *clicking*) the button on the left side of the mouse.

You will be introduced to many commands and procedures, but we cannot hope to cover all the capabilities of SPSS. Similarly, we cannot anticipate all the questions you might have as we proceed, so this is a good time to tell you that SPSS for Windows, Student Version comes with extensive tutorials and Help features. If you run into problems or have questions that haven't been dealt with in this text, click on the word **Help** (use the mouse to move the arrow on the screen over the word *Help* and click the left button on the mouse), and SPSS provides the assistance you need.

Now we are ready to start up SPSS for Windows, Student Version and take the first step in the research process. The program runs in many different situations, far too numerous for us to anticipate, so we assume that SPSS for Windows, Student Version has already been installed on the computer you are using (if not, see the manual that comes with the software) and that you are looking at the main Windows screen: a rectangular box that shows Program Manager [SPSS] along its top.[1] If you don't see this window, get help from your local "computer guru" before continuing.

---

1. If you are using Windows 95, the words "Program Manager" will not appear at the top of the screen but the basic procedures for launching SPSS for Windows are the same as those described in the text.

The **Program Manager** window has different *icons* (or pictures), each of which activates a different program. Look for the SPSS for Windows, Student Version icon, which looks like this:

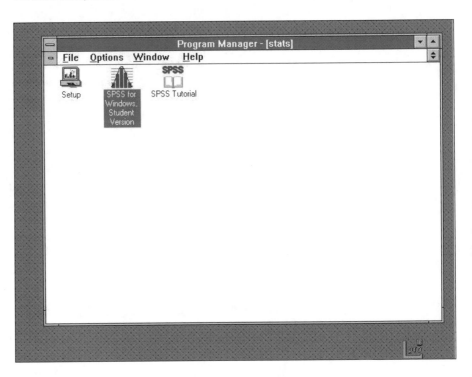

With your mouse, move the arrow over the SPSS icon and double-click (press twice) the left button, and the program will begin to run. There may be a brief pause while SPSS sorts itself out, but you will soon be looking at a screen with three, superimposed windows or rectangular boxes:

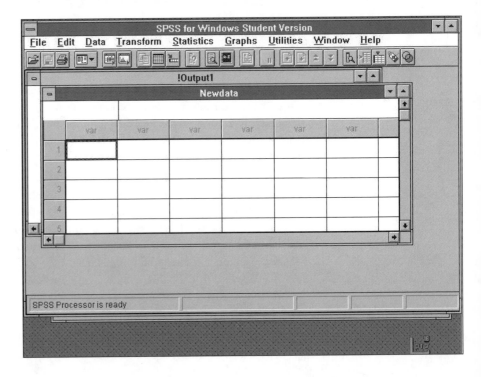

The windows can be distinguished from each other by the titles printed along the top. The closest is the **Newdata** window, behind which is the **!Output1** window. The largest window, farthest in the background, is the **SPSS for Windows, Student Version** window. This is the main window, and everything we do with SPSS begins here.

At the top of the screen is a *menu bar* (a set of menus), running from **File** on the left to **Help** on the right. These menus are the control system and commands by which you will operate SPSS. As a preview, click on the word **File** (use the mouse to move the arrow on the screen over the word *File* and press the left button on the mouse) on the menu bar. A list of commands will drop down below the title, with some of the commands in dark, black letters and some in gray:

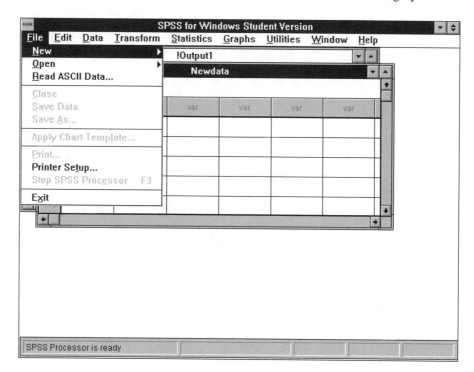

The commands in black are currently available for use; they can be executed by clicking on them. Right now, for example we can **Open** but not **Save** a data set, because we have nothing to save yet.

Click on the word **File** again to make the menu disappear. Now look in the upper-right corner of the **SPSS for Windows, Student Version** window and you'll find two arrows, one pointing up and the other pointing down.[2] Click the up-arrow, and the **SPSS for Windows, Student Version** window fills the screen. Notice that the up-arrow has now changed to a two-headed, up–down arrow. Clicking on this kind of arrow returns the window to its former self. Try this now, and you are back to the original arrangement of three superimposed windows.

Now click the down-arrow in the upper-right corner of the **SPSS for Windows, Student Version** window. The window has vanished! Looks like you're in big trouble, but you're not. If you look along the bottom of the screen,

---

2. In Windows 95, these arrows have been replaced by a set of three icons in the upper-right corner of the screen. The ⊠ icon closes the window, the ☐ icon replaces the up-arrow, and the — icon replaces the down-arrow.

you'll find an icon labeled SPSS for Windows, Student Version, like the one you used to first start SPSS. What you have done is move SPSS temporarily out of the way, in case you want to work on something else for awhile.

If you click the **SPSS for Windows, Student Version** icon once, you will be presented with a short menu, the top entry of which is Restore.

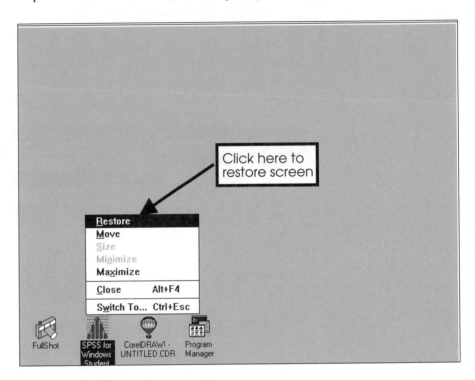

This has the same effect as the up–down arrow we saw a minute ago: It will restore the original arrangement of three windows. You can accomplish the same thing by double-clicking the icon. However you do it, get back to the SPSS for Windows, Student Version window.

The !Output1 Window

Notice the !Output1 window, hidden behind the Newdata window; this is where SPSS stores the results of the commands you give it. Click anywhere on the **!Output1** window, either along the top or down the left side, which is also peeking out from behind the Newdata window. Clicking on any window other than the SPSS for Windows, Student Version window will bring it to the front of the screen.

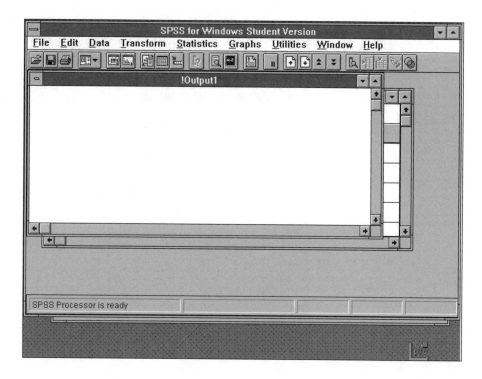

Right now, the output window is blank because we haven't given SPSS any commands that produce results. Before long, however, you will see results here, and you will become very familiar with this window. You might notice in passing that the output window has up- and down-arrows in its upper-right corner. These operate just like the ones we discussed earlier, and you can experiment with them if you want. If you do, be careful because more than one set of arrows will often be on the screen at a time, and it's important to click the arrow on the particular window you want to shrink or expand.

The Newdata Window

The window originally "nearest" to you was entitled **Newdata**. You can see its right-hand border and bottom behind the output window. Click anywhere on it to bring it back to the front of the screen. This is the window that will contain the data for SPSS to analyze, although right now it is empty. If you want, you can begin entering data for analysis. In fact, if you decide to conduct your own survey later on (see Appendix C), this is where you would enter data. As a quick preview of this feature, type a **1** and press the Enter key on your keyboard. Note that SPSS automatically represents the score you entered as 1.00.

You have now created the world's smallest *data set:* with one piece of information about one person. The "1" on the left of the *matrix* represents "Person 1." If you had entered another number as you just did, you would have brought "Person 2" into existence—with one piece of information. Why don't you do that now? Enter a **2** for that person. Your screen should look like the following:

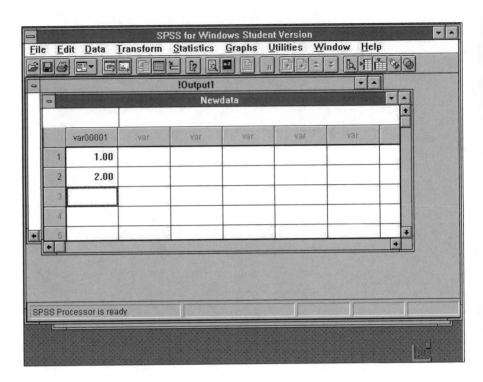

The **var00001** at the top of the column in the matrix identifies the specific information we are storing. The numbers in this column might represent gender, for example, and a value of 1.00 might mean "male" and value of 2.00 might mean "female." Therefore, we would have indicated that Person 1 is male and Person 2 is female.

If we were actually entering data, we would continue in this manner until we had recorded all scores for all cases. We would then save our data set so that it would be available for analysis in the future. As you can probably imagine, entering the data for a large sample can be time-consuming and painstaking because we want to enter our results carefully and without error. The good news is that you can avoid this chore (until you conduct your own survey) because data sets (the General Social Survey) have been supplied with this text. The next exercise describes how to access the GSS.

If you need to stop at this point, click **File** on the menu bar and then click **Exit**. This closes the SPSS program and brings you back to Windows. Before closing, SPSS will ask if you want to "save the contents of data window Newdata." The question refers to the "world's smallest data set," which we began to create in Exercise 1.1. We do not need to keep our fictitious data, so just click **No**. When you are ready for Exercise 1.2, click on the SPSS icon again, to start up the SPSS program.

EXERCISE 1.2   **Loading a Data File**

In this exercise, you will load one of the data sets supplied with this text. From the menu bar across the top of the **SPSS for Windows, Student Version** screen, click on the word **File**, and its menu will open up below it. The second command in that menu is the one we want: Open. Click on **Open**, and another menu appears to the right, asking us to specify the kind of file we want to open. We want to open a data file, so click **Data**. Your screen should look like this:

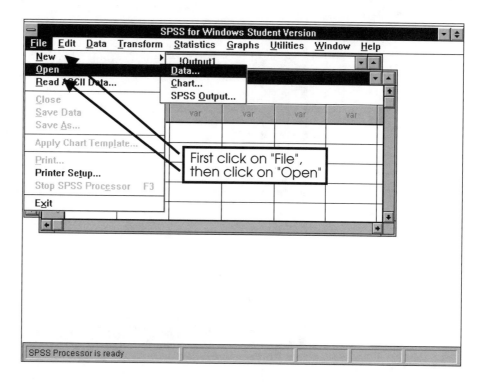

In the future, we will present instructions for using SPSS commands in numbered command blocks like this:

COMMAND BLOCK 1.1   Opening a Data File

> Click **File** → **Open** → **Data. . .**

This will make it easier for you to locate instructions. The first time a command or action is presented, it will also have a label explaining the purpose of the commands. Any new commands introduced in a chapter are also listed at the end of the chapter, and all SPSS commands used in this text, grouped by function, are listed in Appendix B.

If you closed SPSS at the end of Exercise 1.1, you are now looking at the **Open Data File** window. If you continued straight through from Exercise 1.1 without closing SPSS, you will be asked at this point if you want to "save the contents of data window Newdata." This question refers to the data set we began to create in Exercise 1.1. We were just doodling and don't need to keep this data, so click **No**.

Either way, you should be looking at the **Open Data File** window now. This window lists data files that might be loaded into SPSS. Locate the file called GSS94TAB.SAV. You may have to insert a disk in drive a: or b: and then adjust the **Drives** indicator to select the a: or b: drive. With your cursor, click the file name GSS94TAB.SAV; then click the **OK** button. As an alternative, rapidly double-click on the file name.

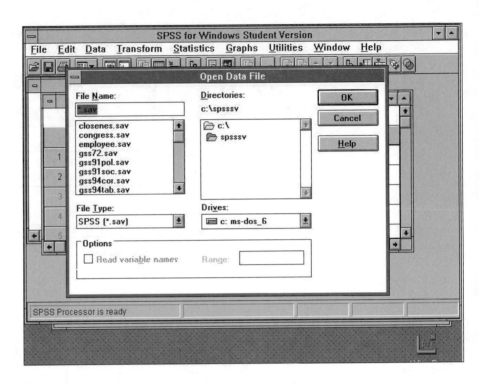

Now you should be looking at the data in the GSS94TAB.SAV file, one of the three data sets included with this book.

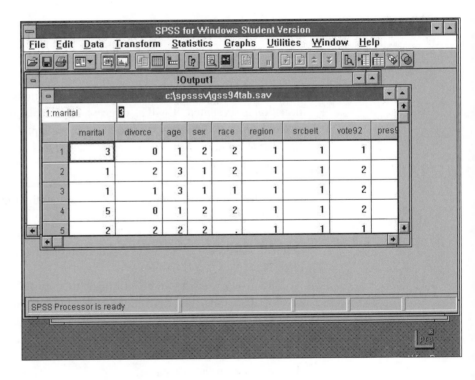

There are *variable name*s (MARITAL, DIVORCE, AGE, and so on) across the top of the matrix and numbers in the cells. Each variable name refers to a specific item on the 1994 General Social Survey. For example, MARITAL records each respondent's marital status. Other variable names (for example, SEX, RACE, AGE) are easy to figure out. Remember that SPSS uses these names to refer to specific variables. SPSS also limits variable names to eight characters, so many of the names that appear along the top row of the matrix may be highly abbreviated. An alphabetical list of variable names, along with the full text of the item or question from the 1994 General Social Survey, is included in Appendix A.

Notice that respondent 1 (the case numbers run down the left side of the matrix) has a score of 3 in the column for MARITAL. This score means that this respondent is divorced. The score of respondent 2, on the other hand, is a 1, and this means that he or she is married. [Codes for all variables can be found in Appendix A. SPSS also provides an on-screen procedure for deciphering codes (using the Utilities command), which will be explained shortly.]

To move around in the data window, use the arrows at the bottom and right-hand margins of the matrix. Why not experiment with this? The two arrows on the bottom margin let you *scroll* (move) left and right to look at different variables, and the two arrows on the right side of the matrix let you move up and down through the list of respondents.

You can also move around in this window with the *scroll button* located next to the left-pointing arrow on the bottom margin and just below the up-pointing arrow on the right-hand margin. Click on either button and *drag* it (move it with the left button of the mouse pressed down) along the margin. Moving the button on the bottom margin moves you left and right through the variables in the data set. Moving the button on the right-hand margin moves you up or down through the cases.

Using either the arrows or the scroll button, find the religion (RELIG) of respondent 10. You should find that this respondent has a score of 3 on RELIG, but what does that mean? In addition to using Appendix A, you can find out the meaning of scores with the *Utilities command*. Click **Utilities** on the menu bar and the Utilities menu will drop down. Click on **Variables. . .**, the third command on this menu.

COMMAND BLOCK 1.2   Finding Information on Variables

> Click **Utilities → Variables. . .**

Now you are looking at a two-part window. On the right is some information about the variable ABANY, including the meaning assigned to each score. On the left is an alphabetical list of variables. When you move the highlight (or cursor) over a variable name in this list, the window at the right displays information about that variable.

There are four ways to move the highlight through the list of variable names:

1. Click on the up- and down- pointing arrows on the right-hand margin of the variable-list window.
2. Move the scroll button located on the same margin.
3. Use the arrow keys on your keyboard to move up and down through the list.

4. Find a variable by clicking on the first letter of the variable's name. The highlight will move to the first variable in the list that begins with that letter, and then you can use any of the other three methods to move the highlight to your variable name.

Use any of these methods to find RELIG, and the following screen will appear:

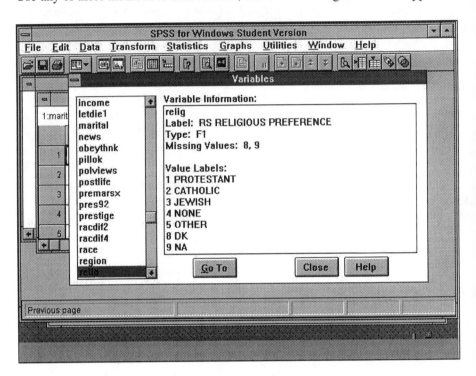

This window tells us that a code of 3 means that the respondent is Jewish.

Spend a little time poking around in the list of variables and examining the information provided. When you finish, close this window by clicking the small box in the upper-left corner. A short menu appears; choose **Close** in that menu to close the window.

When you are finished for this session, click **File** on the menu bar, and the File menu drops down. At the very bottom, click on the command **Exit**; this instructs the computer to terminate the SPSS session and returns you to the Windows desktop.

COMMAND BLOCK 1.3   Ending Your SPSS Session

Click **File** → **Exit**

Before executing this command and closing the SPSS program, however, you will be asked if you want to "save contents of data window Newdata." Recall that we have loaded the file GSS94TAB.SAV into that window. Because the data set is already saved and has not been changed, click the **No** button. If you had entered additional data or otherwise changed the data set, you definitely would have clicked Yes.

Frequency Distributions

At this point, you are familiar enough with SPSS commands to actually begin some research. You will perform some simple data analyses in Exercise 1.3 and then build on your skills in chapters to come. The goal of this exercise is to get some basic information about the respondents in the 1994 GSS. First, we will guide you through the SPSS commands needed to produce a table showing the number and percentage of males and females in the sample. Then you will be on your own to get similar information on the racial, religious, and age composition of the sample.

EXERCISE 1.3   **Frequency Distributions**

Assuming that you are starting from the Windows **Program Manager** screen, click the **SPSS for Windows, Student Version** icon. Open the GSS94TAB.SAV data file, as we did in Exercise 1.2 (see Command Block 1.1).

You are going to instruct SPSS to construct a type of table called a **frequency distribution** for the variable SEX. A frequency distribution reports the number of times (frequency) each score of a variable occurred in the sample, along with some other information. In this case, the table tells us the number of males and females in the 1994 GSS sample. Begin by clicking on **Statistics** from the menu bar and then click **Summarize** and **Frequencies**. Do this now, and you should be looking at the following screen:

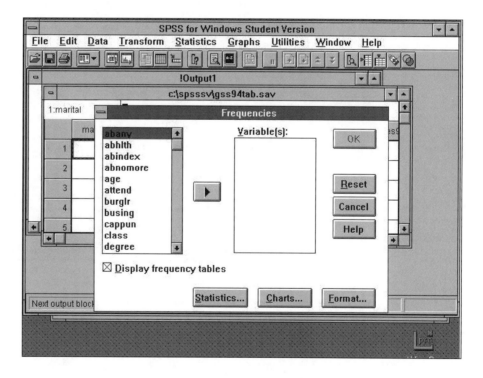

Note that the **Frequencies** dialog box has two windows. To the left of the screen is a box listing all the survey items by their SPSS variable names.[3] As before, there are four ways to move through the list of variables: Click on (1) the

---

3. It is possible that the list of variable names that appears on your screen will not be in alphabetical order.

arrows or (2) the scroll button on the right-hand margin, (3) use the up- or down-arrow keys on your keyboard, or (4) type the first letter of the variable name. Use any or all of these methods to highlight SEX, the variable in which we are interested. Now, click on the arrow to the right of the variable-list window, and the variable name SEX moves to the other window in this dialog box, which is titled **Variable(s):**. You can transfer more than one variable to this window; SPSS processes all the variables listed in the **Variables(s):** window at one time. If you change your mind about which variables you want to process, highlight the variable name and click the left-pointing arrow in the middle of the screen. This will move the variable name back to the original list.

For now, let's confine our attention to SEX. Click the **OK** button, and SPSS rushes off to construct a frequency distribution for this variable. The commands for getting a frequency distribution are listed in Command Block 1.4.

COMMAND BLOCK 1.4   Constructing Frequency Distributions

> Click **Statistics** → **Summarize** → **Frequencies** →
> Highlight the first variable name →
> Click the arrow pointing to the **Variable(s):** box →
> Highlight the second variable name →
> Click the arrow pointing to the **Variable(s):** box →
> Continue until all variables have been moved to the **Variable(s):** box →
> Click **OK**

Soon, the !Output1 window moves to the front of the screen, with a summary table for gender. Figure 1.1 displays the output window.

FIGURE 1.1   **Partial Output Window for Frequencies Procedure**
(1994 General Social Survey)

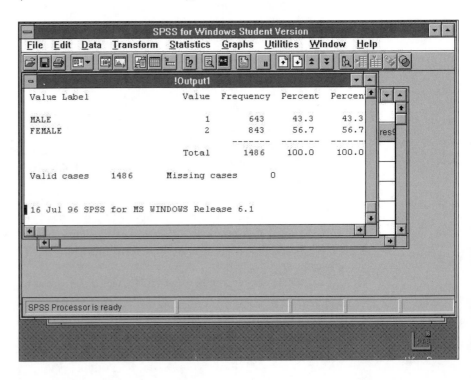

It is likely that you will be looking at only part of the output, as in Figure 1.1. To see the whole table, click the up-pointing arrow in the upper-right corner of the !Output1 window (*not* the SPSS window). To return to the smaller window, click the double-headed arrow (one pointing up, one pointing down) in the upper-right corner of the !Output1 window.

If the entire table is still not visible (this will be the case with bigger tables or output that includes more than one table), you can move around in the output window in a number of different ways: using a mouse, the arrow keys, and the scroll button on the right-hand and lower margins of the output window; using a keyboard, the arrow keys, or the Page Up and Page Down keys. Figure 1.2 shows the entire table.

FIGURE 1.2   **Output for Frequencies Procedure**
(1994 General Social Survey)

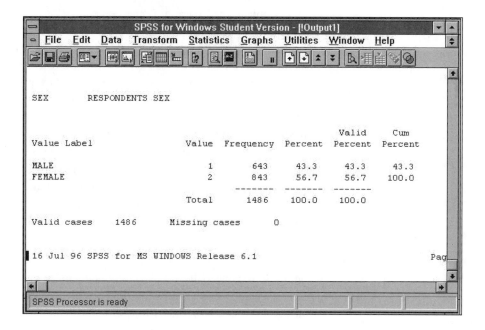

Reading Frequency Distributions

Let's analyze this table (Figure 1.2) piece by piece. At the top left of the window, we see the SPSS variable name SEX (if you don't see this, scroll up until it is visible). Remember that this is the name by which SPSS refers to this variable: If you want to have SPSS do something with a specific variable, you must refer to the variable by its SPSS name. (SPSS variable names for our data set are listed in alphabetical order in Appendix A.)

To the right of the variable name is a descriptive label. Although not necessary in this case, long labels are essential for the many variables that have SPSS names more esoteric than SEX. Because SPSS limits variable names to eight characters, they can sometimes be difficult to decipher. For example, what do you think PREMARSX stands for? (See Appendix A or use the Utilities procedure as presented in Command Block 1.2 for the answer.)

Now move to the far left-hand column, Value Label, where the categories of the variable (MALE and FEMALE) are listed. To the right is a column labeled Value, which tells us that the score of "male" was recorded as a 1 and the score of "female" was recorded as a 2. Move one more column to the right, and you find the **Frequency** column, which reports the number of cases in each category. There are 643 males and 843 females in our sample.[4]

The **Percent** column reports the percentages of all cases in each category of the variable, including **missing values**, or responses such as "Don't Know" (DK), when the respondent didn't have the information requested, and "No Answer" (NA), when the respondent may have had the requested information but chose not to answer. We usually ignore missing values and therefore usually ignore this column.

Move to the next column to the right, **Valid Percent**. This column reports the percentages of cases in each category of the variable, *not* including missing values. For the table displaying SEX, the two percentage columns are identical because gender was determined by interviewer observation and thus there are no missing values. For virtually all other variables, the two percentage columns will be different and, again, we will use the **Valid Percent** column only.

The column on the far right is titled **Cum** (for cumulative) **Percent**. This column is constructed by adding the percentage of cases in a category to previous categories, as you move down the table. The information in this column is used for certain types of graphs and to make statements about the percentage of cases greater than or less than a particular score. For SEX, this column is not very useful and can be ignored. You should realize, however, that statistical packages like SPSS often produce more information than you actually need, and sometimes they produce useless information. Part of the challenge of using software like SPSS is to learn what information can be ignored.

So, after all this, what do we know about the sample? Simply this: Females outnumber males by 56.7% to 43.3%. Although this information may not seem very interesting now, it is important to understand the makeup of the sample. Most research projects begin with an inspection of frequency distributions, or similar summary information, for all variables.

Saving Frequency Distributions

Once you've gone to the trouble of producing information about the sample, you will usually want to save the output for future reference. The frequency distribution of the variable SEX can be saved by following the instructions in Command Block 1.5:

COMMAND BLOCK 1.5   Saving Your Output

Click **File → Save SPSS Output**

The **Save Output** window opens, and SPSS prompts you for a *file name*; this is the name under which your output is stored in the computer's memory. Using abbreviations that help you remember the contents of the file is good practice. In this case, a file name such as SEXFREQ (although perhaps a tad risqué) might do.

---

4. This table indicates that this sample is *not* representative of the population on sex. In the United States, females are only about 51% of the population (U.S. Bureau of the Census, 1993, p. 14).

Why the discrepancy between sample and population? Part of the overrepresentation of females may be due to sampling error. Remember that random sampling always carries a margin of error and it is unlikely that samples will be exact *microcosms,* or reproductions, of populations. The discrepancy may also reflect the higher death rate for males over age 18 and the fact that males are more likely to be transient, homeless, imprisoned, or otherwise unavailable for interviewing.

As a safeguard, if you try to exit the program without saving your output, SPSS asks if you really want to do this. There will be instances in which you do not need to save your results and, if this is the case, simply click No to SPSS's question. *Be careful and be sure about your decision.* Once you click **NO**, your results disappear (although they can always be reconstructed).

Printing Frequency Distributions

Having a hard copy of your results is frequently useful. To have SPSS print your output, follow the instructions in Command Block 1.6:

COMMAND BLOCK 1.6   Printing Your Output

> Click **File → Print**

A new window now appears with information about your printer setup. Click **OK**, and you will soon have a hard copy of the frequency distribution for SEX.

EXERCISE 1.4   **Producing Frequency Distributions for the 1994 GSS**

Now it's your turn to apply what you have learned in this chapter by completing Research Reports 1.1 and 1.2. To do this, you will need to produce and analyze frequency distributions following the procedures established in Exercise 1.3. Assuming that the SPSS for Windows, Student Version program has been started and the GSS94TAB.SAV data file has been loaded, execute the command for frequency distributions (see Command Block 1.7). Choose RELIG (religious affiliation), RACE, and AGE from the variable list.

COMMAND BLOCK 1.7

> Click **Statistics → Summarize → Frequencies →**
> Highlight **RELIG**
> Click the arrow pointing to the **Variable(s):** box →
> Highlight **RACE**
> Click the arrow pointing to the **Variable(s):** box →
> Highlight **AGE**
> Click the arrow pointing to the **Variable(s):** box →
> Click **OK**

Use your output to fill in the blanks in Research Report 1.1. You may want to save or print these frequency distributions or just copy the relevant information from the screen.

When you finish with Research Report 1.1, choose five more variables from the GSS94TAB.SAV data file and have SPSS construct a frequency distribution for each. In the space provided in Research Report 1.2, write a sentence or two summarizing each table. (You may use Research Report 1.1 as a guide.)

NAME   _____

INSTRUCTOR   _____

DATE   _____

1. (RELIG) For the 1994 GSS sample, the most common religious affiliation was _____with _____% of the sample. The second most common was _____ with _____%. The least common religious affiliation was _____ with _____% of the sample. About _____% of the respondents have no religious affiliation ("None").

2. (RACE) The larger racial grouping was _____ with _____%.

3. (AGE) Most respondents (_____%) were in the _____ age range. The _____ age range was second largest with _____% of the sample. The _____ age range was the smallest with _____% of the sample.

NAME _____

INSTRUCTOR _____

DATE _____

Describe, in a sentence or two, each of the five variables you selected. Use Research Report 1.1 as a guide.

Name of Variable 1:
Description:

Name of Variable 2:
Description:

Name of Variable 3:
Description:

Name of Variable 4:
Description:

Name of Variable 5:
Description:

Main Points

■ This textbook is an introduction to the practice of social science research. State-of-the-art statistical software (SPSS for Windows, Student Version) is used to analyze real-life data (the General Social Survey).

■ The General Social Surveys supplied with this text were administered to representative samples of the U.S. population. With certain limitations, the responses and characteristics of the sample are also those of the entire society.

■ This chapter covered how to use SPSS for Windows, Student Version to create, save, and print frequency distributions.

SPSS Commands Introduced in This Chapter

COMMAND BLOCK 1.1   *Opening a Data File*

> Click **File** → **Open** → **Data. . .** →
> Click the name of the data file →
> Click **OK**

1.2   *Finding Information on Variables*

> Click **Utilities** → **Variables. . .**

1.3   *Ending Your SPSS Session*

> Click **File** → **Exit**

1.4   *Constructing Frequency Distributions*

> Click **Statistics** → **Summarize** → **Frequencies** →
> Highlight the first variable name →
> Click the arrow pointing to the **Variable(s):** box →
> Highlight the second variable name →
> Click the arrow pointing to the **Variable(s):** box →
> Continue until all variables have been moved to the **Variable(s):** box →
> Click **OK**

1.5   *Saving Your Output*

Click **File → Save SPSS Output**

1.6   *Printing Your Output*

Click **File → Print → OK**

Chapter 2

Theory and Research: The Scientific Method

Sociologists, like everyone, wonder about all kinds of things: What causes divorce? Why do some parents abuse their children? Can poverty be eliminated? Why are there wars? In a way, answers to questions like these are easy to come by. Everyone—talk-show hosts, sociology instructors, news commentators, your best friend, ministers, politicians—has an opinion about what causes violence, poverty, unhappiness, and other social problems. The challenge is to *evaluate* all these answers: How can we tell which are worthwhile and which are off the mark?

One very powerful way to seek answers is provided by *science*, a method for thinking critically and clearly, evaluating facts, and reaching conclusions. The key to the scientific approach is that conclusions are based on *research*, the careful gathering and evaluation of empirical evidence. Nonscientists might seek answers in common sense, conventional wisdom, tradition, or simple intuition, but science relies on research as a guide to the truth.

Sociologists use the scientific method to study violence, poverty, divorce, crime, and thousands of other issues. We develop **theories**, or explanations of human behavior, and conduct research to test those theories. If the theory is consistent with observations and evidence, the theory is supported. If research produces observations that cannot be explained by the theory, the theory may be revised or, perhaps, discarded. By constantly comparing theories with "the facts," sociologists hope to improve their understanding of the social world.

Theory and Research

To illustrate how sociologists do research, consider a specific problem: What causes divorce? Are people with certain characteristics more prone to divorce? One way to research this problem is to start with a theory that can be tested. Because theories are general and abstract, researchers usually develop more specific **hypotheses**, or statements about what they expect to find in their observations, to guide their research.

You probably have your own ideas about what causes divorce (and you will get a chance to test your ideas soon), but, for purposes of illustration, we will supply this hypothesis: Divorce is less common among people who have strong religious beliefs. Although extremely simplistic, this hypothesis serves to illustrate the process of social research.

Causation

Before conducting the test, we need to establish some ground rules and make some decisions. First, our hypothesis asserts that a **causal relationship** exists between the strength of religious conviction (or religiosity) and divorce. Scientific research tends to focus on causal relationships between variables, and we need to be clear about what these relationships are. A causal relationship exists if one variable (religiosity, in our case) *makes* the other variable (divorce) occur or, at least, changes the value, intensity, or rate of the other variable. In the language of science, the variable that is presumed to be the cause is called the **independent variable** and the "effect" variable is called the **dependent variable**.

Causal relationships can take several different forms. Some causal relationships are very certain and predictable. For example, when you drop an object, the law of gravity always causes the object to fall *down*, not sideways or up.

Other causal relationships are more tenuous and uncertain, and the connection between cause and effect is less predictable. Other factors may affect the predictability of the relationship and make it less certain than the behavior of a dropped object. These types of relationships are called **probabilistic causal relationships**, and they are described using words like *tendency* or *trend* or *likelihood*.

In the social sciences, we are almost always concerned with probabilistic cause-and-effect relationships. The social world is exceedingly complex, and causal relationships are never perfect. In the case of our hypothesis, it is extremely unlikely that every highly religious person would be immune from divorce or that every divorced person would be nonreligious. Our theory will still be supported, however, if we find that the *more* religious persons in our sample are *less likely* to divorce. If we find a probabilistic relationship of this sort, we would have identified one apparent cause of divorce, even though we would not have accounted for all causes of divorce.

Measuring Concepts

Next, we need to make some decisions: How will we measure divorce and religiosity? This process of deciding how to measure concepts is called **operationalization**; this can be one of the most problematic and challenging phases of a research project, especially when our concepts are abstract and general.

For our research situation, whether or not a person has ever been divorced is a pretty concrete piece of information and should not be too difficult to measure. Religiosity, on the other hand, seems much more abstract and ambiguous. What exactly is religiosity? Your definition might vary from mine, and we might even disagree about whether a specific person is religious.

If we were doing an original research project, starting from scratch, we could develop our own techniques for measuring divorce and religiosity. We might, for example, write several different survey questions to measure each concept. For the situation at hand, however, our choices are limited to the items included in the General Social Survey. We must search through the actual survey items and hope that we can find questions that match our concepts.

EXERCISE 2.1   **Finding Measures**

To begin the process of matching survey items to concepts, launch the SPSS for Windows program and load the GSS94TAB.SAV data file:

COMMAND BLOCK 2.1

Click **File** → **Open** → **Data. . .** →
Highlight the **GSS94TAB.SAV** file →
Click **OK**

There are 46 variables in this file and we can examine each in turn by clicking on the **Utilities** procedure in the menu bar and then selecting **Variables**:

COMMAND BLOCK 2.2

Utilities → **Variables. . .**

Scroll through the list and find all items that might be used to measure either religiosity or divorce. Write the variable names in the space provided in Research Report 2.1. Then, select the items that match the concepts most closely and explain your selections. We explain our selections following the research report. (Don't cheat—make your selections without considering ours.)

NAME _____

INSTRUCTOR _____

DATE _____

List the variable names of all items in the GSS94TAB.SAV data set that measure marital status or divorce and religion or religiosity:

Divorce _____ *Religiosity*_____

_____ _____

_____ _____

Which items should be selected to measure our concepts? From these lists, choose one variable for each concept and explain why you made that selection.

For Divorce

For Religiosity

We found two variables related to martial status and three related to religion and religiosity:

Divorce	*Religiosity*
MARITAL	RELIG
DIVORCE	RELITEN
	ATTEND

We choose DIVORCE because MARITAL records only *current* marital status (married, widowed, divorced), not whether the respondent has ever been divorced. (That is, if someone had divorced and remarried, we would only know from MARITAL that he or she was currently married.) Religiosity is a little trickier (because the concept is more abstract and ambiguous), but we quickly eliminated RELIG because it records *religious preference* (see the wording of the question in Appendix A), not *strength of religiosity*.

Building a case for both of the remaining items is possible, but we selected RELITEN as the measure of religiosity. Our thinking was that ATTEND measures church *attendance*, not strength of religious convictions. Although it is logical to assume that highly religious people go to church more often than less religious people, people may also attend church for other reasons (as a social activity or to conform to local or family practices, for example). Thus, RELITEN seems more directly and clearly related to religiosity than ATTEND.

In making our decision to use RELITEN, we had in mind a criterion for measurement called **validity**: A measurement is valid if it actually taps the concept intended. Had we tried to measure religiosity with a survey item that asked for a person's age or height or even his or her religious preference (RELIG), we would have had an obvious problem with validity. We would be measuring apples while theorizing about oranges. As we find measures for the concepts in our hypotheses, we need to be very careful about matching abstract concepts like religiosity to concrete variables and about maintaining the validity of our research project.

EXERCISE 2.2   **Testing the Theory**

With our variables selected, we can test our theory. RELITEN has four responses:[1]

1. Strong
2. Somewhat Strong
3. Not Very Strong
4. Not Religious

A typical first step in the research process is to get a frequency distribution of the variables of interest. We can do this by using the **Frequencies** procedure introduced in Chapter 1. Follow Command Block 1.4 at the end of Chapter 1 to produce the table and use the output to complete item 1 of Research Report 2.2.

---

1. In preparing the data set for this text, we changed the original coding of this variable and switched "somewhat" and "not very" strong. If you are using the full 1994 GSS data set, you will need to recode these scores to be consistent with our coding. See the SPSS manual or consult your local computer guru for information about recoding.

Next, we need to see if the respondents who are stronger in their religious convictions are less likely to be divorced. We can use a procedure called **Crosstabs** to produce **crosstab tables** that display the number of people who answer Yes and No on DIVORCE for each category of RELITEN. Comparisons are easier to make if we also ask for the percentages of the people who are divorced for each level of religiosity. Percentages calculated in this manner are called **column percentages**. Remember that our theory will be supported if the percentage of divorced people is lower among respondents who are "Strong" on RELITEN than those who are "Somewhat Strong," and so forth.

To start the procedure, click on **Crosstabs** from the **Statistics** menu, and the following dialog box appears:

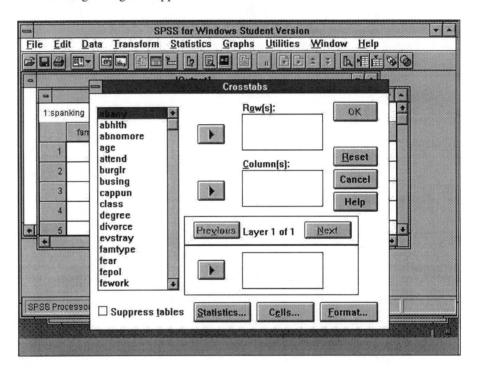

Variables for the procedure are selected from the window on the left. In our hypothesis, DIVORCE is the dependent variable and, by convention, the scores of dependent variables are recorded in the rows (or horizontal dimension) of crosstab tables. Highlight the variable name and click on the arrow pointing to the box titled Row(s):, and DIVORCE will be transferred to that box. Then, transfer RELITEN, our independent variable, to the box titled Column(s):.

Remember that we want to calculate column percentages or the percentages of divorced people for each category of RELITEN. We can instruct SPSS to do this by clicking on the **Cells** button at the bottom of the Crosstabs window. The Crosstabs: Cell Display window then appears:

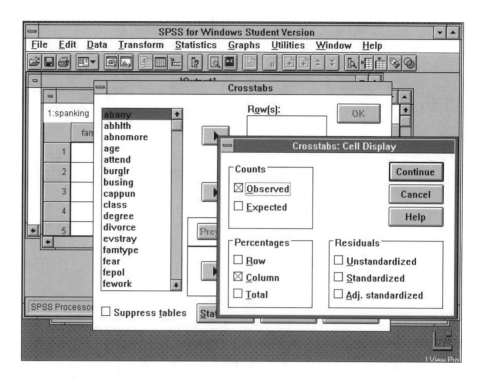

In the **Percentages** window on the lower left, click on the box next to **Column**. Click **Continue** to return to the **Crosstabs** window, click **OK** and SPSS produces the table in seconds.

The Crosstabs procedure is summarized in Command Block 2.3:

COMMAND BLOCK 2.3   Producing Crosstab Tables with Column Percentages

> Click **Statistics** → **Summarize** → **Crosstabs** →
> Highlight the name of the dependent variable(s) →
> Click the arrow pointing to the **Row(s):** box →
> Highlight the name of the independent variable(s) →
> Click the arrow pointing to the **Column(s):** box →
> Click **Cells** in the **Crosstabs** dialog box →
> Click **Columns** in the **Percentages** box →
> Click **Continue** →
> Click **OK**

When the !Output1 window appears, you will probably be looking at the bottom of the table. Click the up-arrow in the upper-right corner of the box to enlarge the window, and then you can move around by using the arrow keys and the scroll buttons.

The percentage of divorced people ("Yes" on DIVORCE) for each level of religiosity can be found by looking along the top row in the table. To clarify results, we constructed Table 2.1, an abbreviated table from the SPSS output:

TABLE 2.1   **Divorce by Religiosity (RELITEN)**

	Religiosity			
	Strong	Somewhat Strong	Not Very Strong	Not Strong At All
Divorce = Yes	17.6%	21.2%	26.6%	32.4%

This table shows the percentage of respondents at each degree of religiosity who have ever been divorced. The pattern of results seems consistent with our hypothesis: The percentage divorced is lowest for people who answer "strong" and increases steadily as religiosity declines. The lower the degree of religiosity, the higher the percentage of divorced respondents.

EXERCISE 2.3   **Other Causes of Divorce**

Now it's your turn to analyze the causes of divorce. Scroll through the items available in the GSS94TAB.SAV database (use the **Utilities** procedure) and find another item (besides ATTEND) that you think might be related to divorce. What, besides religiosity, might affect the likelihood that a person would divorce? A person's level of education (DEGREE)? Age or social class (CLASS)? Some other factor?

In item 2 in Research Report 2.2, state a hypothesis about how you expect these variables to be related. Your hypothesis should identify the category of the independent variable that you expect to be associated with a higher rate of divorce (for example, "less religious people will be *more* likely to divorce"). Use Command Block 2.3 to execute the procedure but replace RELITEN with the independent variable you selected. Use the table in the output window to complete Research Report 2.2. You can copy the necessary information from the monitor screen or print a hard copy of the table (select **Print** from the **File** menu). You may also want to save the table for future reference by selecting **Save SPSS Output** from the **File** menu and giving the table a name.

The research report asks you to evaluate your results in terms of your hypothesis and to compare these results with the relationship between DIVORCE and RELITEN. To evaluate results, compare the pattern of percentages in the table with those you predicted in your hypothesis. Is the percentage of divorced respondents higher (or lower) for the predicted category of your independent variable? If the patterns in the table are consistent with your predictions, your hypothesis is supported, and you may have identified one of the causes of divorce. (Congratulations!) If there is no difference in the percentage divorced from column to column or if the pattern is not consistent with your predictions, your hypothesis is not supported and may need to be discarded.

One simple way to compare your results with the relationship between DIVORCE and RELITEN is to look at the difference between the values of the percentages from column to column. Find the largest and smallest percentages in either row and subtract the smaller from the larger. The result is a statistic called **epsilon**. For DIVORCE and RELITEN, epsilon was 32.4 – 17.6, or 14.8. If epsilon is greater than this for your table, you may conclude that your independent variable has a stronger relationship with DIVORCE than did our independent variable (RELITEN).

NAME _____

INSTRUCTOR _____

DATE _____

1. In 1994 the percentage of respondents who have been divorced is _____ .

2. State your hypotheses linking DIVORCE to your independent variable.

3. Briefly explain why you expect these results.

4. Present your results by completing the summary table below. On line 1, fill in the blank with the name of your independent variable. On line 2, write in the names of the categories of your independent variable, using as many blanks as necessary. On line 3, fill in the blanks with the percentage divorced ("Yes" on DIVORCE) for each category of the independent variable.

   Line 1   DIVORCE by _____

   Line 2   _____   _____   _____   _____

   Line 3 Divorce = Yes _____   _____   _____   _____

5. Are your results consistent with your hypothesis? How?

6. Compute epsilon (= _____) and compare your results with the table showing the relationship between DIVORCE and RELITEN. Which independent variable (RELITEN or yours) seems to have the more important relationship with DIVORCE? Are both variables causes of DIVORCE?

A Final Caution: Association and Causation

When we find relationships between variables that are consistent with our hypotheses, it is very tempting to say that our theory is thereby *proven*. It is extremely important to recognize, however, that two variables can have a strong relationship but not be causally related. Variables may be related for a number of reasons besides causation. For example, the variables may represent different aspects of the same underlying concept. Although strong associations may be taken as *evidence* of a causal relationship, they cannot *prove* that two variables are causally related. Some techniques for dealing with questions of causation will be introduced later in the text. For now, it is sufficient that you restrain your natural enthusiasm when your hypothesis is confirmed and refrain from making rash statements about causation.

NAME _____

INSTRUCTOR _____

DATE _____

Continue to research the causes of DIVORCE by selecting two more potential independent variables. As before, produce crosstab tables with column percentages for each independent variable you select and DIVORCE. Use Command Block 2.3 as a guide and substitute the names of your independent variables for RELITEN.

1. State and briefly explain the hypotheses linking your independent variables with DIVORCE.

   Independent Variable 1:

   Independent Variable 2:

2. Present your results in a summary table, using Table 2.1 as a guide.
   a. *For independent variable 1:* On line 1, fill in the blank with the name of your independent variable. On line 2, write in the names of the categories of your independent variable, using as many blanks as necessary. On line 3, fill in the blanks with the percentage divorced ("Yes" on DIVORCE) for each category of the independent variable.

   Line 1   DIVORCE by _____

   Line 2   _____ _____ _____ _____

   Line 3 Divorce = Yes _____ _____ _____ _____

b. *For independent variable 2:* On line 1, fill in the blank with the name of your independent variable. On line 2, write in the names of the categories of your independent variable, using as many blanks as necessary. On line 3, fill in the blanks with the percentage divorced ("Yes" on DIVORCE) for each category of the independent variable.

Line 1   DIVORCE by _____

Line 2   _____   _____   _____   _____

Line 3 Divorce = Yes _____   _____   _____   _____

3. Compare these results with the earlier efforts to explain DIVORCE. Remember to compute epsilon. Which independent variable seems to have the more important relationship with DIVORCE? Which seem to be causes of DIVORCE?

NAME _____

INSTRUCTOR _____

DATE _____

Conduct a comparative analysis of the causes of divorce using the 1972 and 1994 GSS databases. Load the 1972 database (see Command Block 2.1 and substitute the GSS72 file for the GSS94TAB.SAV file) and run a frequency distribution for DIVORCE (see Command Block 1.4 at the end of Chapter 1).

1. The percentage of respondents who were divorced in 1972 was _____. The comparable percentage for 1994 was _____ . (See item 1 of Research Report 2.2.)

2. Were more religious people less likely to divorce in 1972? Use ATTEND as a measure of religiosity (RELITEN is not available). Run the **Crosstabs** procedure with DIVORCE as the dependent variable (in the rows) and ATTEND as the independent variable (in the columns). Use Command Block 2.3 as a guide. Present the results in the form of a summary table:

Divorce by ATTEND

	Attendance			
	Never	**Rarely**	**Monthly or more**	**Weekly or more**
Divorce = Yes	_____	_____	_____	_____
Compute epsilon:	_____			

3. Compare these results with those presented in Table 2.1. Was religiosity a cause of divorce in 1972? Was the relationship between these concepts substantially the same, or are there important differences? Keeping in mind that we are measuring religiosity with a different variable in 1972, what conclusions can you make about the causes of divorce?

Main Points

■ Sociologists use the scientific method to conduct research and test their theories. The causal relationships between our independent and dependent variables are almost always probabilistic. To measure our theoretical concepts, we must match them with concrete variables, such as the survey items on the GSS.

■ Crosstab tables and percentages were used to test some hypotheses about divorce and to illustrate the scientific method.

SPSS Commands Introduced in This Chapter

COMMAND BLOCK 2.3   *Producing Crosstab Tables with Column Percentages*

> Click **Statistics** → **Summarize** → **Crosstabs** →
> Highlight the name of the dependent variable(s) →
> Click the arrow pointing to the **Row(s):** box →
> Highlight the name of the independent variable(s) →
> Click the arrow pointing to the **Column(s):** box →
> Click **Cells** in the **Crosstabs** dialog box →
> Click **Columns** in the **Percentages** box →
> Click **Continue** →
> Click **OK**

Chapter 3   Describing the Sample

In this chapter, we continue the task of describing the 1994 GSS sample, which we began in Chapter 1. In that chapter, you used the Frequencies procedure to summarize the racial, sexual, religious, and age composition of the sample. Here, you will produce similar information in the form of bar charts. Also, you will be introduced to a new SPSS procedure and to a second version of the 1994 GSS data set.

The SPSS procedures in this chapter are typically used at the beginning of a research project to produce background information about the sample. These procedures work with one variable at a time and, because we are almost always concerned with *relationships* between two or more variables, they cannot answer our research questions. Still, they can provide useful information about the sample, which in turn can provide a context for interpreting the responses to the questions asked on the GSS.

Bar Charts

It is often said that a picture is worth a thousand words; SPSS gives us many ways to present results graphically. In Exercise 3.1, you use one of these procedures to construct a **bar chart** for RELIG (religious affiliation). Bar charts display a rectangular bar for each category or score of the variable, and the height of the bar is proportional to the number (or percentage) of cases in the category. Thus, bar charts are the graphic equivalents of frequency distributions.

EXERCISE 3.1   **A BAR CHART FOR RELIG**

Launch SPSS for Windows Student Version and load the GSS94TAB.SAV data set. (See Command Block 2.1 or Appendix B if you need a reminder about how to load a data file.) To request a bar chart, select **Graphs** from the menu bar across the top of the main SPSS window, click on **Bar** and the Bar Charts dialog window opens:

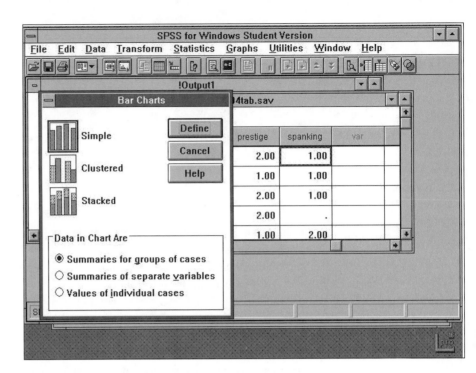

Note the three types of bar charts listed on the left. We have only one variable, so we want the **Simple** bar chart, which is already highlighted. Click the **Define** button, and a new window opens:

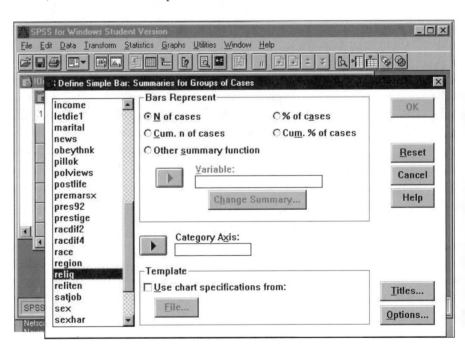

Scroll through the list of variables on the left until you highlight RELIG, and then click on the arrow pointing to the rectangle labeled **Category Axis:**. This tells SPSS to construct the chart with the categories of RELIG (Protestant, Catholic, and so on) arrayed along the horizontal axis.

Note that several choices are listed in the **Define Simple Bar** dialog box. For example, the Bars Represent rectangle at the top of the screen contains radio buttons that allow us to choose a format for the vertical axis of the bar chart. This axis of the chart can display frequencies (N of cases), percentages (% of cases), cumulative frequencies (Cum. n of cases), or cumulative percentages (Cum. % of cases). Use the frequencies option for now, but you should experiment with the other options at your convenience.

You can also add titles, subtitles, and footnotes to the table by clicking the **Titles. . .** button in the lower-right corner of the Define Simple Bar window. Feel free to explore these possibilities now or when you have completed this exercise.

One choice you have in designing charts and graphs is how to handle cases with missing scores (that is, respondents who did not, for whatever reason, supply the requested information). Usually, we want to eliminate these cases from the analysis. For charts and graphs, you can do this by clicking the **Options. . .** button in the lower-right portion of the screen and then making sure that the box next to the Display groups defined by missing values option is *not* checked. If the box has an x in it, eliminate the x by clicking the box. If the box is already blank, click on the **Continue** button and return to the Define Simple Bar dialog box.

Now you are ready to have SPSS produce the chart. Click on **OK** in the Define Simple Bar window, and the bar chart for RELIG appears on the screen in seconds. Command Block 3.1 summarizes the steps involved in producing a bar chart:

COMMAND BLOCK 3.1   Producing a Bar Chart

> Click **Graphs** → **Bar** →
>
> Highlight the variable name (for example, **RELIG**) →
>
> Click the arrow pointing to the **Category Axis:** box →
>
> Click **Options. . .** →
>
> Make sure the **Display groups defined by missing values** option is *not* checked →
>
> Click **Continue** →
>
> Click **OK**

The bar chart first appears in a window labeled Chart Carousel. To change the appearance of the chart, click **Edit**; the chart moves to a Chart window. Do this now and observe the array of commands available along the top of the window. SPSS provides a variety of choices for editing the chart. For example, you can change the "fill patterns" of the bars from solid colors to diagonal stripes or a variety of other designs. Explore these options now or at your leisure.

At this point, you almost certainly want to save or print the bar chart. To save the chart, click **File** and then **Save As** and give the chart a name. To get a hard copy, click **File** and then **Print**. When you are finished with the chart, click the small box in the upper-left corner of the window and choose **Close**.

The bar chart for religious affiliation is reproduced here as Figure 3.1. The fact that Protestants are the most common religious affiliation in the United States, followed by Catholics, is readily apparent from this chart.

FIGURE 3.1   **Religious Affiliations**
(1994 GSS)

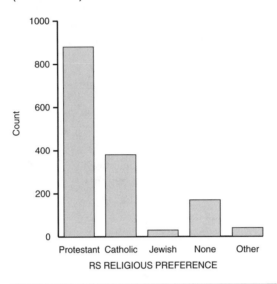

EXERCISE 3.2   **More Bar Charts**

Now it's your turn to produce bar charts. Using Command Block 3.1 as a guide, get bar charts for the variables marital status (MARITAL), place of residence (SRCBELT), and social class (CLASS). From the Bars Represent dialog box, choose percentages instead of frequencies for the vertical axis of the chart by clicking the button next to % of cases. Use the charts to complete the statements in Research Report 3.1. You may print or save the chart if you wish, or you can read the necessary information from the monitor screen.

NAME _____

INSTRUCTOR _____

DATE _____

1. About _____ % of the sample are married, and about _____% are widowed.

2. The most common place of residence for the sample is _____, and the least common is _____.

3. The largest social class is the _____ class, and the smallest is the _____ class.

Types of Variables and Data Sets

The SPSS procedures introduced to this point (frequency distributions, crosstab tables, and bar charts) are not equally useful or appropriate for all variables. For example, crosstab tables work well for variables with only a few scores (like RELIG or SEX) but not for variables that have many scores, like years of age. SPSS provides many procedures for the latter type of variable, and Exercise 3.3 introduces you to one such technique. Before proceeding, however, the distinctions between different types of variables need to be clarified, as does the rationale for including two different data sets for the 1994 GSS.

Variables

One crucial difference between variables lies in the mathematical nature of their scores. The scores of some variables are just labels rather than actual numbers. For example, SEX has two scores: 1 for males and 2 for females. These scores are arbitrary codes, which could be easily changed. We could make males "2" and females "1" and not lose information or violate logic or common sense. The scores for SEX are not really numbers and they cannot be added, subtracted, multiplied, divided, or otherwise treated as if they had an arithmetic nature. Variables that do not have numeric scores are sometimes called **nominal variables**.

Other variables, like age in years, do have actual numbers for scores. These scores can be treated mathematically and used to calculate statistics such as the **mean**, or the average, which involves addition and division. That is, to compute an average, you *add* the scores and *divide* the total by the number of scores. Variables that have scores with true numbers are sometimes called **interval-ratio variables**.

There is a third class of variables between nominal and interval-ratio. **Ordinal variables**, like CLASS, have scores that can be ranked higher or lower but that are not fully numerical. For example, on CLASS, a 1 indicates membership in the lower class, a 2 identifies a working-class person, and so forth. Although we know that a person with a higher score on CLASS belongs to a higher social grouping, we do not know exactly *how much* higher, and the distance from one score to the next is undefined.

As researchers, we have to keep the distinction between numerical and non-numerical variables in mind because SPSS does not: The program does not distinguish actual numbers (for age in years) from mere labels (for SEX). If you tell SPSS to compute a mean for SEX, it will do so happily and rapidly. It is up to us, not SPSS, to make sure that we are treating variables sensibly and choosing procedures that are appropriate for the mathematical nature of the variable.

Data Sets

Although you need to be aware of the mathematical differences between variables, the distinction will not be a major issue in this text because we have included two data sets for the 1994 GSS. The two data sets include exactly the same respondents, but the GSS94TAB.SAV data set includes mostly nominal and ordinal variables that have few scores and some interval-ratio variables in collapsed format (for example, the scores for AGE are collapsed into three broad categories in this data set). The GSS94COR.SAV data set, on the other hand, includes numerical variables with many scores—like years of education, AGE in years, and number of children—along with some background variables like SEX and RACE. Thus, we load the GSS94TAB.SAV data set when we consider SPSS techniques designed for non-numerical variables and switch to the more numerical GSS94COR.SAV data set as appropriate.

Some further explanation for the separate data sets may be useful. First, the Student Version of SPSS for Windows has a 50-variable limit for all data sets, and this can create problems of flexibility. For example, depending on the research situation, we will sometimes need to use a variable like AGE in a collapsed format, whereas at other times the uncollapsed, multiple-score "years of age" format will be more useful. We could have supplied a single data set with AGE in both formats, but because we are limited to 50 variables in a data set, other equally important variables would have to be excluded.

An alternative to providing variables like AGE in two different formats would be to explain how to use an SPSS command called RECODE to change the format for yourself. This command is not difficult to learn or use, but it would require a number of pages to present the necessary information and some expenditure of energy on your part to learn the techniques. This brings us to a second reason for having two data sets: by avoiding lengthy (and tedious) explanations of the RECODE command, you have that much more time to spend *doing* social research—so, let's return to the central purpose of this text.

EXERCISE 3.3

Descriptive Statistics

The SPSS procedure **Descriptives** produces summary statistics, like the mean, for numerical variables such as those in the GSS94COR.SAV data set. Load this data set now by following the instructions in Command Block 3.2:

COMMAND BLOCK 3.2

> Click **File → Open → Data →**
> Highlight the **GSS94COR.SAV** file →
> Click **OK**

We will demonstrate the use of the Descriptives procedure with AGE. Click **Statistics**, **Summarize**, and **Descriptives**; a window that looks very much like the Frequencies window opens. Locate and highlight AGE, click the arrow to the right of the variable-list window to select this variable, and then click **OK**. These commands are summarized in Command Block 3.3:

COMMAND BLOCK 3.3   Producing Descriptive Statistics

> Click **Statistics → Summarize → Descriptives →**
> Highlight the variable name →
> Click the arrow pointing to the **Variable(s):** box →
> Click **OK**

A new output window appears with several descriptive statistics, as presented in Figure 3.2.

FIGURE 3.2   **Output of Descriptives Procedure for AGE**
(1994 GSS)

```
Number of valid observations (listwise) =      1483.00

                                             Valid
Variable      Mean     Std Dev   Minimum   Maximum    N   Label

AGE           46.11     17.49        18        89   1483   AGE OF RESPONDENT
```

Reading Descriptive Statistics

This procedure produces the mean (or average) score, a standard deviation (Std
Dev), the lowest and highest scores, and the number of cases included in the computations (Valid N). We will ignore the standard deviation and concentrate on the
other statistics. The mean age of the sample is 46.11. This gives us information
about our typical (or average) respondent, but we also want to know something
about the amount of variety in the sample. Is everyone about 46 years old, or do
the respondents represent a variety of ages? One measure of diversity is the
range, or the distance from the high score to the low score. The minimum and
maximum scores are listed to the right of the screen and can be used to compute
the range. In our sample, the youngest respondent is 18 and the oldest is 89, so
the range is $89 - 18 = 71$.

Printing and Saving Output from Descriptives

You can print or save your Descriptives output using the same commands we used
for Frequencies. Click the **Save** or **Print** command from the **File** menu.

EXERCISE 3.4   **More Descriptive Statistics**

Now, it's your turn. With the GSS94COR.SAV data file still loaded, get descriptive statistics for three more variables: EDUC (number of years of education completed), CHILDS (number of children), and TVHOURS (number of hours per day
watching television). Follow the instructions in Command Block 3.3 and transfer
the names of all three variables into the Variable(s): window and then click **OK**.
Remember that SPSS processes all variables included in this window at one time.
Save or print the output or copy the relevant information from the screen to complete the statements in Research Report 3.2.

NAME   _____

INSTRUCTOR   _____

DATE   _____

1. The sample has completed an average of _____ years of schooling. The most educated respondents completed _____ years, and the least educated finished _____ years. The range of the scores was _____.

2. On the average, the sample had _____ children. The highest number of children was _____ , and the lowest was _____. The range of this variable was _____.

3. The sample watched an average of _____ hours of television a day. The heaviest viewers watched _____ hours, and the lowest number of hours was _____ for a range of _____.

Line Charts

For variables with many scores like AGE, **line charts** work well as "pictures" of the overall distribution of scores on the variable. These graphs display the scores of the variable along the horizontal axis and frequencies or percentages along the vertical axis. The scores are represented by a single line that begins at the lowest score of the variable (on the far left of the graph) and continues to the highest score. The height of the line indicates, with either frequencies or percentages, how common the score was. Common scores are indicated by high peaks, and the line dips toward the horizontal axis for less common scores. Thus, we can get an overall idea of the shape of the distribution for a variable with a quick glance at the chart.

EXERCISE 3.5   **A Line Chart for AGE**

To request a line chart, click **Graphs** on the main menu bar and then click **Line**, and this dialog box opens:

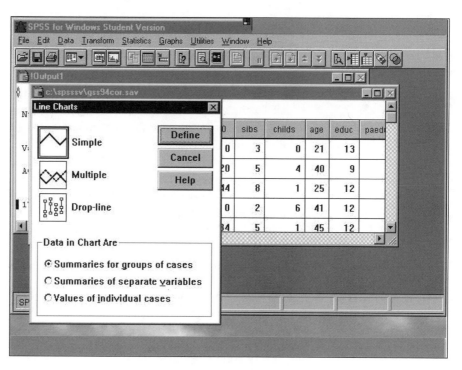

Three types of graphs are listed to the left with Simple already highlighted. We only have one variable, so this is the type we want; click the **Define** button, and the Define Simple Line dialog box opens:

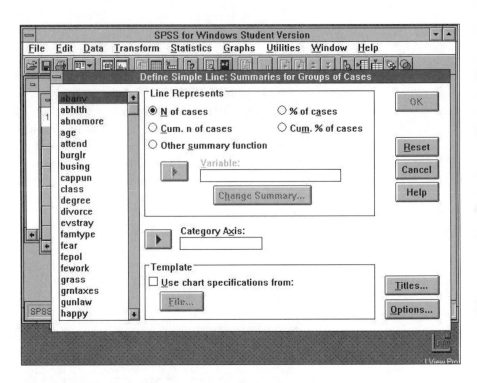

Scroll through the variable list until you highlight AGE and click the arrow to transfer the variable name to the Category Axis: box. Note that you can choose among various options for the content and titles of the graph. Explore the possibilities now or at your leisure. Make sure you eliminate cases with missing scores, however, by clicking the **Options. . .** button and making sure that the Display groups defined by missing values option is *not* checked. When you have made your selections, click **OK** to have SPSS produce the line chart. As was the case with bar charts, you can save or print the line graph by making the appropriate selections from the File menu. When you are finished with the line chart, click on the small box in the upper-left corner of the window and choose **Close**. These procedures are summarized in Command Block 3.4:

COMMAND BLOCK 3.4 Producing a Line Chart

> Click **Graphs** → **Line** →
>
> Highlight a variable name →
>
> Click the arrow pointing to the **Category Axis:** box →
>
> Click **Options. . .** →
>
> Make sure the **Display groups defined by missing values** option is *not* checked →
>
> Click **Continue** →
>
> Click **OK** →
>
> **Save** or **Print** the chart (if you wish)

The line chart for AGE is presented in Figure 3.3.

FIGURE 3.3   **Line Chart for AGE**
(1994 GSS)

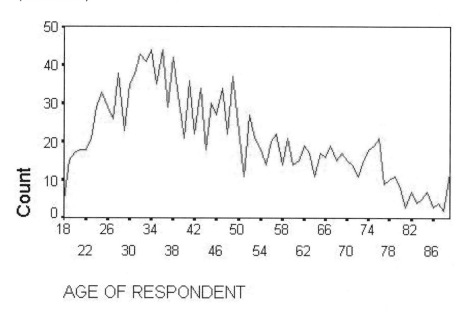

AGE OF RESPONDENT

Take a moment to observe how the scores are spread from the youngest respondent (age 18) to the oldest (age 89). You can see that the sample includes people of all ages over 18 and that the sample is concentrated in the late 20s to about age 50. For ages over 50, the number of respondents gradually decreases.

EXERCISE 3.6   **Line Charts for Other Numerical Variables**

Now it's your turn to produce line charts and use them to complete Research Report 3.3. Repeat the procedure in Command Block 3.4 for EDUC, CHILDS, and TVHOURS. You can save or print each chart as you produce it or read the information necessary to complete the report from the monitor screen.

NAME _____

INSTRUCTOR _____

DATE _____

1. For years of education (EDUC), the highest peak (most common score) was _____ . The lowest point of the graph was at _____ years of education. Most cases seemed to be grouped around _____ years of schooling.

2. The most common score for number of children (CHILDS) was _____ , and the least was _____. Most people had about _____ children.

3. Most people watched about _____ hours of television (TVHOURS) each day. The least common number of hours of television watching was _____ .

NAME _____

INSTRUCTOR _____

DATE _____

Continue to produce summary tables and statistics for the variables in the 1994 General Social Survey. Pick three more variables from the **GSS94TAB.SAV** data set and produce frequency distributions and bar charts for each. In the section below, identify the variable by its SPSS name and, if necessary, explain what the variable measures. Use the **Utilities** procedure or consult Appendix A as necessary. Briefly describe the distribution of each variable. You should identify the largest and smallest categories for the variable and note any other interesting information.

Variable 1

Name: _____

Description:

Variable 2

Name: _____

Description:

Variable 3

Name: _____

Description:

NAME _____

INSTRUCTOR _____

DATE _____

Get descriptive statistics (use the Descriptives procedure) and line charts for three more variables from the GSS94COR.SAV data set. Identify the variable by its SPSS name and, if necessary, explain what the variable measures. Use the **Utilities** procedure or consult Appendix A as necessary. Record the mean and range for each variable. Using these statistics and the line charts, briefly describe the distribution of each variable.

Variable 1

    Name: _____

    Mean = _____   Range = _____

    Description:

Variable 2

    Name: _____

    Mean = _____   Range = _____

    Description:

Variable 3

    Name: _____

    Mean = _____   Range = _____

    Description:

COMPARATIVE ANALYSIS 3.1

HAVE THE CHARACTERISTICS OF THE U.S. POPULATION CHANGED OVER TIME?

NAME _____

INSTRUCTOR _____

DATE _____

Load the **GSS72.SAV** data set and get frequency distributions (see Command Block 1.4) and bar charts (see Command Block 3.1) for CLASS and SRCBELT. Compare these results with the 1994 patterns for CLASS and SRCBELT, which you used to complete Research Report 3.1.

1. What changes can you detect in class structure over the time period? The _____ class has grown the most in relative size, and the _____ class has lost the most members. On the whole, these results indicate that the U.S. population has _____ (become richer/become poorer/not shown any economical change).

2. What changes can you detect in residential patterns? The _____ (urban/suburban/small town/rural) area has grown the most, whereas the _____ (urban/suburban /small town/rural) has declined in relative size. On the whole, the United States has become _____ (more/less) urban.

   Get descriptive statistics (see Command Block 3.3) and line charts (see Command Block 3.4) for EDUC, AGE, and CHILDS for the 1972 GSS. Compare these results with those from 1994, which you used to complete Research Reports 3.2 and 3.3. Patterns for AGE were presented in Exercise 3.3.

1. The average years of education in 1972 was _____ years, and the range was _____ . In 1994, average years of education had (increased/decreased) to _____ years, a (gain/loss) of _____ years.

2. The average age of the sample in 1972 was _____ years, and the range was _____ . In 1994, average age had _____ (increased/decreased) to _____ years. U.S. society had grown _____ (older/younger)

3. The average number of children in 1972 was _____ , with a range of _____ . In 1994, Americans averaged _____ children. Americans in 1994 were having _____ (fewer/more) children than they were in 1972.

Main Points

- Research projects often begin with an inspection of frequency distributions, charts, and descriptive statistics for all variables. This information can provide an important context for interpreting the responses of the sample.

- Two versions of the 1994 GSS are included with this text. One, the GSS94TAB.SAV data set, includes nominal and other variables suitable for use in tables. The other, GSS94COR.SAV, includes variables with numerical scores for which other procedures are appropriate.

- Bar charts provide a visual display of the frequency distribution of variables with few scores. Line charts can be used to display the distributions of numerical variables with many scores.

- The Descriptives procedure produces summary statistics for numerical variables.

SPSS Commands Introduced in This Chapter

COMMAND BLOCK 3.1   *Producing a Bar Chart*

> Click **Graphs** → **Bar** →
>
> Highlight the variable name →
>
> Click the arrow pointing to the **Category Axis:** box →
>
> Click **Options. . .** →
>
> Make sure the **Display groups defined by missing values** option is *not* checked →
>
> Click **Continue** →
>
> Click **OK**

3.3   *Producing Descriptive Statistics*

> Click **Statistics** → **Summarize** → **Descriptives** →
>
> Highlight the variable name →
>
> Click the arrow pointing to the **Variable(s):** box →
>
> Click **OK**

3.4   *Producing a Line Graph*

Click **Graphs** → **Line** →

Highlight a variable name →

Click the arrow pointing to the **Category Axis:** box →

Click **Options. . .** →

Make sure the **Display groups defined by missing values** option is *not* checked →

Click **Continue** →

Click **OK**

Chapter 4   Culture: What Do Americans Value?

Culture includes everything associated with the way of life or heritage of a society: Language, eating utensils, etiquette, jokes, and ideas about the meaning of life and death—all are part of culture. Culture tells us how we should organize our families and communities, live our lives, and relate to one another. You might think of culture as a kind of blueprint for human society and human relationships.

The culture of even the simplest human society is complex and has many components. Some cultural elements (like hammers, dresses, diesel engines, and bagels) have a physical presence and are referred to as *material culture*. Other elements are less tangible. These include information, rules of conduct, *values* (ideas about what is moral and desirable), and *beliefs* (ideas about what is true).

The United States includes many different groups and types of Americans and thus many different cultural values and beliefs. Members of this society can belong to the Catholic church, an organized-crime family, a professional sports teams, a college fraternity, a labor union, or thousands of other groups, each of which might maintain a different set of values and beliefs. Furthermore, Americans can be recent immigrants, Boston blue bloods, southerners or westerners, baby boomers, or members of generation X. Each different type of American and each different group may have a unique *subculture* or variation on the overall culture.

In this chapter, we will use SPSS and the General Social Survey (GSS) to explore some of the values and beliefs in U.S. culture. We'll use the Frequencies routine to see if members of U.S. society agree in their values and then use the Crosstabs procedure to explore the diversity of values in our society. Along the way, you will learn some useful techniques for data analysis.

How Religious Are Americans?

Because values have a moral component, one obvious place to look for them is in religion. In Chapter 1, we saw that the vast majority of the GSS sample (about 90%) affiliate themselves with a religious denomination (see Research Report 1.1), and this indicates that religion is an important component of U.S. culture.

Claiming membership in a religion is not, of course, the same thing as being religious. If we want to know how religious Americans really are—not just their affiliation—a more valid indicator would measure the strength of their commitment. As we saw in Chapter 2, the GSS includes several items that can be used as indicators of the strength of religious beliefs. One is attendance at religious services (ATTEND), and the other is the extent to which the respondent claims to be a "strong" member of their faith (RELITEN). We will show you how to analyze the first of these and you can analyze the second on your own.

The ATTEND variable, as originally administered in the survey, had nine different scores, which we collapsed into four categories for the GSS94TAB.SAV data set. A frequency distribution and bar chart for this variable should give us an idea about how involved Americans are in their religions.

EXERCISE 4.1   **Measuring Religiosity**

Launch SPSS for Windows, load the GSS94TAB.SAV data file, and run the **Frequencies** procedure for ATTEND. Command Block 4.1 presents the commands needed to load the data set and run the Frequencies procedure.

COMMAND BLOCK 4.1

> Click **File** → **Open** → **Data. . .** →
> Highlight the **GSS94TAB.SAV** file →
> Click **OK** →
> Click **Statistics** → **Summarize** → **Frequencies** →
> Highlight **ATTEND** in the list of variables →
> Click the arrow pointing to the **Variable(s): box** →
> Click **OK**

Remember to maximize the size of the output window by clicking the up-arrow (or the box with the line in it if you are using Windows 95) in the upper-right corner. Use the arrow keys or the scroll buttons to move around in the window. Figure 4.1 shows the full output.

FIGURE 4.1   **Output of Frequencies Procedure for ATTEND**
(1994 GSS)

```
ATTEND    HOW OFTEN R ATTENDS RELIGIOUS SERVICES


                                              Valid      Cum
Value Label             Value  Frequency  Percent  Percent  Percent

Never                     0       247      16.6     16.9     16.9
Rarely                    1       494      33.2     33.8     50.7
Monthly                   2       330      22.2     22.6     73.3
Weekly                    3       390      26.2     26.7    100.0
DK,NA                     9        25       1.7   Missing
                               -------   -------  -------
                       Total     1486     100.0    100.0

Valid cases    1461    Missing cases     25
```

The most common level of attendance (called the **mode**), with about 33% of the respondents, was "rarely." In terms of the original coding for this variable, this category includes respondents who attend services "several times a year" or less. However, note that weekly and monthly attendance patterns are also very common and that the percentage of Americans who "never" attend is not that far below the other categories. It seems that Americans are quite variable in their attendance at religious services and, at best, this table suggests that the degree of religiosity in our society is mixed.

For a visual display of the distribution of this variable, request a bar chart by clicking **Graphs** from the menu bar and then **Bar**. The necessary commands are presented in Command Block 4.2. If you want, you may choose from the options in the Bars Represent rectangle at the top of the screen of the Define Simple Bar dialog box or add titles, subtitles, or footnotes to the table by clicking the **Titles** bar in the lower-right corner of the window. Remember to eliminate cases with missing values. Click **Options. . .** and make sure that the box next to the Display groups defined by missing value option is *not* checked.

COMMAND BLOCK 4.2

Click **Graphs** → **Bar** →
Click **Define** →
Highlight **ATTEND** →
Click the arrow pointing to the **Category Axis:** box→
Click **Options. . .** →
Make sure the **Display groups defined by missing values** option is *not* checked →
Click **Continue** →
Click **OK**

The bars in the chart will be similar in height, reflecting the roughly equal size of the categories of ATTEND. You may choose to Save or Print the bar chart by clicking the **File** menu.

EXERCISE 4.2   **Another Measure of Religiosity**

We can also measure religiosity with RELITEN, the respondent's answer to the question "Would you call yourself a strong (*stated religious preference*) or a not very strong (*stated religious preference*)?" Use the **Frequencies** procedure to get a frequency distribution for this variable. Follow the commands in Command Block 4.1 but substitute RELITEN for ATTEND. Use the output to complete Research Report 4.1.

NAME _____

INSTRUCTOR _____

DATE _____

1. _____ % of the respondents are "strong" in their religious convictions, _____ % are "somewhat strong," _____% are "not very strong," and _____ % are "not religious."

2. Compare the frequency distribution for RELITEN with the one for ATTEND. Do the tables present similar pictures of religiosity? Explain. What conclusions can you make about the strength of religiosity in the United States? That is, would you say that these variables indicate that the society is "deeply religious"? Somewhat religious? Not religious? Variable in religiosity? Explain your conclusion.

Analyzing Bivariate Tables

The Frequencies procedure is very useful in the early phases of a research process, but it cannot be used to examine *relationships* between variables, and relationships are almost always the primary focus of our theories and hypotheses. In Chapter 2, we introduced the Crosstabs procedure and bivariate tables as one technique for exploring relationships. In this section, we examine bivariate tables in more detail and explore some new analytical techniques. In Exercise 4.3, we will use these techniques to test a theory of religiosity.

To begin, consider Table 4.1, which shows the relationship between SEX and RELITEN for the *entire* 1994 GSS sample of almost 3000 respondents, not the smaller data set included in GSS94TAB.SAV.

TABLE 4.1 **Religious Intensity by SEX, Full 1994 GSS Sample** (Frequencies)

		SEX		
		Male	Female	Total
RELITEN	Strong	403	699	1102
	Somewhat strong	127	187	314
	Not very strong	552	636	1188
	Not religious	155	119	274
	Total	1237	1641	2878

The body of a bivariate table consists of **cells**, each of which shows the number (or percentage) of cases that had a certain combination of scores. Since SEX has two scores and RELITEN has four, there are a total of eight (2 × 4) possible combinations of scores and eight cells in the table. In Table 4.1, the upper-left cell shows the number of strongly religious males, whereas the lower-right cell displays the number of females who are not religious. The table also shows *univariate* frequency distributions. By reading the totals, we see that 1237 males and 1641 females were in the sample and 1102 people were "strong," 314 were "somewhat strong," and so forth.

The Format of Bivariate Tables

Bivariate tables have two dimensions: **columns** go up and down (the vertical dimension), and **rows** go across (the horizontal dimension). Usually, the independent (or causal) variable is placed in the columns. This means that each column represents a category of the independent variable. In Table 4.1, we have one column for males and one for females. Similarly, the dependent variable (or the effect) is placed in the rows and each row is a category of the dependent variable (one row for people who are "strong," one for those who are "somewhat strong," and so on).

Exploring Causal Relationships

We can use bivariate tables to analyze causal relationships between variables by following two steps:

1. Calculate the column percentages, or percentages within each column (see Chapter 2). For each value of the independent variable (for each column of the table), divide the frequency in each cell by the total number of cases in the column and multiply the resulting fraction by 100.
2. Compare the columns with each other.

Comparing the column percentages with each other will show the effect, if any, of the independent variable on the dependent variable. If the variables are related—that is, if SEX is a cause of RELITEN—the column percentages will vary, and men will display different patterns on RELITEN than women. The greater the difference from column to column, the greater the impact of the independent variable on the dependent variable. Table 4.2 displays the column percentages for SEX and RELITEN.

TABLE 4.2   **Religious Intensity by SEX, Full 1994 GSS Sample (Percentages)**

		SEX	
		Male	Female
RELITEN	Strong	33%	43%
	Somewhat strong	10%	11%
	Not very strong	45%	39%
	Not religious	12%	7%
	Total	100%	100%

Comparing from column to column (or, comparing men and women), we see that the distribution of percentages varies. A higher percentage of women are "strong," whereas men have a higher percentage of cases in the "not very strong" and "not religious" categories. These results suggest that women are more religious and support the hypothesis that SEX and RELITEN are related.

Determining Cause and Effect

How can we decide which variable is the cause (independent) and which is the effect (dependent)? Usually, the role of each variable will be obvious from our research question or hypothesis. For Tables 4.1 and 4.2, the question would be: Does religious intensity vary *as a result of* a person's gender? SEX must therefore be the independent or causal variable.

For this particular relationship, we can also use the logic of time to determine which variable is cause (independent) and which is effect (dependent). Because gender is determined at birth and does not change over the course of a person's life, a person's "score" on SEX is determined before their religious beliefs are developed. Thus, gender may affect religious beliefs, but the reverse cannot be true.[1]

A Test of the Deprivation Theory of Religiosity

What types of Americans are the most religious? Does religiosity vary by social class, gender, or race? What would you hypothesize? One idea that we can use to guide an analysis of these questions comes from the deprivation theory of religiosity (Glock, Ringer, and Babbie, 1967). According to this theory, people who are blocked from success and gratification in the secular society are more likely to turn to religion as an alternative source of comfort and gratification. Because the United States remains largely a white, male-dominated society in which material wealth is equated with success, we can use this theory to hypothesize that religiosity will be higher for women, nonwhites, and people in the lower social classes. Our dependent variable will be RELITEN, and our independent variables will be SEX, RACE, and CLASS. We will check out the first relationship and you can investigate the others.

EXERCISE 4.3   **What Are the Correlates of Religiosity?**

Launch the SPSS program and load the **GSS94TAB.SAV** data set. We will use the Crosstabs procedure to test our hypothesis. SEX will be in the columns, RELITEN will be in the rows, and we will request column percentages. Command Block 4.3 presents the relevant commands:

---

1. OK, if you want to be picky, it is probably true that a person's religious beliefs would affect a decision about undergoing a sex-change operation. In that highly unusual circumstance, religious intensity would be the independent variable, and gender would be the dependent variable. Such rare situations need not concern us for this example.

COMMAND BLOCK 4.3

> Click **Statistics** → **Summarize** → **Crosstabs** →
> Highlight **RELITEN** →
> Click the arrow pointing to the **Row(s):** box →
> Highlight **SEX** →
> Click the arrow pointing to the **Column(s):** box →
> Click **Cells** →
> Click **Columns** in the **Percentages** box →
> Click **Continue** to close this dialog box →
> Click **OK** in the Crosstabs dialog box

When the Output window appears, you will probably be looking at the bottom of the table. Click the up-arrow in the upper-right corner of the Output box (or the box with the square in it if you are using Windows 95) to enlarge the window, and then you can move around by using the arrow keys and the scroll buttons. Figure 4.2 shows the output of the Crosstabs procedure.

FIGURE 4.2 **Output from Crosstabs for RELITEN and SEX**
(1994 GSS)

```
RELITEN   STRENGTH OF AFFILIATION   by   SEX   RESPONDENTS

                              SEX              Page 1 of 1
                   Count
                   Col Pct  MALE       FEMALE
                                                 Row
                              1          2      Total
    RELITEN
                   1        212        356        568
       STRONG               34.3       43.8       39.7

                   2         54         88        142
    somewhat strong          8.7       10.8        9.9

                   3        269        306        575
    not very strong         43.5       37.6       40.2

                   4         83         63        146
    NO RELIGION             13.4        7.7       10.2

                   Column   618        813       1431
                   Total    43.2       56.8      100.0
```

The variables being analyzed are identified by a title above the table, each column represents a different category of SEX, and each row is a category of RELITEN. Recall that the entries in each cell are the number of cases in the cell (for example, the upper-left cell shows that there are 212 men who are "strong") and the percentage of all cases in the column in the particular cell. Thus, looking across the top row, we see that about 34% of all men are strong while about 44% of women are strong.

   As was the case with the full sample of all 1994 GSS respondents (see Tables 4.1 and 4.2), the column percentages for our smaller sample are different from each other. Furthermore, as predicted by the theory of deprivation, there is a higher percentage of women in the "strong" and "somewhat strong" categories and a higher percentage of men in the "not very strong" and "no religion" categories. These results support the hypothesis that sex is a cause of religiosity and the idea that women are more religious than men. You may, at this point, wish to Save or Print this table for future reference. Both commands are listed under the File menu.

As noted previously, social science theories incorporate concepts, like religiosity, that are abstract, somewhat ambiguous, and open to various interpretations. Because addressing all possible meanings of a concept at once is difficult, multiple tests of a theory are common. Additional tests might be conducted by using different concrete variables to take the place of the abstract concept. In the case of the deprivation theory of religiosity, the theory can be tested further by examining relationships between RELITEN and other measures of deprivation. The greater the extent to which a theory is supported over a series of trials, the greater the confidence that can be placed in the validity of the theory.

EXERCISE 4.4

Further Tests of the Deprivation Theory of Religiosity

Conduct additional tests of the deprivation theory by using RACE and CLASS as independent variables in place of SEX. Use **Crosstabs** (see Command Block 4.4) and name RELITEN as the dependent variable and *both* RACE and CLASS as independent variables. SPSS will produce a bivariate table for each combination of variables named in the Row(s) and Column(s) windows. In this case, the output will consist of two tables, one for RELITEN and RACE and one for RELITEN and CLASS. Don't forget column percentages. Use the output to complete Research Report 4.2.

COMMAND BLOCK 4.4

Click **Statistics** → **Summarize** → **Crosstabs** →
Highlight **RELITEN** →
Click the arrow pointing to the **Row(s):** box →
Highlight **RACE** →
Click the arrow pointing to the **Column(s):** box →
Highlight **CLASS** →
Click the arrow pointing to the **Column(s):** box →
Click **Cells** to get the **Cell Display** window →
In the **Percentages** box, choose **Columns** →
Click **Continue** →
Click **OK**

NAME _____

INSTRUCTOR _____

DATE _____

1. _____ % of white respondents are strong in their religious faith vs. _____ % of the black respondents. RELITEN is strongest for _____ (blacks/whites) and there _____ (is/is not) a relationship between these two variables. This table _____ (does/does not) support the deprivation theory. Explain.

2. _____% of the lower class, _____% of the working class, _____% of the middle class , and_____% of the upper class are strong in their religious faith. RELITEN is strongest for the _____ (lower/working/middle/upper) class, and there _____ (is/is not) a relationship between RELITEN and CLASS. This table _____ (does/does not) support the deprivation theory. Explain.

3. What are your conclusions about the deprivation theory of religiosity? Do the bivariate tables support the theory? How strongly? Could you conclude that the theory is definitely true or not true? Why, or why not? (Remember that association is *not* the same thing as causation. See Chapter 2.)

Assessing the Significance and Strength
of Bivariate Relationships

Comparing the distribution of column percentages in a bivariate table is normally only a first step in analysis; two more important questions must be asked: Is the relationship statistically significant? How strong is the relationship? We will deal with these questions one at a time.

Statistical Significance

Remember that when we analyze the GSS94TAB.SAV data set, we are working with a random sample of about 1500 respondents, not with the population of all Americans. It's really the population we are interested in, and the GSS sample is only a means to the end of learning more about American society. Recall from Chapter 1 that, almost always, properly selected samples will be representative of the population. That is, the sample will reproduce the important characteristics of the population, and the patterns and relationships we observe in the sample will reflect what is true for the population. If women are more religious than men in the 1994 GSS sample, we can assume with great confidence that the same is true for the entire U.S. population.

However, even the most carefully selected sample, on rare occasion, will be unrepresentative of the population from which it was drawn, and the patterns we observe in the sample will *not* be true for the population. Particularly when percentage differences from column to column are small, it is possible that the sample outcomes were produced by random chance and do not reflect actual relationships in the society at large.

Fortunately, SPSS gives us a convenient way to estimate the **statistical significance** of our results, or the probability that the sample patterns were produced by mere random chance and do not exist in the population. When we construct bivariate tables with Crosstabs, we can request a statistic called **chi square**, which can be used to estimate the probability that random chance is at work. When we request this statistic, SPSS will conduct several different chi square tests, each based on a different mathematical model or set of assumptions. The results of these tests are reported as part of the Crosstabs output, directly below the table. The result of interest to us is the **significance** associated with the Pearson chi square. This value, which is the probability that our results were produced by random chance, can range from 0.00000 to 1.0000; and the *lower* the significance value, the *less likely* that our results were produced merely by random chance.

As a rule of thumb, social scientists generally accept significance values of .05 or less as indicating a statistically significant result (or one that is unlikely to have been produced by mere random chance). To summarize: If the value reported for the significance of the Pearson chi square is *less than* .05 (5 out of 100, or 20 to 1), we can assume that our results are statistically significant and reflect what is true about the population.

The Strength of the Association

Besides statistical significance, we also want to know the *strength* of the relationship: To what extent does one variable affect the other? If a relationship is strong, we will see large differences in the percentage distributions from column to column of the bivariate table. In weak relationships, the differences will be small or nonexistent.

Social scientists use statistics called **measures of association** to assess the strength of a relationship. Most measures of association vary between 0.00 and 1.00. The closer to 1.00, the stronger the relationship; the closer to 0.00, the weaker the relationship. SPSS can calculate many different measures of association, but for now we will use just one: a statistic called **Cramer's *V*.**

What values of Cramer's *V* indicate that the bivariate relationship is "strong" (or "moderate" or "weak")? Other than the extremes (a value of 0.00 means no relationship, and a value of 1.00 means a perfect or the strongest possible relationship), there are no agreed-upon conventions for describing the strength of bivariate relationships. Any words we use to characterize strength are bound to be somewhat arbitrary. In most social science research situations, however, we can say that measures of association less than .10 indicate weak and uninteresting relationships between the variables. Values between .10 and .30 would be regarded as moderate in strength and worth noting, whereas those over .30 would generally be regarded as extremely interesting and evidence of a strong relationship between the variables.

This scale may strike you as too low. If Cramer's *V* has an upper limit of 1, how could values as low as .30 be regarded as "strong"? Remember that, in the social sciences, we deal with *probabilistic* causal relationships (see Chapter 2). We do not propose that our independent variable is *the* cause of the dependent variable but merely *a* cause. A variable like religiosity has many causes. When examining bivariate relationships and independent variables one at a time, expecting measures of association to approach 1 is unreasonable. Given the complexity of the social world, the (admittedly arbitrary) guideline presented is serviceable in most instances.

Summary: Analyzing Bivariate Relationships

Figure 4.3 lists three questions about the output from the Crosstabs procedure that can be used to determine if a particular relationship is noteworthy and worth pursuing. If the answer to either of the first two questions is no, we do not need to go on to the third question. As a rule, we pay attention only to relationships that are statistically significant and reasonably strong. Remember that the *lower* the value for significance (less than .05) and the *higher* the value for Cramer's *V*, the more significant and the stronger the relationship.

FIGURE 4.3   **Assessing the Strength and Significance of a Bivariate Relationship**

1. Do the column percentages change?
2. Is the relationship statistically significant? (Is the significance of chi square *less than* .05?)
3. How strong is the relationship? (What is the value of Cramer's *V*?)

EXERCISE 4.5   **Is There a Heaven?**

Let's put our new statistical tools to use and examine another aspect of religiosity. The sample was asked "Do you believe there is a life after death?" (POSTLIFE); about 80% said yes. You can confirm this with a frequency distribution (click **Statistics → Summarize → Frequencies**) for the variable POSTLIFE.

What type of person would be most likely to believe in an afterlife? Earlier in this chapter, we tested the deprivation theory of religiosity using RELITEN as the dependent variable and SEX, RACE, and CLASS as independent variables. In a further test of the theory, we will use the same independent variables but use POSTLIFE in place of RELITEN as the dependent variable. If we find that relationships with POSTLIFE are similar to those with RELITEN, the deprivation theory will be supported.

We analyze the relationship between POSTLIFE and SEX, using all of our statistical tools, and leave the other potential independent variables to you. All commands for Crosstabs, including column percentages, chi square, and Cramer's *V*, are presented in Command Block 4.5:

COMMAND BLOCK 4.5   Producing Crosstab Tables with Column Percentages, Chi Square, and Cramer's *V*

> Click **Statistics → Summarize → Crosstabs →**
> Highlight **POSTLIFE →**
> Click the arrow pointing to the **Row(s):** box →
> Highlight **SEX →**
> Click arrow pointing to the **Column(s):** box →
> Click **Cells** to get the **Cell Display** window →
> In the **Percentages** box, choose **Columns →**
> Click **Continue** to close this dialog box →
> In the **Crosstabs** dialog box, click **Statistics →**
> Select **Chi square** and **Cramer's V →**
> Click **Continue →**
> Click **OK**

Figure 4.4 shows the output.

FIGURE 4.4   **Output from Crosstabs for POSTLIFE and SEX with Chi Square and Cramer's *V*** (1994 GSS)

```
POSTLIFE   BELIEF IN LIFE AFTER DEATH   by   SEX   RESPONDENTS SEX

                       SEX             Page 1 of 1
              Count
              Col Pct  MALE    FEMALE
                                            Row
                        1        2        Total
   POSTLIFE  ────────
                 1      272      428        700
       YES            80.2     82.8       81.8

                 2       67       89        156
        NO            19.8     17.2       18.2

              Column   339      517        856
              Total    39.6     60.4      100.0


        Chi-Square              Value        DF        Significance
   --------------------       ----------    ----       ------------

   Pearson                      .89287        1           .34470
   Continuity Correction        .73000        1           .39288
   Likelihood Ratio             .88680        1           .34635
   Mantel-Haenszel test for     .89182        1           .34498
        linear association

   Minimum Expected Frequency -    61.780


                                                           Approximate
        Statistic              Value      ASE1   Val/ASE0  Significance
   --------------------      ---------  --------  --------  ------------

   Phi                        -.03230                       .34470 *1
   Cramer's V                  .03230                        .34470 *1


   Gamma                      -.08449    .08905   -.93489


   *1 Pearson chi-square probability

   Number of Missing Observations:   630
```

Use the questions in Figure 4.3 to help you analyze the table. Do the column percentages change? A higher percentage of women (about 83%) than men (about 80%) believe in an afterlife. Once again, women seem more religious than men, as predicted by the deprivation theory. However, the difference is less than 3 percentage points, and a large majority of both sexes believe in an afterlife.

Is this relationship statistically significant, or did it occur by random chance? You will find the significance for Pearson chi square in the first row of the right-hand column in the information printed below the crosstab table. This value of .34 is much higher than the .05 value usually used to identify significant results. Therefore, the pattern of cell frequencies which we observe in the table did occur by random chance. There is no relationship between SEX and POSTLIFE in the population.

Normally, when a relationship is not statistically significant, the analysis would end. To finish the demonstration, however, find Cramer's *V* in the block of information below chi square. The value of *V* is .03, which indicates that the relationship between POSTLIFE and SEX is weak (almost zero).

To summarize, the column percentages suggest a (very weak) relationship between gender and belief in the afterlife. Women are slightly more religious than men. The relationship is not statistically significant, however, and weak (Cramer's *V* is low). Remember that we usually look for *statistically significant* and *strong* relationships. In this case, the relationship is not strong enough to merit much further attention, and the idea that belief in an afterlife is related to sex is not supported. This test does not support the deprivation theory of religiosity.

EXERCISE 4.6 **More Tests of the Deprivation Theory**

Now it's your turn. Rerun **Crosstabs** with POSTLIFE as the row variable and RACE and CLASS as the column variables. Request column percentages, chi square, and Cramer's *V*. Use Command Block 4.5 as a guide, substituting RACE and CLASS for SEX. Use the output from these two tables and the output in Figure 4.4 to complete Research Report 4.3.

Another Caution: Association and Causation

At the risk of nagging, we repeat the warning that *association and causation are two different things*. Even when we find very strong and highly significant relationships that are consistent with our theory, we cannot conclude that our theory is thereby proven. Strong and significant relationships between variables can be caused by many things other than causal relationships. When we find strong and significant relationships, probably the strongest conclusion we should permit ourselves is that the theory is *supported* (not proven).

NAME _____

INSTRUCTOR _____

DATE _____

1. Record the percentage of respondents who said "yes" to POSTLIFE for each independent variable. Record the significance of chi square and the value of Cramer's V in the space provided.

	Percentage (Yes)	Significance (Chi Square)	Strength (Cramer's V)
RACE			
White	____		
Black	____	____	____
CLASS			
Lower	____		
Working	____		
Middle	____		
Upper	____	____	____

2. For RACE: The column percentages _____ (do/do not) change, so there _____ (is/is not) a relationship between these variables. The significance of chi square is _____ (less than/more than) .05, so the relationship between RACE and POSTLIFE _____ (is/is not) statistically significant. The value of Cramer's V for RACE and POSTLIFE is ____ , so this is a _____ (weak/moderate/strong) relationship.

3. For CLASS: The column percentages _____ (do/do not) change, so there _____ (is/is not) a relationship between these variables. The significance of chi square is _____ (less than/more than) .05, so the relationship between CLASS and POSTLIFE _____ (is/is not) statistically significant. The value of Cramer's V for CLASS and POSTLIFE is ____ , so this is a _____ (weak/moderate/strong) relationship.

(Research Report continues)

4. Of the three potential independent variables, which has the *most significant* relationship (lowest value for significance of chi square) with POSTLIFE? ———————— (SEX/RACE/CLASS). Of the three potential independent variables, which has the *strongest* relationship (highest value for Cramer's *V*) with POSTLIFE? ———————(SEX/RACE/CLASS).

5. Do these results support the deprivation theory of religiosity? Explain.

NAME _____

INSTRUCTOR _____

DATE _____

Choose two more variables from the **GSS94TAB.SAV** data set that seem to be indicators of deprivation (like SEX, RACE, and CLASS). Run **Crosstabs** with RELITEN as the row (dependent) variable and your independent variables in the columns. Don't forget to get column percentages, chi square, and Cramer's *V*. Use Command Block 4.5 as a guide.

1. *Summarize results for your first independent variable*. Complete the following summary table. On line 1, fill in the blank with the name of your independent variable. On line 2, write in the names of the categories of your independent variable, using as many blanks as necessary. On line 3, fill in the blanks with the percentage who were "strong" on RELITEN for each category of the independent variable.

   Lines

   1.   RELITEN by _____

   2.   _____ _____ _____ _____ _____

   3. RELITEN =
         Strong   _____ _____ _____ _____ _____

   Significance of chi square = _____

                   Cramer's *V* = _____

   The column percentages _____ (do/do not) change, so there _____ (is/is not) a relationship between these variables. The significance of chi square for this relationship is _____ (less than/ more than) .05, so the relationship between _____ (name of your independent variable) and RELITEN _____ (is/is not) statistically significant. According to Cramer's *V*, this is a _____ (weak/moderate/strong) relationship.

2. *Summarize results for your second independent variable*. Complete the following summary table. On line 1, fill in the blank with the name of your independent variable. On line 2, write in the names of the categories of your independent variable, using as many blanks as necessary. On line 3, fill in the blanks with the percentage who were "strong" on RELITEN for each category of the independent variable.

Lines

1.   RELITEN by _____

2.   _____ _____ _____ _____ _____

3. RELITEN =

    Strong   _____ _____ _____ _____ _____

Significance of chi square = _____

              Cramer's V = _____

The column percentages _____ (do/do not) change, so there _____ (is/is not) a relationship between these variables. The significance of chi square for this relationship is _____ (less than/more than) .05, so the relationship between _____ (name of your independent variable) and RELITEN _____ (is/is not) statistically significant. According to Cramer's V, this is a _____ (weak/moderate/strong) relationship.

3. Do your results support the deprivation theory of religiosity? Explain.

NAME _____

INSTRUCTOR _____

DATE _____

What social factors *other than deprivation* might be causes of religiosity? Select a potential independent variable from the GSS94TAB.SAV data set that does *not* measure deprivation.

1. State and explain an hypothesis about religiosity and your independent variable.

2. Run **Crosstabs** with RELITEN as the row (dependent) variable and your independent variable in the columns. Use Command Block 4.5 as a guide and get column percentages, chi square, and Cramer's *V*. Complete the summary table below. On line 1, fill in the blank with the name of your independent variable. On line 2, write in the names of the categories of your independent variable, using as many blanks as necessary. On line 3, fill in the blanks with the percentage who were "strong" on RELITEN for each category of the independent variable.

   Lines

   1.   RELITEN by _____

   2.   _____ _____ _____ _____ _____

   3. RELITEN =

          Strong   _____ _____ _____ _____ _____

        Significance of chi square = _____

                Cramer's *V* = _____

   The column percentages _____ (do/do not) change, so there _____ (is/is not) a relationship between these variables. The significance of chi square for this relationship is _____ (less than/more than) .05, so the relationship between _____ (name of your independent variable) and RELITEN _____ (is/is not) statistically significant. According to Cramer's *V*, this is a _____ (weak/moderate/strong) relationship.

3. Compare these results with those for deprivation theory as presented in Research Reports 4.2 and 4.3 and Independent Project 4.1. Which theory has more support: yours or deprivation theory? Explain.

(Use the back of this page for additional space)

NAME _____

INSTRUCTOR _____

DATE _____

Test the deprivation theory of religiosity, using the **GSS72.SAV** data set. Use ATTEND as a measure of religiosity and SEX, RACE, and CLASS as independent variables. Run the **Crosstabs** procedure with column percentages, chi square, and Cramer's *V*. Use Command Block 4.5 as a guide.

1. Record the percentage of respondents who were "strong" on RELITEN for each independent variable. Record the significance of chi square and the value of Cramer's *V* in the space provided.

	Percentage "Strong"	Significance (Chi Square)	Strength (Cramer's *V*)
SEX			
Male	____		
Female	____	____	____
RACE			
White	____		
Black	____	____	____
CLASS			
Lower	____		
Working	____		
Middle	____		
Upper	____	____	____

2. For SEX: The column percentages _____ (do/do not) change, so there _____ (is/is not) a relationship between these variables. The significance of chi square is _____ (less than/more than) .05, so the relationship between RACE and POSTLIFE _____ (is/is not) statistically significant. The value of Cramer's *V* for SEX and RELITEN is ____ , so this is a _____ (weak/moderate/strong) relationship.

3. For RACE: The column percentages _____ (do/do not) change, so there _____ (is/is not) a relationship between these variables. The significance of chi square is _____ (less than/more than) .05, so the relationship between RACE and POSTLIFE _____ (is/is not) statistically significant. The value of Cramer's *V* for RACE and RELITEN is ____ , so this is a _____ (weak/moderate/strong) relationship.

4. For CLASS: The column percentages _____ (do/do not) change, so there _____ (is/is not) a relationship between these variables. The significance of chi square is _____ (less than/more than) .05, so the relationship between CLASS and POSTLIFE _____ (is/is not) statistically significant. The value of Cramer's *V* for CLASS and RELITEN is _____ , so this is a _____ (weak/moderate/strong) relationship.

5. Of the three independent variables, which has the most *significant* relationship (lowest value for significance of chi square) with RELITEN? _____ (SEX/RACE/CLASS). Of the three potential independent variables, which has the strongest relationship (highest value for Cramer's *V*) with RELITEN? _____ (SEX/RACE/CLASS).

6. Do these results support the deprivation theory of religiosity? Why, or why not?

Main Points

■ Culture encompasses everything associated with the heritage of a society, including religious values and beliefs. Americans are highly variable in their religious practices and the strength of their religiosity.

■ The deprivation theory, tested in this chapter, proposes that religiosity will be stronger among people who are blocked from achievement in secular society.

■ Relationships between variables can be examined with the Crosstabs procedure. Useful statistics include column percentages to assess the effect of the independent variable, chi square to test for statistical significance, and Cramer's *V* to measure the strength of a relationship.

■ Figure 4.3 lists three questions that should be asked about every bivariate relationship. In general, we concentrate on relationships that are statistically significant and reasonably strong.

SPSS Commands Introduced in This Chapter

COMMAND BLOCK 4.5   *Producing Crosstab Tables with Column Percentages, Chi Square, and Cramer's V*

Click **Statistics** → **Summarize** → **Crosstabs** →
Highlight the name of the dependent variable(s)→
Click the arrow pointing to the **Row(s):** box →
Highlight the name of the independent variable(s)→
Click the arrow pointing to the **Column(s):** box →
Click **Cells** to get the **Cell Display** window →
In the **Percentages** box, choose **Columns** →
Click **Continue** to close this dialog box →
In the **Crosstabs** dialog box, click **Statistics** →
Select **Chi square** and **Cramer's V** →
Click **Continue** →
Click **OK**

Chapter 5

A Controversy in Values: Attitudes about Abortion in 1994

Americans disagree about all sorts of moral, religious, and political issues, but few debates are as intense and as bitter as the controversy surrounding abortion. In this chapter, we will continue our analysis of American values by exploring the responses of the GSS sample to a series of questions about the conditions under which legal abortions should be available. We will also search for causal relationships and see if we can identify some of the reasons why abortion attitudes vary from person to person. The Frequency and Crosstabs procedures and percentage distributions, chi square, and Cramer's *V* will continue to be our primary analytical tools.

Objectivity and Scientific Research

Feelings about abortion are so strong that a word of caution about objectivity and science may be in order before we begin. In the context of scientific research, **objectivity** means that the investigator's personal opinions and values are not allowed to affect his or her procedures or conclusions. Obviously, if objectivity is not maintained, the usefulness of a research project will be compromised.

In reality, it is sometimes difficult for even the most dedicated scientist to achieve complete objectivity, especially when the topic involves emotionally charged issues such as abortion. Social scientists recognize this difficulty and maintain a number of protections against bias and value judgments. For example, before the results of a research project are published in a professional journal, they are critically and anonymously reviewed by colleagues who look for biased or unjustified conclusions, faulty logic, and other problems.

As a student, you will not have the benefit of professional reviews of your thinking as you complete the projects in this chapter. Still, you need to keep the ideal of objectivity in mind and pay close attention to what the data say (not what you wish they would say). Above all, remember that the goal of this chapter is to measure and analyze public opinion on abortion, *not* to resolve the issue or to say which side is right or wrong.

EXERCISE 5.1   **Do Americans Believe That Abortion Should Be a Legal Right?**

The GSS94TAB.SAV data set includes three items that measure attitudes about abortion. The items are listed, along with their SPSS variable names, in Table 5.1. Note that, rather than asking a single, general question (for example, "Do you favor or oppose abortion?"), these three items ask people to react to different circumstances. One advantage of this multi-item format is that it permits researchers to see if attitudes are absolute and unchanging (if people *always* support or oppose abortion regardless of circumstance) or if attitudes are contingent and change as situations change. It may be that people have more than one attitude or set of feelings about abortion and, if so, these complex reactions could only be captured with multiple survey items.

TABLE 5.1 **Three Items Measuring Approval of The Right to a Legal Abortion**

Situation	Variable Name
A legal abortion should be available if:	
1. The woman's health is seriously endangered.	ABHLTH
2. She is married and does not want any more children.	ABNOMORE
3. The woman wants it for any reason.	ABANY

As a first step in the analysis, we can measure the extent to which the sample opposes or supports the right to a legal abortion by running the Frequencies procedure for each variable in Table 5.1. See Command Block 5.1 for the necessary commands and use the output to complete Research Report 5.1. You may want to save or print the output, or you can just copy the relevant information from the screen.

COMMAND BLOCK 5.1

Statistics → Summarize → Frequencies →
Highlight **ABANY** →
Click the arrow pointing to the **Variable(s):** box →
Highlight **ABHLTH** →
Click the arrow pointing to the **Variable(s):** box →
Highlight **ABNOMORE** →
Click the arrow pointing to the **Variable(s):** box →
Click **OK**

NAME _____

INSTRUCTOR _____

DATE _____

1. Record the percentage of respondents who said "yes" to each item:

	Percentage
Item	*Yes*
ABHLTH	_____
ABNOMORE	_____
ABANY	_____

2. Are Americans generally in favor of the legal right to an abortion or generally opposed? Explain.

The patterns presented in Research Report 5.1 suggest that people do change their attitudes about abortion as situations change. The great majority of the sample felt that legal abortion should be available when the mother's health was in danger (ABHLTH), but the other two, more open-ended situations met with much lower levels of support.

Are people consistent and logical in their judgments about these various situations? If they are, then the respondents who approve of the right to a legal abortion in the most permissive circumstance (ABANY) should also approve in the more restrictive circumstances (ABNOMORE and ABHLTH). By the same token, people who oppose the right even when the health of the mother is at stake (ABHLTH) should also oppose it in all less restrictive situations (ABNOMORE and ABANY).

The Structure of Attitudes

EXERCISE 5.2

Is There Consistency in Attitudes about Abortion as a Legal Right?

Explore the structure of abortion attitudes by examining the relationship between ABANY and ABHLTH, the variables that stipulate the most and least permissive situations. Run **Crosstabs** twice, once with ABHLTH as the column variable and ABANY in the rows and once with the positions reversed. Get column percentages for both tables, but don't bother with other statistics. See Command Block 5.2 for the necessary commands:

COMMAND BLOCK 5.2

Click **Statistics** → **Summarize** → **Crosstabs** →
Highlight **ABHLTH** →
Click the arrow pointing to the **Row(s):** box →
Highlight **ABANY** →
Click the arrow pointing to the **Column(s):** box
Click **Cells** →
In the **Percentages** box, select **Columns** →
Click **Continue** →
Click **OK**

Click **Statistics** → **Summarize** → **Crosstabs** →
Highlight **ABANY** →
Click the arrow pointing to the **Row(s):** box →
Highlight **ABHLTH** →
Click the arrow pointing to the **Column(s):** box →
Click **OK**

From the bivariate tables, we can tell what percentage of respondents who say "yes" to ABANY also say "yes" to ABHLTH and what percentage of those who say "no" to ABHLTH also say "no" to ABANY. If people are consistent in their attitudes, these percentages should be high. Use the **Crosstabs** output to complete Research Report 5.2.

NAME _____

INSTRUCTOR _____

DATE _____

1. What percentage of respondents who said "yes" to ABANY also said "yes" to ABHLTH?_____ (Look at the table that has ABANY as the column variable. The percentage you want is in the upper-left cell.)

2. What percentage of respondents who said "no" to ABHLTH also said "no" to ABANY?_____ (Look at the table that has ABHLTH as the column variable. The percentage you want is in the lower-right cell.)

3. Are people consistent in their attitudes? Do people who support a legal right to abortion in the most permissive situation also support the right in other situations? Do people who oppose a legal right to an abortion in the most restricted situation also oppose the right in other situations? Explain.

Summarizing Attitudes about the Right to a Legal Abortion

In Exercise 5.1, we pointed out that having three separate measures of attitudes about abortion allows us to examine how attitudes change as situations change. There is also a disadvantage to having multiple measures: They make it difficult to get a sense of "overall" attitudes or how the sample feels about abortion "in general." Fortunately, SPSS provides a technique, called the *Compute command*, by which we can use the three separate variables to create a summary variable, or an **index**, which will measure these overall feelings.

EXERCISE 5.3

Using the Compute Command to Create an Index

The Compute command uses the scores of existing variables to create new variables. The new variables can then be added to the data set and used just like any other variable. For example, they can be included in the Frequencies or Crosstabs procedures.

The Compute command is extremely flexible and permits all mathematical operations (addition, multiplication, and so on) in the creation of new variables. In the present instance, however, our use of the Compute command will be relatively simple. We will tell SPSS to add the scores of the three abortion items together to create a new variable, which we will then use as an overall measure of people's attitudes. We'll call the new variable ABINDEX, short for ABortion INDEX. We can choose any name for a new variable as long as it is no more than eight characters long and begins with a letter.

Consider the three abortion items. On each, a score of "1" means yes, or approval of a legal right to abortion, and a score of "2" means disapproval. When we add the three variables together, ABINDEX will have a low score of "3" (when a person says "yes" to all three items), and the high score will be "6" ("no" to all three). We can label the score of 3 as "strongly in favor" and the score of 6 as "strongly opposed."

The intermediate score of "4" would be earned when people answered "yes" for any two items and "no" for the third (1 + 1 + 2). The score of "5" would be assigned to anyone who answered "no" to any two items and "yes" to the third (2 + 2 + 1). These intermediate scores can be labeled "moderately in favor" (4) and "moderately opposed" (5). Scores and labels for ABINDEX are presented in Table 5.2. Note the direction of the variable: *higher* scores indicate *greater opposition* to abortion.

TABLE 5.2   **Scores and Labels on ABINDEX**

Score	Label
3	Strongly in favor
4	Moderately in favor
5	Moderately opposed
6	Strongly opposed

The Compute command is accessed from the **Transform** menu. Instructions for computing new variables are given to SPSS in the **Compute Variable** window:

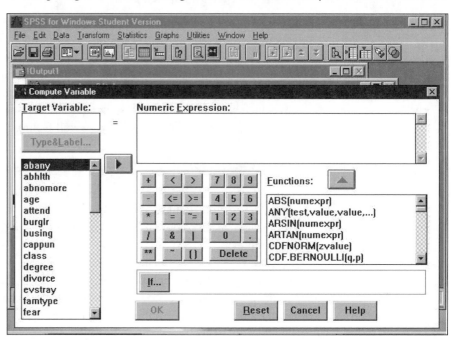

The first step in computing a variable is to give it a name. Do this by typing ABINDEX in the **Target Variable:** box in the upper-left corner of the window. The value of our computed variable (ABINDEX) will be the summation of the three abortion items. We can state this computation as

ABINDEX = ABHLTH + ABNOMORE + ABANY

and we need to create this expression in the **Numeric Expression:** box in the upper-right corner of the **Compute Variable** window. Select (highlight) ABANY from the variable list on the left; click the arrow to transfer the variable to the **Numeric Expression:** window. Click the plus sign (**+**) from the calculator pad in the middle of the screen and then select ABHLTH; click the **+** sign again and repeat this operation for ABNOMORE and then click **OK**. These commands are presented in Command Block 5.3:

COMMAND BLOCK 5.3   Computing an Abortion Attitude Index (ABINDEX)

> Click **Transform** → **Compute** →
> Click **Target Variable:** → type **ABINDEX** →
> Highlight **ABANY** →
> Click the arrow pointing to the **Numerical Expression:** box →
> Click the **+** sign →
> Highlight **ABHLTH** →
> Click the arrow pointing to the **Numerical Expression:** box →
> Click the **+** sign →
> Highlight **ABNOMORE** →
> Click the arrow pointing to the **Numerical Expression:** box →
> Click the **+** sign →
> Click **OK**

When you click **OK**, SPSS computes the new variable and adds it to the data set. You can check to see if the variable has been added by moving to the far right-hand column of the window in which the GSS94TAB.SAV data set is displayed. (See Exercise 1.1 for instructions on how to move around in this window.)

Saving the Data Set with the Computed Variable   At this point, the computed variable ABINDEX is only temporary; if you leave the SPSS program without saving the data set, ABINDEX will disappear. To save the data file with the new variable included, click the **Save Data. . .** option from the **File** menu. Do this now and you will be able to access ABINDEX in the future.

Missing Cases   When computing new variables, SPSS automatically deletes any case that is missing a score on any of the constituent variables. Thus, a respondent who failed to answer *any* of the three abortion items would be omitted from the computations. If cases with missing scores were not eliminated, the scores might not reflect actual opinions. For example, suppose someone said no to ABANY and ABHLTH but did not respond to ABNOMORE. Unless eliminated from the computations, this person would have a score of 4 (2 + 2) on ABINDEX and would look like someone who was "moderately in favor" when the only information we have shows that she or he strongly opposes the legal right to an abortion. Because cases with missing scores are dropped from computations, computed variables typically have fewer cases than any of their constituent variables.

Checking the Computed Variable   It is always a good idea to check computed variables before using them. You can do this with a frequency distribution; the commands are presented in Command Block 5.4:

COMMAND BLOCK 5.4

> Click **Statistics** → **Summarize** → **Frequencies** →
> Highlight **ABINDEX** →
> Click the arrow pointing to **Variable(s):** box →
> Click **OK**

Use the Valid Percent column of this frequency distribution to complete Research Report 5.3.

What Are the Causes of Attitudes about the Right to a Legal Abortion?

Now that we have a sense of attitudes about abortion in the United States, it's time to analyze the sources of these opinions. What might cause support or opposition to the legal right to an abortion? Given the biology of pregnancy and abortion, is it reasonable to suppose that men and women might have different attitudes? Do you suppose that men or women would be more supportive of the legal right to abortion? We will test the relationship between SEX and ABINDEX, and you can follow up by testing the power of other potential independent variables in Exercise 5.5.

EXERCISE 5.4   **Testing the Relationship between ABINDEX and SEX**

Follow the commands in Command Block 5.5 to run the Crosstabs procedure, with percentages and statistics, to produce a table with ABINDEX as the dependent variable and SEX as the independent variable.

COMMAND BLOCK 5.5

> Click **Statistics** → **Summarize** → **Crosstabs** →
> Highlight **ABINDEX** →
> Click the arrow pointing to the **Row(s):** box →
> Highlight **SEX** →
> Click the arrow pointing to the **Column(s):** box →
> Click **Cells** →
> In the **Percentages** box, select **Columns** →
> Click **Continue** →
> In the **Crosstabs** dialog box, click **Statistics** →
> Select **Chi square** and **Cramer's V** →
> Click **Continue** →
> Click **OK**

The output will look like that shown in Figure 5.1.

NAME _____

INSTRUCTOR _____

DATE _____

1. What percentage of the sample is:

Label	Score	Percentage
Strongly in favor	3	_____
Moderately in favor	4	_____
Moderately opposed	5	_____
Strongly opposed	6	_____

2. Summarize these results. Compare them with the earlier discussion of the complexity and "situation-specific" nature of attitudes. Can the sample be characterized as generally "in favor of" or generally "opposed to" the legal right to an abortion? Why?

FIGURE 5.1   **Crosstabs Output for ABINDEX and SEX**

```
ABINDEX  by  SEX  RESPONDENTS SEX

                      SEX              Page 1 of 1
            Count
            Col Pct | MALE     FEMALE
                    |                    Row
                    |   1        2      Total
ABINDEX    ---------+-------------------
            3.00    |  180      222      402
                    | 43.9     42.5     43.1
                    |
            4.00    |   46       50       96
                    | 11.2      9.6     10.3
                    |
            5.00    |  149      203      352
                    | 36.3     38.9     37.8
                    |
            5.00    |  149      203      352
                    | 36.3     38.9     37.8
                    |
            6.00    |   35       47       82
                    |  8.5      9.0      8.8
                    |
            Column     410      522      932
            Total     44.0     56.0    100.0
```

Chi-Square	Value	DF	Significance
Pearson	1.15233	3	.76446
Likelihood Ratio	1.15030	3	.76495
Mantel-Haenszel test for linear association	.47194	1	.49210

Minimum Expected Frequency -   36.073

Statistic	Value	ASE1	Val/ASE0	Approximate Significance
Phi	.03516			.76446 *1
Cramer's V	.03516			.76446 *1

*1 Pearson chi-square probability

Number of Missing Observations: 554

It might seem like common sense to suppose that men and women will hold different opinions about abortion, but the bivariate table shows that this is not the case. If you compare the responses for men with those for women (compare the male column with the female column for each row of the table), you will see that the two sexes are virtually identical in their attitudes on this issue. That is, for each row (score on ABINDEX), there is hardly a difference in the percentage of men and women who hold that position.

The value for the significance of chi square (.77, which is much greater than .05) tells us that the small differences between men and women in the table are trivial and the results of random chance. The conclusion that there is no relationship between SEX and ABINDEX is further reinforced by the minuscule value for Cramer's V (.04). Thus, sex and attitudes on abortion are not related, and sex is not an important cause of abortion attitudes. The reasons attitudes vary on this issue must be sought in an area other than simple biology.

EXERCISE 5.5   **Testing Hypotheses about Support for Legal Abortion**

What other factors might shape attitudes about abortion? Use your textbook or other course materials, if relevant, to help you select two potential independent variables and develop hypotheses about the cause of attitudes about abortion. Make sure that variables permitting you to test your ideas are available in the GSS94TAB.SAV data set. Some variables you might consider include religious denomination (RELIG) and religiosity (RELITEN or ATTEND). Also, because abortion has been a prominent political issue for years, difference in attitudes might exist among liberals, moderates, and conservatives (POLVIEWS). What about the effect of level of education (DEGREE) or social class (CLASS)?

After you have developed hypotheses and identified your independent variables, use Command Block 5.5 to produce bivariate tables. Substitute the names of your independent variables for SEX and transfer them both to the Column(s) box. Use the tables to complete Research Report 5.4.

Main Points

■ Attitudes about abortion comprise one of the most intense and divisive differences in cultural values among Americans. When analyzing such emotionally charged issues, social scientists need to be especially careful to maintain objectivity.

■ We examined the degree of opposition and support for the right to a legal abortion and the structure of abortion attitudes.

■ With the Compute command, new variables can be created from the scores of variables already in the data set. We created an index (ABINDEX) to measure overall feelings about abortion.

■ A number of hypotheses were tested about the causes of attitudes about abortion.

SPSS Commands Introduced in This Chapter

COMMAND BLOCK 5.3   *Computing an Index or Summary Variable*

Click **Transform** → **Compute** →
Click **Target Variable:** →
Type a name for the new variable →
Use existing variables and mathematical procedures to state an
expression that defines the new variable in the Numerical
Expression: box →
Click **OK** →
Save the data file

NAME _____

INSTRUCTOR _____

DATE _____

State and briefly explain your hypotheses.

1. Name your first independent variable:_____ . State a hypothesis linking this variable to ABINDEX. Which category of this variable will be most in favor of the legal right to abortion? _____ Why?

2. Name your second independent variable:_____ . State an hypothesis linking this variable to ABINDEX. Which category of this variable will be most in favor of the legal right to abortion? _____ Why?

Summarize your results.

3. *For your first independent variable:* On line 1 of the following summary table, fill in the blank with the name of your independent variable. On line 2, write in the names of the categories of your independent variable, using as many blanks as necessary. On line 3, fill in the blanks with the percentage "strongly in favor" (a score of 3) for each category of the independent variable.

   Lines

   1. ABINDEX by _____

   2. _____ _____ _____ _____ _____

   3. % Strongly in Favor _____ _____ _____ _____ _____

The column percentages _____ (do/do not) change, so there _____ (is/is not) a relationship between these variables. The significance of chi square for this relationship is _____ (less than/more than) .05, so this relationship _____ (is/is not) statistically significant. The value of Cramer's V is _____, so this is a _____ (weak/moderate/strong) relationship.

4. *For your second independent variable:* On line 1 of the following summary table, fill in the blank with the name of your independent variable. On line 2, write in the names of the categories of your independent variable, using as many blanks as necessary. On line 3, fill in the blanks with the percentage "strongly in favor" (a score of 3) for each category of the independent variable.

Lines

1.   ABINDEX by _____

2.   _____ _____ _____ _____ _____

3. % Strongly in Favor   _____ _____ _____ _____ _____

The column percentages _____ (do/do not) change, so there _____ (is/is not) a relationship between these variables. The significance of chi square for this relationship is _____ (less than/more than) .05, so this relationship _____ (is/is not) statistically significant. The value of Cramer's V is ____, so this is a _____ (weak/moderate/strong) relationship.

5. Were your hypotheses confirmed? Why, or why not?

NAME _____

INSTRUCTOR _____

DATE _____

What other variables might be related to attitudes on abortion? Choose two more potential independent variables from the GSS94TAB.SAV data set. Use Command Block 5.5 to produce bivariate tables for ABINDEX and each of the two new independent variables you choose. Substitute the names of your independent variables for SEX and transfer them both to the Column(s) box.

1. Name your first independent variable: _____ . State a hypothesis linking this variable to ABINDEX. Which category of this variable will be most in favor of the legal right to abortion? _____ Why?

2. Name your second independent variable: _____ . State a hypothesis linking this variable to ABINDEX. Which category of this variable will be most in favor of the legal right to abortion?_____ Why?

Summarize your results.

3. *For your first independent variable:* On line 1 of the following summary table, fill in the blank with the name of your independent variable. On line 2, write in the names of the categories of your independent variable, using as many blanks as necessary. On line 3, fill in the blanks with the percentage "strongly in favor" (a score of 3) for each category of the independent variable.

Lines

1.   ABINDEX by _____

2.   _____ _____ _____ _____ _____

3. % Strongly in Favor _____ _____ _____ _____ _____

(Independent Project continues)

The column percentages _____ (do/do not) change, so there

_____ (is/is not) a relationship between these variables.

The significance of chi square for this relationship is _____

(less than/more than) .05, so this relationship _____ (is/is

not) statistically significant. The value of Cramer's V is _____, so this

is a _____ (weak/moderate/strong) relationship.

4. *For your second independent variable:* On line 1 of the following summary table, fill in the blank with the name of your independent variable. On line 2, write in the names of the categories of your independent variable, using as many blanks as necessary. On line 3, fill in the blanks with the percentage "strongly in favor" (a score of 3) for each category of the independent variable.

Lines

1.   ABINDEX by _____

2.   _____ _____ _____ _____ _____

3. % Strongly in Favor _____ _____ _____ _____ _____

The column percentages _____ (do/do not) change, so there

_____ (is/is not) a relationship between these variables. The

significance of chi square for this relationship is _____

(less than/more than) .05, so this relationship _____ (is/is

not) statistically significant. The value of Cramer's V is _____ , so this

is a _____ (weak/moderate/strong) relationship.

5. Were your hypotheses confirmed? Why, or why not?

NAME _____

INSTRUCTOR _____

DATE _____

The GSS72.SAV data set includes two of the three abortion items used in this chapter (ABHLTH and ABNOMORE). Load this data set and run the **Frequencies** distribution for each of these variables. Use the Valid Percents column to complete this report.

1. What percentage of respondents said "yes" to each item in 1972?

	Percentage
Item	*Yes*
ABHLTH	_____
ABNOMORE	_____

2. Compare these percentages to those that you produced in Research Report 5.1. Has the nation grown more pro- or more anti-abortion? Describe the extent of the change.

COMPARATIVE ANALYSIS 5.2

HAVE THE CAUSES OF ATTITUDES ABOUT ABORTION CHANGED OVER TIME?

NAME _____

INSTRUCTOR _____

DATE _____

Choose an independent variable from those you used for Research Report 5.4 or Independent Project 5.1. All other things being equal, choose the independent variable that had the strongest, more significant relationship with ABINDEX. From the GSS72.SAV data file, choose *either* ABHLTH or ABNOMORE as a measure of attitude about abortion and use the **Crosstabs** procedure to test the relationship for strength and significance. See Command Block 5.5 for guidance.

1. Summarize your results. On line 1 of the following summary table, fill in the blanks with the names of your independent and dependent variables. On line 2, write in the names of the categories of your independent variable, using as many blanks as necessary. On line 3, fill in the blanks with the percentage who supported the right to a legal abortion ("yes") for each category of the independent variable.

Lines

1. _____ by _____

2. _____ _____ _____ _____ _____

3. % Yes _____ _____ _____ _____ _____

The column percentages _____ (do/do not) change, so there _____ (is/is not) a relationship between these variables. The significance of chi square for this relationship is _____ (less than/more than) .05, so this relationship _____ (is/is not) statistically significant. The value of Cramer's V is _____ , so this is a _____ (weak/ moderate/strong) relationship.

2. Are these results consistent with the hypothesis you stated earlier between your independent variable and support of the right to a legal abortion? Explain.

Chapter 6   Socialization: What Kinds of Children Do Americans Want?

In this chapter, we focus on **socialization**: the process by which people learn the culture of their society. Several aspects of this complex, lifelong process are considered. First, we'll examine what people say when they are asked to describe the "ideal child." These responses will identify some of the values and ideals that shape the process of growing up in the United States. Second, we'll examine spanking as a form of punishment in the United States. Is there any relationship between what people say they desire in the "ideal child" and the techniques they use to discipline their children? What other factors are associated with support for spanking? Along the way, some new techniques for analyzing bivariate relationships will be introduced.

Before beginning, a (probably obvious) point needs to be made: The items we will analyze reflect the personality traits people *say* they want in their children, and there are some sharp limitations on the conclusions that can be reached. On one hand, we have no way of knowing (from the GSS, at least) if people actually live by these ideals and successfully produce children with the desired traits. On the other hand, even expectations and ideals will affect socialization, parenting styles, and personality development.

What Do Americans Want in Children?

The respondents to the 1994 General Social Survey were asked to rank order five qualities in children from most to least important. The actual wording and the percentage of the full 1994 sample (*not* the smaller data set included with this text), which ranked each item first, are presented in Table 6.1.

TABLE 6.1   **Ideal Qualities for Children, Full 1994 GSS Sample**

Quality	Percentage Ranking the Quality First
To think for himself or herself	53
To obey	18
To work hard	15
To help others when they need help	13
To be well-liked or popular	<1

As you can see, "to think for himself or herself" was ranked first by a much higher percentage of the sample than any other value. Three ideals—to obey, to work hard, and to help others—are ranked first by smaller but roughly equal percentages, and popularity was ranked first by less than 1% of the respondents. These results suggest that there is some consensus in U.S. society about the "ideal child."

Unfortunately, there is not enough space in the data set supplied with this workbook to include all five of the variables in Table 6.1. Instead, we'll use a single item (OBEYTHNK), which captures the more detailed rankings presented above, even though it uses slightly different wording. On this item, respondents were asked to choose between "to think for themselves" and "to be obedient"—the two top ranked ideals in Table 6.1—as the most important trait in a child.

The responses of the full 1994 GSS sample to OBEYTHNK were comparable to the five-item ranking in Table 6.1. More than twice as many respondents selected "to think for themselves" (69%) as "to be obedient" (31%). (For both ideals, percentages are higher for the single item because fewer choices were available to respondents.) These results reinforce our earlier conclusion that some consensus about the most desirable traits in children exists in U.S. society.

EXERCISE 6.1   **Why Do Socialization Values Vary?**

What independent variables might explain why some people choose "to think for themselves" while others choose "to be obedient"? One possible causal factor is social class or, more specifically, the jobs associated with the different social classes (Kohn, 1959, 1969, 1983; Kohn, Slimczynski, & Schooler, 1986). People in the higher social classes tend to be in occupations that stress individual initiative and motivation. These jobs are not highly supervised, and success is correlated with the ability to work (and think) independently.

Lower-status occupations, on the other hand, tend to stress conformity to the work routine (obedience). Blue-collar and manual labor jobs tend to be regimented and routinized, and success is associated with following established rules.

Based on this reasoning, an hypothesis linking social class and socialization would be: Child rearing reflects everyday work experiences, and people from different classes will stress different personality characteristics in their children. People from the middle and upper social classes will more often choose "to think for themselves," whereas those from the working and lower classes will more commonly choose "to be obedient." We can use the Crosstabs procedure, with column percentages, chi square, and Cramer's *V*, to test this hypothesis. Command Block 6.1 lists the necessary commands. The dependent variable is OBEYTHNK and the independent variable is social class (CLASS).

COMMAND BLOCK 6.1

Click **Statistics** → **Summarize** → **Crosstabs** →
Highlight **OBEYTHNK** →
Click the arrow pointing to the **Row(s):** box →
Highlight **CLASS** →
Click the arrow pointing to the **Column(s):** box →
Click **Cells** →
Click **Columns** in the **Percentages** box
Click **Continue** →
Click **Statistics** →
Select **Chi square** and **Cramer's V** →
Click **Continue** →
Click **OK**

The bivariate table is presented in Figure 6.1. Comparing the percentages from column to column, we can see that the hypothesis is generally supported. While over half of the lower-class and one-third of the working-class respondents chose "to be obedient," only 25% of the middle-class and 29% of the upper-class respondents did likewise. On the other hand, the majority of respondents of all classes except the lower class chose "to think for themselves." This is consistent with the fact that the sample chose independent thinking over obedience by a 2 to 1 margin and perhaps reflects changes in the workplace associated with a post-industrial, information-based economy.

FIGURE 6.1   **Output of Crosstabs Procedure for OBEYTHNK and CLASS**

```
OBEYTHNK   SHOULD CHLDRN BE OBEDIENT OR THINK FOR S
by  CLASS   SUBJECTIVE CLASS IDENTIFICATION

                      CLASS                               Page 1 of 1
              Count
              Col Pct |LOWER CL WORKING  MIDDLE C UPPER CL
                      |ASS       CLASS   LASS     ASS       Row
                      |   1        2       3        4      Total
OBEYTHNK      --------
           1  |    34      201     146      12       393
TO BE OBEDIENT|  54.8     33.1    25.6    28.6      30.7

           2  |    28      406     424      30       888
TO THINK FOR THE| 45.2     66.9    74.4    71.4      69.3

         Column     62      607     570      42      1281
         Total      4.8     47.4    44.5     3.3     100.0

     Chi-Square            Value          DF         Significance
-----------------------    ----------     ----       ------------

Pearson                    25.67174        3             .00001
Likelihood Ratio           24.36885        3             .00002
Mantel-Haenszel test for   18.57584        1             .00002
    linear association

Minimum Expected Frequency -   12.885


                                                       Approximate
      Statistic           Value      ASE1    Val/ASE0  Significance
-----------------------   --------- -------- --------  ------------

Phi                         .14156                       .00001  *1
Cramer's V                  .14156                       .00001  *1
```

Chi square (significance = .00001) shows that the relationship between social class and desired trait in children is statistically significant. That is, the probability that the patterns in the table were caused by random chance is small (less than .05, or 1 out of 20), and the relationship between OBEYTHNK and CLASS in the sample almost certainly reflects relationships in the population. Cramer's V is only moderate in strength (because independent thinking was so popular at all class levels) but does indicate that the variables are related.

EXERCISE 6.2

A Further Test of the Hypothesis: Social Class Is a Cause of Socialization Ideals

A concept like social class is fairly general and could be measured or operationalized (see Chapter 2) with variables other than CLASS. In the GSS94TAB.SAV data set, find another variable that measures social class and repeat the analysis of OBEYTHNK in Exercise 6.1. Use Command Block 6.1 as a guide and run **Crosstabs** with the measure of social class you selected as the column variable and OBEYTHNK as the row variable. Don't forget column percentages, chi square, and Cramer's V. Use the output to complete Research Report 6.1.

RESEARCH REPORT 6.1

IS THERE A RELATIONSHIP BETWEEN SOCIAL CLASS AND SOCIALIZATION IDEALS?

NAME _____

INSTRUCTOR _____

DATE _____

1. Name of the variable you selected to measure social class: _____ .

2. *Summarize your results.* On line 1 of the following summary table, fill in the blank with the name of your independent variable. On line 2, write in the names of the categories of your independent variable, using as many blanks as necessary. On line 3, fill in the blanks with the percentage who chose "to think for themselves" for each category of the independent variable.

   Lines

   1.   OBEYTHINK by _____

   2.   _____ _____ _____ _____ _____

   3. % Think for
      Themselves   _____ _____ _____ _____ _____

   The column percentages _____ (do/do not) change, so there

   _____ (is/is not) a relationship between these variables. The

   significance of chi square is _____ (less than/more than) .05,

   so this relationship _____ (is/is not) statistically significant.

   The value of Cramer's V is _____ , so this is a _____

   (weak/moderate/strong) relationship.

3. Was the hypothesis confirmed? Explain.

EXERCISE 6.3   **What Other Factors Might Affect the Qualities People Desire in Children?**

Besides social class, what other characteristics or experiences might affect how people think about desirable qualities in children? Are there potential independent variables in the GSS94TAB.SAV data set that might have a stronger relationship with OBEYTHNK than social class? If relevant, consult your textbook or other course materials for ideas about possible causes of opinions about the qualities children should possess. (Make sure that your causal variable is included in the GSS94TAB.SAV data set.) Otherwise, consider age, political ideology, religion, or some other variable as a possible independent variable.

However you do it, select a new independent variable and state a hypothesis that links the variable to OBEYTHNK. Using Command Block 6.1 as a guide, test your hypothesis with the Crosstabs procedure. Substitute the name of the new independent variable for CLASS and be sure to get column percentages, chi square, and Cramer's *V*. Use the results to complete Research Report 6.2.

NAME _____

INSTRUCTOR _____

DATE _____

1. What is the name of your independent variable?_____

2. State and briefly explain your hypothesis.

3. *Summarize your results*. On line 1 of the following summary table
   in the blank with the name of your independent variable. On line 2
   write in the names of the categories of your independent variable,
   using as many blanks as necessary. On line 3, fill in the blanks wit
   the percentage who chose "to think for themselves" for each categ
   of the independent variable.

   Lines

   1.   OBEYTHINK by _____

   2.   _____ _____ _____ _____ __

   3. % Think for
      Themselves   _____ _____ _____ _____ __

   The column percentages _____(do/do not) change, so t
   _____ (is/is not) a relationship between these variables.
   significance of chi square is _____ (less than/more than)
   so this relationship _____(is/is not) statistically significa
   The value of Cramer's V is _____, so this is a _____
   (weak/moderate/strong) relationship.

4. Was your hypothesis supported? Explain.

5. Compare your results with the earlier attempt to link OBEYTHNK
   social class. Which relationship was the most significant? (See the
   significance of chi square.) Which was the *strongest*? (See Cramer
   V.) Which hypothesis has the most support? Explain.

EXERCISE 6.4   **To Spank or Not to Spank?**

Is spanking regarded as a legitimate or necessary form of discipline in our society? According to the General Social Survey for 1994, the answer is yes: Over 70% of the full sample agreed or strongly agreed with the statement that it is "sometimes necessary to discipline a child with a good hard spanking."

What factors might account for why people do or do not support the use of corporal punishment? One possibility is that support for spanking is linked to desired qualities in children. Do people who want obedient children support spanking more than those who want children who think independently? Is spanking used to enforce obedience?

Test this idea with Crosstabs, using Command Block 6.1 as a guide. SPANKING is the dependent variable and should be the row variable; OBEYTHNK, as the independent variable, should go in the columns. (Note that the role of OBEYTHNK has changed: In previous exercises, it was the dependent variable. Most variables could be either cause or effect, depending on the logic of the hypothesis.) Record and analyze your results in Research Report 6.3.

RESEARCH REPORT 6.3

IS SUPPORT FOR SPANKING RELATED TO DESIRED QUALITIES IN CHILDREN?

NAME _____

INSTRUCTOR _____

DATE _____

1. Complete the following table by filling in the cells with column percentages.

SPANKING by OBEYTHNK

Support for Spanking	Socialization Ideal	
	Obey	Think
Agree	_____ %	_____%
Disagree	_____%	_____%
Total	100%	100%

2. The column percentages _____ (do/do not) change, so there _____ (is/is not) a relationship between these variables. The significance of chi square is _____ (less than/more than) .05, so this relationship _____ (is/is not) statistically significant. The value of Cramer's V is _____, so this is a _____ (weak/moderate/strong) relationship.

3. Is support for spanking linked to desire for obedience? Explain.

EXERCISE 6.5   **Other Causes of Support for SPANKING**

What other factors might be a cause of support for spanking? What experiences or characteristics might be related to this variable? State a hypothesis (with SPANKING as the dependent variable) that can be tested using the GSS94TAB.SAV data set. If relevant, use your textbook or other course materials to help you identify possible causes of support for spanking. Using Command Block 6.1 as a guide, run **Crosstabs** with SPANKING as the row variable and your selected independent variable in the columns. Use the output to complete Research Report 6.4.

NAME _____

INSTRUCTOR _____

DATE _____

1. What is the name of your independent variable?_____

2. State and briefly explain your hypothesis.

3. *Summarize your results.* On line 1 of the following summary table
   in the blank with the name of your independent variable. On line 2
   write in the names of the categories of your independent variable,
   using as many blanks as necessary. On line 3, fill in the blanks wit
   the percentage who "strongly agree" that spanking is necessary for
   each category of the independent variable.

   Lines

   1.   SPANKING by _____

   2.   _____ _____ _____ _____ ____

   3. % Strongly
      Agree   _____ _____ _____ _____ ____

   The column percentages _____ (do/do not) change, so t

   _____ (is/is not) a relationship between these variables

   The significance of chi square is_____ (less than/more

   than) .05, so this relationship_____ (is/is not) statistica

   significant. The value of Cramer's *V* is _____ , so this is a _____

   (weak/moderate/strong) relationship.

4. Was your hypothesis supported? Explain.

The Direction of Relationships

Up to this point, Cramer's *V* has been used to characterize the *strength* of the association between two variables. Some bivariate relationships can also be analyzed in terms of the *direction* of the relationship. That is, we can determine whether one variable increases or decreases when the other variable changes values. Relationships between variables can be either *positive* (when the variables change in the *same* direction) or *negative* (when they change in *opposite* directions).

For example, a positive relationship is often found between education and income: The variables change in the same direction, and income increases as education increases—the greater the years of education, the higher the income. In contrast, a negative relationship is usually found between education and racial prejudice: As education increases, racial prejudice decreases—the greater the years of education, the lower the prejudice.

Under what conditions can we analyze the direction of a relationship as well as its strength? Bivariate relationships have a direction *only* when *both* variables are numerical. If *either* variable has scores that are only labels (like SEX or RACE), the relationship cannot have a direction. Scores for non-numerical variables are arbitrary codes (for example, 1 for males, 2 for females). Though the scores are different from each other, they are not "less than" or "greater than" each other. Because these scores cannot be rank ordered or treated mathematically, they cannot be characterized in terms of direction.

When we are dealing with two numerical variables, we can use a new type of measure of association rather than Cramer's *V* to help us understand the association. These new measures will give us two pieces of information: they will indicate not only the strength of the relationship (like Cramer's *V*) but also its direction.

SPSS can produce a variety of measures of association for numerical variables, but we will use only **gamma**: a measure of association that varies from −1.00 to +1.00.[1] The closer the value of gamma to either plus or minus 1, the stronger the relationship and, as was the case with Cramer's *V*, values close to zero indicate weak relationships. The sign of the gamma tells us whether the overall relationship is positive or negative. Direction and strength are independent of each other, and a bivariate association may be weak and negative, positive and strong, positive and weak, and so forth.

Figure 4.3 presented three questions that should always be asked about bivariate relationships. Now, we can add to this list of questions, at least for relationships in which both variables are numerical. Figure 6.2 presents the revised list of questions. Both questions 3 and 4 can be answered with gamma.

---

1 The decision to focus on gamma is arbitrary, and some instructors may wish to substitute another measure of association in its place. In general, however, all measures of association designed for numerical variables in tabular format will produce broadly similar values in terms of the direction and strength (weak, moderate, strong) of a relationship.

FIGURE 6.2   **Assessing the Strength, Significance, and Direction of a Bivariate Relationship**

1. Do the column percentages change?
2. Is the relationship statistically significant? (Is the significance of chi

3. How strong is the relationship?
4. What is the direction of the relationship?

EXERCISE 6.6   **Support for Spanking and Social Class: Interpreting Gamma**

Let's illustrate the use and interpretation of gamma by examining the relationship between SPANKING and CLASS. Does support for spanking vary by social class? As shown in Command Block 6.2, you can add gamma to the output for bivariate tables by simply clicking on the appropriate box when choosing statistics.

COMMAND BLOCK 6.2   Producing Crosstab Tables with Column Percentages, Chi Square, and Gamma

> Click **Statistics → Summarize → Crosstabs →**
> Highlight **SPANKING →**
> Click the arrow pointing to the **Row(s):** box →
> Highlight **CLASS →**
> Click the arrow pointing to the **Column(s):** box →
> Click **Cells →**
> Click **Columns** in the **Percentages** box →
> Click **Continue** to close this dialog box →
> In the Crosstabs dialog box, click **Statistics →**
> Select **Chi square** and **Gamma →**
> Click **Continue →**
> Click **OK**

The output from this procedure is presented in Figure 6.3.

FIGURE 6.3   **Output of Crosstabs Procedure for SPANKING and CLASS**

```
SPANKING   spanking to discipline child?
by  CLASS  SUBJECTIVE CLASS IDENTIFICATION

               CLASS                                Page 1 of 1
          Count
          Col Pct |LOWER CL WORKING  MIDDLE C UPPER CL
                  |ASS       CLASS    LASS     ASS        Row
                  |    1        2        3        4       Total
SPANKING  ───────
          1.00  |   35       343      285       23        686
   Agree        |  77.8      76.6     65.5     63.9       71.2

          2.00  |   10       105      150       13        278
   Disagree     |  22.2      23.4     34.5     36.1       28.8

          Column    45       448      435       36        964
          Total    4.7      46.5     45.1      3.7       100.0


       Chi-Square              Value        DF        Significance
  --------------------      ----------      ----      ------------

Pearson                     15.00872         3           .00181
Likelihood Ratio            15.05547         3           .00177
Mantel-Haenszel test for    12.98276         1           .00031
   linear association

Minimum Expected Frequency -   10.382


       Statistic             Value       ASE1     Val/ASE0
  --------------------      ---------   --------  --------



Gamma                         .23985     .06116   3.81934


Number of Missing Observations:  522
```

Gamma is reported below chi square in the column labeled "Value." If the relationship is positive, gamma will have no sign (a plus sign is understood). If the relationship is negative, the value of gamma will be preceded by a minus sign.

In the case of the relationship between SPANKING and CLASS, gamma has a value of .24, which indicates a positive relationship of moderate strength. As scores on CLASS increase (as we move from left to right across the table), scores on SPANKING also increase (moving from the top to the bottom of the table). Note that on SPANKING higher scores mean greater *dis*agreement with the statement that "spanking is sometimes necessary." We can express the positive direction of this relationship by saying: As class increases, disapproval of spanking also increases.

We need to deal with one more issue. A positive gamma tells us that the *scores* of the two variables change in the same direction. Sometimes, however, the numerical coding of variables is arbitrary, and higher scores could indicate *either* greater or lesser amounts of the variable.

For example, SPANKING is coded so that higher scores indicate greater disapproval of spanking. We interpreted the positive sign of gamma to mean that "as class increases, disapproval of spanking increases." However (this is the tricky part), we could also say that "as class increases, approval of spanking decreases," thus characterizing the relationship as negative. Both characterizations are correct. Remember that gamma tells us how the scores of the variables are related, and we will always have to examine the meanings of the scores to be sure that we are interpreting the relationship correctly.

EXERCISE 6.7

An Additional Test for a Relationship Between Social Class and SPANKING

Now it's your turn to interpret gamma. Choose either DEGREE, INCOME, or PRESTIGE as a measure of social class. The scores of all three of these potential independent variables are numerical, so gamma is an appropriate measure of association. Using Command Block 6.2 as a guide, run the **Crosstabs** procedure with SPANKING in the rows and your choice of independent variable in the columns. Use the output to complete Research Report 6.5.

Main Points

- Socialization is affected by the ideals and values of the culture, the techniques of discipline that are used, and many other factors.

- Several hypotheses about the desired traits in children and support for spanking were tested.

- Bivariate relationships in which *both* variables are numerical have direction as well as strength. Gamma is one of several measures of association that are appropriate in this research situation.

SPSS Commands Introduced in This Chapter

COMMAND BLOCK 6.2   *Producing a Crosstab Table with Column Percentages, Chi Square, and Gamma*

Click **Statistics** → **Summarize** → **Crosstabs** →
Highlight the name of the dependent variable →
Click the arrow pointing to the **Row(s):** box →
Highlight the name of the independent variable →
Click the arrow pointing to the **Column(s):** box →
Click **Cells** →
Click **Columns** in the **Percentages** box →
Click **Continue** to close this dialog box →
In the Crosstabs dialog box, click **Statistics** →
Select **Chi square** and **Gamma** →
Click **Continue** →
Click **OK**

NAME _____

INSTRUCTOR _____

DATE _____

1. What is the name of your independent variable? _____

2. *Summarize your results*. On line 1 of the following summary table, fill in the blank with the name of your independent variable. On line 2, write in the names of the categories of your independent variable, using as many blanks as necessary. On line 3, fill in the blanks with the percentage who "strongly agree" that spanking is necessary for each category of the independent variable.

Lines

1. SPANKING by _____

2. _____ _____ _____ _____ _____

3. % Strongly
    Agree _____ _____ _____ _____ _____

The column percentages _____ (do/do not) change, so there _____ (is/is not) a relationship between these variables. The significance of chi square is _____ (less than/more than) .05, so this relationship _____ (is/is not) statistically significant. The value of gamma is _____, so this is a _____ (weak/moderate/strong) relationship. The sign of gamma indicates that this is a _____ (positive/negative) relationship. As the independent variable increases, disapproval of spanking _____ (increases/decreases).

3. Which is the more important cause of support for spanking: the independent variable you selected for this research report or CLASS (see Exercise 6.6)? Which relationship is most significant? Strongest? Are both relationships in the same direction?

NAME _____

INSTRUCTOR _____

DATE _____

Test the hypothesis that approval of spanking reflects traditional or "old-fashioned" child-rearing practices and traditional cultural values. Use POLVIEWS (political ideology) or RELITEN (strength of religious beliefs) as the independent variable and SPANKING as the dependent. (If you have already used one of these as an independent variable in Research Report 6.4, use the other.) Use **Crosstabs** with column percentages, chi square, and gamma to test the hypothesis.

1. Which variable did you select to measure "old-fashioned" or traditional values?_____. Justify your choice in terms of validity (see Chapter 2). Which variable more closely fits your idea of "old-fashioned" or "traditional"?

2. *Summarize your results*. On line 1 of the following summary table, fill in the blank with the name of your independent variable. On line 2, write in the names of the categories of your independent variable, using as many blanks as necessary. On line 3, fill in the blanks with the percentage who "strongly agree" that spanking is necessary for each category of the independent variable.

   Lines

   1.   SPANKING by_____

   2.   _____ _____ _____ _____ _____

   3. % Strongly
      Agree   _____ _____ _____ _____ _____

   The column percentages _____ (do/do not) change, so

   there _____ (is/is not) a relationship between these vari-

   ables. The significance of chi square is _____ (less

   than/more than) .05, so this relationship _____ (is/is not)

   statistically significant. The value of gamma is_____, so this is a

   _____ (weak/moderate/strong) relationship. The sign of

gamma indicates that this is a _____ (positive/negative) relationship. As the independent variable increases, disapproval of spanking _____ (increases/decreases).

3. Was the hypothesis confirmed? Explain.

NAME _____

INSTRUCTOR _____

DATE _____

Develop and state your own hypothesis about the causes of support for spanking, using your textbook or other course materials if relevant. Run **Crosstabs** with your independent variable in the columns and SPANKING in the rows. Follow Command Block 6.2, but choose *either* gamma or Cramer's *V*. Look at the scores of your independent variable (click **Utilities** on the menu bar to get variable information or consult Appendix A) and decide if they are merely labels (like the scores of SEX) or are numerical. If the scores are not numerical, get Cramer's *V*. If the scores are numerical, get gamma.

1. What is the name of your independent variable?_____

2. State and explain your hypothesis.

3. *Summarize your results*. On line 1 of the following summary table, fill in the blank with the name of your independent variable. On line 2, write in the names of the categories of your independent variable, using as many blanks as necessary. On line 3, fill in the blanks with the percentage who "strongly agree" that spanking is necessary for each category of the independent variable.

Lines

1.　　　　　　　SPANKING by _____

2.　　　　　　　_____ _____ _____ _____ _____

3. % Strongly
   Agree　　　　_____ _____ _____ _____ _____

The column percentages _____ (do/do not) change, so there _____ (is/is not) a relationship between these variables.

The significance of chi square is _____ (less than/more than) .05, so this relationship _____ (is/is not) statistically significant. The value of _____ (Cramer's *V*/gamma) is _____, so this is a _____ (weak/moderate/strong) relationship. *If you are using gamma*: The sign of gamma indicates that this is

(Independent Project continues)

a _____ (positive/negative) relationship. As the independent variable increases, disapproval of spanking _____ (increases/decreases).

4. Was the hypothesis confirmed? Explain.

Chapter 7   Crime, Fear, and Punishment

In this chapter, you will use your research tools and computer skills to answer some questions about crime in the United States: Who is most likely to become a victim of crime? Who is most fearful of crime? Who is most supportive of the death penalty, the ultimate punishment available? The first two of these questions will be the subjects of the chapter research reports, and the third question will be the basis for some independent projects. This chapter will also introduce multivariate analysis, a research technique that allows us to examine relationships between more than two variables.

Defining Crime

Our options for researching crime are limited because the 1994 GSS included only a few relevant items. Of these, only one has been included in the GSS94TAB.SAV data set: a question that asks people if they have been the victims of burglary during the past year (BURGLR). Unfortunately, this item is less than ideal because it was given to only half of the respondents. Thus, you will be working with a relatively small sample in these exercises.

Before beginning the analysis, we need to consider crime in general and burglary in particular. Burglary, like rape and assault, falls into the category of "street crimes" or criminal activities that have obvious victims and result in clear, easily measurable injury or loss. Actually, crime in the United States encompasses activities in addition to street crime, including so-called victimless crimes (for example, prostitution and sale of illegal drugs), white collar and corporate crimes (such as embezzlement and tax fraud), and other types of illegal activity. Thus, street crimes are only a portion of the total volume of crime committed yearly in the United States, and burglary is only a fraction of all street crime. By focusing on this single crime, we are taking a rather narrow view of the subject and we will have to be especially careful in our conclusions to avoid making sweeping generalizations about the totality of crime in the United States.

Measuring Crime

Crime, by its nature, is difficult to measure. Various methods have been used to estimate the U.S. crime rate and none of them are completely satisfactory.

When people discuss "the crime rate," they are usually referring to a set of statistics compiled by the Federal Bureau of Investigation. This "official" crime rate is based on eight types of serious crimes (including homicide, rape, robbery, arson, and burglary) reported to local police departments. A major weakness of this method for measuring crime is that the authorities sometimes are not notified when a crime has been committed. Rape, for example, is substantially underreported; thus, the "official" rate of rape underestimates the true extent of this crime by an unknown—but large—margin.

A second method for measuring crime is the "self-report," in which people are asked to list the offenses they have committed, usually over a specific span of time. Although this method has been successfully used, it has some obvious limitations. It is self-incriminating and some people may not admit their past criminality for fear of being exposed and arrested. Others may exaggerate their deviance and boast of crimes they did not commit.

The General Social Survey takes a third approach, asking respondents if they have been the victims of crime. This methodology avoids the problem of self-incrimination and some of the underreporting associated with the official, FBI-compiled crime rates. Because it includes incidents that were not reported to the police, this method may yield better estimates of the true volume of criminal activity than the official crime rates, at least for some crimes.

Victimization surveys have their own limitations, of course. Their accuracy varies by type of crime (and they don't work at all for homicide), and they can tell us relatively little about the *causes* of crime because victims often cannot provide reliable information about perpetrators. Also, people may forget or exaggerate their victimization. The same pressures that stop some people (for example, some rape victims) from notifying the police may also prevent them from discussing their victimization with interviewers and poll takers.

Given these limitations and qualifications, it is clear that we will not be able to unlock all of the mysteries of crime in America in these brief pages. Nonetheless, we can still use the information in the GSS data set to test some important hypotheses and establish some meaningful relationships.

EXERCISE 7.1 | **Victimization**

Who is most likely to be the victim of burglary? What would you guess? Would the typical victim of this crime be rich or poor? Black or white? A resident of a city, a suburb, or a rural area? Male or female? Older or younger? Use your textbook and other course materials, if relevant, to develop hypotheses linking burglary victimization to INCOME (total family income), RACE, SEX, and one more potential independent variable of your own choosing. State your hypotheses in Research Report 7.1.

Choosing a Measure of Association

Should we use Cramer's *V* or gamma to measure the strength of the relationships between BURGLR and the independent variables? Recall (see Chapter 6) that the choice will depend on whether or not *both* variables in a relationship have numerical scores. The scores of BURGLR could be considered numerical in the sense that they rank people as "more or less victimized" by burglary. One of the independent variables, INCOME, is also numeric, and gamma could be used to measure the strength of the association between this variable and BURGLR. On the other hand, Cramer's *V* would be the appropriate measure for relationships involving SEX and RACE because these variables have scores that are merely labels.

Rather than choosing between gamma and Cramer's *V*, it will be more convenient to use both measures. Cramer's *V* will provide a convenient way of comparing the strength of all relationships, regardless of numerical quality. We can look to gamma for additional information about the direction of relationships as appropriate. Remember to interpret the direction of gamma carefully. The sign of gamma shows the direction of the relationship between the *scores* of the variables. In particular, note that BURGLR is scored so that a yes is "1," whereas no has a higher score of "2."

The commands necessary for producing crosstab tables for all independent variables and BURGLR are presented in Command Block 7.1. Use the output to complete Research Report 7.1.

COMMAND BLOCK 7.1   Producing Crosstab Tables for BURGLR

Click **Statistics** → **Summarize** → **Crosstabs** →
Highlight **BURGLR** →
Click the arrow pointing to the **Row(s):** box →
Highlight **INCOME** →
Click the arrow pointing to the **Column(s):** box →
Highlight **RACE** →
Click the arrow pointing to the **Column(s):** box →
Highlight **SEX** →
Click the arrow pointing to the **Column(s):** box →
Highlight the name of the variable you selected →
Click the arrow pointing to the **Column(s):** box →
Click **Cells** →
Click **Columns** in the **Percentages** box →
Click **Continue** →
In the Crosstabs dialog box, click **Statistics** →
Select **Chi square**, **Cramer's V**, and **Gamma** →
Click **Continue** →
Click **OK**

NAME _____

INSTRUCTOR _____

DATE _____

1. State and briefly explain hypotheses linking each independent variable to BURGLR:

   a. INCOME:

   b. RACE:

   c. SEX:

   d. Your variable _____:

2. Record the percentage victimized ("Yes" on BURGLR) and other statistics for each value of the independent variables.

   a. For INCOME:

	INCOME			
BURGLR	**Low**	**Middle**	**High**	**Cramer's *V***
% Yes	____	____	____	____

The column percentages _____ (do/do not) change, so there

_____ (is/is not) a relationship between these variables. The

significance of chi square is _____ (less than/more than) .05,

so this relationship _____ (is/is not) statistically significant.

The value of gamma is _____, so this is a _____ (weak/moder-

ate/strong) relationship. The sign of gamma indicates that this is a

_____ (positive/negative) relationship. As INCOME increases,

victimization _____ (increases/decreases).

(Research Report continues)

b. For RACE:

RACE

BURGLR	Black	White	Cramer's *V*
% Yes	——	——	——

The column percentages —————(do/do not) change, so there ————— (is/is not) a relationship between these variables. The significance of chi square is————— (less than/more than) .05, so this relationship————— (is/is not) statistically significant. The value of Cramer's *V* is ——, so this is a ————— (weak/moderate/strong) relationship.

c. For SEX:

SEX

BURGLR	Males	Females	Cramer's *V*
% Yes	——	——	——

The column percentages —————(do/do not) change, so there ————— (is/is not) a relationship between these variables. The significance of chi square is ————— (less than/more than) .05, so this relationship————— (is/is not) statistically significant. The value of Cramer's *V* is ——, so this is a ————— (weak/moderate/strong) relationship.

d. For your variable—————— , fill in the blanks with the names of the categories of the variable and the percentage of burglary victims, using as many blanks as necessary.

—————

BURGLR				Cramer's *V*
	—— —— ——			——
% Yes	—— —— ——			——

The column percentages —————(do/do not) change, so there ————— (is/is not) a relationship between these variables. The significance of chi square is ————— (less than/more than) .05, so this relationship————— (is/is not) statistically significant.

(Research Report continues)

If your independent variable is **not** *numerical*: The value of Cramer's
V is _____ , so this is a _____ (weak/moderate/strong) relationship.

If your independent variable **is** *numerical*: The value of gamma is _____ ,
so this is a _____ (weak/moderate/strong) relationship. The
sign of gamma indicates that this is a _____ (positive/nega-
tive) relationship. As _____ increases, victimization
_____ (increases/decreases).

3. Were your hypotheses confirmed? Who is most victimized by burglary? Explain.

Multivariate Analysis: What Happens When Variables Are Combined?

In Research Report 7.1, you found higher rates of burglary victimization among black and low-income respondents. For that report, you analyzed relationships one at a time. For example, you looked first at the effect of INCOME on BURGLR and then, in a separate analysis, you looked at the effect of RACE on BURGLR. What would happen if we *combined* these two variables and observed their *joint* effects on BURGLR? What victimization rates would we find for people who were *both* low income and black? How would their rate of victimization compare with people who were high income and black? High income and white? Is the rate of burglary higher for low-income respondents regardless of their race? Or, is the burglary rate higher for black Americans regardless of their income?

These types of questions arise as we realize that social phenomena like crime have multiple causes and that we will not be able to understand very much of the social world if we confine our attention solely to relationships between single independent and dependent variables one at a time. If we are to begin to understand phenomena as complex as crime, we need to develop research techniques that are equally complex.

In this chapter, we begin to develop more sophisticated analytical methods, using a technique by which we can observe the joint effect of two variables on a single dependent variable. **Multivariate analysis** refers to statistical techniques that involve more than two variables. The specific technique we will use is called **elaboration** or **controlling for a third variable**. As you will see, this technique builds on the Crosstabs procedure.

Let's start by looking at the relationship between BURGLR and INCOME, while controlling for RACE. We will have SPSS construct two bivariate tables, one displaying the relationship between INCOME and BURGLR for white respondents only and the other showing the relationship between INCOME and BURGLR for black respondents only. BURGLR is still our dependent variable, INCOME is the independent variable, but RACE now becomes the **control variable**. We control for RACE in the sense that its value is fixed for each of the bivariate tables: one includes all white respondents and only white respondents, and the other includes all black respondents and only black respondents.

From the Crosstab dialog window, select BURGLR as the row variable and INCOME as the column variable in the usual way. Then, select RACE and notice that the arrows activated would let you move RACE to the top box (as a row variable), the middle box (a column variable), or to a third box near the bottom of the window. Transfer RACE to this bottom box to make it a control variable. SPSS will produce a table for the dependent and independent variables for every value of the control variable. The dialog box should look like this after you have selected RACE as the control variable:

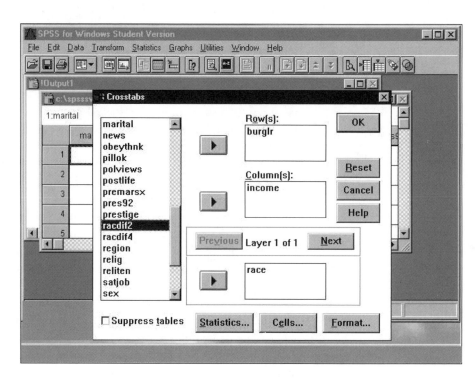

Complete the rest of the Crosstab procedure as usual, as illustrated in Command Block 7.2:

COMMAND BLOCK 7.2   Selecting RACE as a Control Variable

Click **Statistics** → **Summarize** → **Crosstabs** →
Highlight **BURGLR** →
Click the arrow pointing to the **Row(s):** box →
Highlight **INCOME** →
Click the arrow pointing to the **Column(s):** box →
Highlight **RACE** →
Click the arrow pointing to the box at the bottom of the window →
Click **Cells** →
Click **Columns** in the **Percentages** box →
Click **Continue** →
In the Crosstabs dialog box, click **Statistics** →
Select **Chi square** and **Gamma** →
Click **Continue** →
Click **OK**

To view more easily the results of a multivariate analysis, it is often useful to construct a summary table showing the original bivariate relationship and the effect of controlling for the third variable. Table 7.1 shows the percentage of the full sample that had been burglarized and the comparable percentages for each race.

TABLE 7.1   **Victims of Burglary by Income and Race**
(Percentages "Yes" on BURGLR)

	Lower Income	Middle Income	Higher Income	Gamma	
All	10%	5%	2%	.48	(N = 541)
Whites	6%	6%	1%	.34	(N = 439)
Blacks	23%	5%	0%	.82	(N = 74)

Before analyzing these results, note the pattern of missing scores. Only 541 of the 1480 respondents in the GSS94TAB.SAV data set are included in the bivariate table for INCOME and BURGLR (N = 541). Most of the "missing" 939 respondents were given a form of the General Social Survey that did not include the INCOME or BURGLR items. Of these 541, 439 white respondents had scores on RACE as well as INCOME and BURGLR (N = 439); only 74 black respondents had scores on all three variables (N = 74).

This reduced sample size puts us in a rather awkward position, especially when we see the small numbers in some of the combined categories of the tables (for example, there are only 12 higher-income black respondents). These small cells clearly identify the major limitation of elaboration as a multivariate analytical technique: we can quickly run out of cases. For a variety of statistical reasons, low cell frequencies are very undesirable and will make our conclusions especially tentative.

In spite of the need to be extra cautious, there are some clear patterns in these tables that deserve some analytical attention. Note that the percentage of the full sample who were victimized by burglary declines as income increases. Both white and black respondents show a similar pattern but the percentage of victimized low-income black respondents is quite large, much larger, in fact, than any other subgroup in the tables.

Looking at the gammas, we see that the relationship between INCOME and BURGLR has the same direction for all three tables. Remember that a positive gamma indicates that the *scores* of the variables are positively related. BURGLR is coded so that *non*victims (a score of 2) have a higher score than victims (a score of 1); and the relationship between INCOME and BURGLR is actually negative—as income increases, the rate of victimization decreases. Note that the relationship between INCOME and BURGLR is much stronger for black respondents than for white respondents.

What can we conclude? In general, rates of victimization by burglary decrease as income increases. This relationship is very much affected by race, however, and is much stronger for black respondents. Low-income blacks are especially vulnerable to the crime of burglary.

EXERCISE 7.2   **A Multivariate Analysis of BURGLR**

Replicate the preceding multivariate analysis of BURGLR with INCOME as the independent variable and SEX as the control variable. Are INCOME and BURGLR related in the same way for both males and females? Are low-income females more or less vulnerable than low-income males? Follow the commands in Command Block 7.2, but substitute SEX for RACE. Use the output to complete Research Report 7.2.

NAME _____

INSTRUCTOR _____

DATE _____

1. Complete the summary table showing the effect of controlling for SEX.

Victims of Burglary by INCOME and SEX

	Lower Income	Middle Income	Higher Income	Gamma
All	10%	5%	2%	.48
Males	____	____	____	____
Females	____	____	____	____

2. For the full sample, victimization by burglary decreases as income increases. Describe the effect of controlling for SEX.

   a. *For males*: The rate of victimization _____ (increases/decreases) as income increases. The gamma of _____ indicates a _____ (weak/moderate/strong) relationship.

   b. *For females*: The rate of victimization_____ (increases/decreases) as income increases. The gamma of _____ indicates a _____ (weak/moderate/strong) relationship.

   c. Compare the pattern of victimization for males, females, and the full sample. Is the pattern basically the same for all three? Are there any important differences in the relationship between victimization and income for the sexes?

Who's Afraid?

One social cost of crime is fear: fear of victimization, fear of strangers, and fear of walking alone at night. The GSS includes an item that asks, "Is there an area right around here—that is, within a mile—where you would be afraid to walk alone at night?" (FEAR). Almost 50% of the sample said "yes" to this question, indicating that fear is widespread in our society.

What kind of person would be most likely to be fearful? Given the relationships already established in this chapter, an obvious hypothesis would be that fear would be greater for the groups most victimized by crime: greater for blacks than for whites and greater for people with low income than those with middle or higher incomes. It might also occur to you that people who have been victims of crime ("yes" on BURGLR) might be more fearful than nonvictims. We will examine the relationship between income and FEAR, and you can continue the investigation with other potential causes of fear.

Using the Crosstabs procedure, we examine the relationship between FEAR and INCOME. We hypothesized that fear would decrease as income increased, a pattern that parallels the relationship between BURGLR and INCOME. FEAR was the dependent (row) variable and INCOME was the independent (column) variable. The output from Crosstabs is presented in Figure 7.1.

FIGURE 7.1   **Output of Crosstabs for FEAR and INCOME**
(1994 GSS)

```
FEAR  AFRAID TO WALK AT NIGHT IN NEIGHBORHOOD  by  INCOME  Total Family Income

                     INCOME                  Page 1 of 1
            Count
            Col Pct  Lower    Middle   Higher
                                                    Row
                      1.00     2.00     3.00|  Total
      FEAR
                1      210      125       91      426
          YES          53.8     44.2     45.3     48.7

                2      180      158      110      448
          NO           46.2     55.8     54.7     51.3

            Column     390      283      201      874
            Total      44.6     32.4     23.0    100.0
```

```
     Chi-Square              Value        DF       Significance
    --------------------    -----------   ----     ------------

Pearson                      7.40268       2          .02469
Likelihood Ratio             7.41167       2          .02458
Mantel-Haenszel test for     5.25038       1          .02194
   linear association

Minimum Expected Frequency -   97.970
```

```
                                                       Approximate
        Statistic            Value     ASE1   Val/ASE0  Significance
    --------------------   ---------  -------- --------  ------------

Phi                         .09203                        .02469 *1
Cramer's V                  .09203                        .02469 *1
```

```
*1 Pearson chi-square probability

Number of Missing Observations:  612
```

As you can see, this table is generally consistent with our hypothesis but the relationship is not very strong. The low-income group has a higher percentage of fearful people but the percentages for the middle (44%) and higher (45%) income groups are almost identical. The relationship is statistically significant (the significance of chi square is less than .05) and gamma is .14, indicating a weak to moderate association between the variables. Note the coding scheme for FEAR: yes is coded as "1" and no is coded as "2." The positive sign of the gamma means that as the *score* on INCOME increases, so does the *score* on FEAR. In other words, respondents with higher incomes were more likely to say "no" (were less fearful) than respondents with lower incomes.

EXERCISE 7.3   **The Correlates of Fear**

Now it's your turn to analyze the causes of fear by selecting two more potential independent variables. You can select these variables in any of three ways: you can use your textbook or other course materials, if relevant; you can select the variables we suggested previously (RACE or BURGLR); or you can select your own from the GSS94TAB.SAV data set. State a hypothesis linking these independent variables to FEAR in Research Report 7.3 and run **Crosstabs** with FEAR as the dependent variable and your independent variables in the columns. Use Command Block 7.1 as a guide with FEAR as the row variable. Request either Cramer's *V* or gamma as appropriate for the numerical qualities of *both* variables. Use the output to complete Research Report 7.3.

NAME _____

INSTRUCTOR _____

DATE _____

1. Name of your independent variables: _____ and
   _____ . State and briefly explain the hypotheses linking the
   independent variables to FEAR.
   a. For your first independent variable:

   b. For your second independent variable:

2. Summarize your results.
   a. *For your first independent variable*: On line 1 of the following
      summary table, fill in the blank with the name of your independent
      variable. On line 2, write in the names of the categories of your
      independent variable, using as many blanks as necessary. On line
      3, fill in the blanks with the percentage who said "yes" on FEAR
      for each category of the independent variable.

      Lines

      1.   FEAR by _____

      2.   _____ _____ _____ _____ _____

      3. % Yes _____ _____ _____ _____ _____

      The column percentages _____ (do/do not) change, so
      there _____ (is/is not) a relationship between these vari-
      ables. The significance of chi square is _____ (less
      than/more than) .05, so this relationship _____ (is/is
      not) statistically significant.
      If the independent variable is **not** *numerical*: The value of
      Cramer's V is _____, so this is a _____ (weak/moder-
      ate/strong) relationship.

(Research Report continues)

If the independent variable **is** *numerical:* The value of gamma is _____, so this is a _____ (weak/moderate/strong) relationship. The sign of gamma indicates that this is a _____ (positive/negative) relationship. As INCOME increases, victimization_____ (increases/decreases).

b. *For your second independent variable*: On line 1 of the following summary table, fill in the blank with the name of your independent variable. On line 2, write in the names of the categories of your independent variable, using as many blanks as necessary. On line 3, fill in the blanks with the percentage who said "yes" on FEAR for each category of the independent variable.

Lines

1.   FEAR by _____

2.   _____ _____ _____ _____ _____

3. % Yes _____ _____ _____ _____ _____

The column percentages _____ (do/do not) change, so there _____ (is/is not) a relationship between these variables. The significance of chi square is _____ (less than/more than) .05, so this relationship _____ (is/is not) statistically significant.

If the independent variable is **not** *numerical*: The value of Cramer's *V* is _____ , so this is a _____ (weak/moderate/strong) relationship.

If the independent variable **is** *numerical*: The value of gamma is _____, so this is a _____ (weak/moderate/strong) relationship. The sign of gamma indicates that this is a _____ (positive/negative) relationship. As INCOME increases, victimization _____ (increases/decreases).

3. Were your hypotheses confirmed? Explain.

EXERCISE 7.4   **A Multivariate Analysis of FEAR**

What will happen to FEAR if we combine variables and conduct a multivariate analysis? We investigated the relationship between FEAR (the dependent variable) and INCOME (the independent variable) while controlling for RACE. Table 7.2 summarizes our results.

TABLE 7.2   **Fear by Income and Race**
(Percentages "Yes" on FEAR)

	Lower Income	Middle Income	Higher Income	Gamma
All	54%	44%	45%	.14 (*N* = 874)
Whites	50%	42%	43%	.11 (*N* = 710)
Blacks	69%	56%	63%	.16 (*N* = 120)

Note that, once again, we are working with a sample that is much reduced in size. The numbers are not as low as they were with BURGLR, however, and there are no empty cells in the tables.

In all tables, the percentage of respondents who said "yes" on FEAR was highest for the lowest income group. The level of fear in the middle- and upper-income groups is very similar for whites; in the case of black respondents, it is higher for the highest income group than for the middle-income group. For each income group, the level of fear for blacks was higher than for whites. As was the case for victimization, this burden of crime falls more heavily on blacks than on whites.

EXERCISE 7.5   **An Additional Multivariate Analysis of FEAR**

Now it's your turn: replicate the multivariate analysis of FEAR and INCOME using SEX and a variable of your own choosing as control variables. Make sure that your control variable has no more than two or three possible scores (preferably two). Using Command Block 7.2 as a guide, run the **Crosstabs** procedure with FEAR substituted for BURGLR and first SEX and then the control variable you selected substituted for RACE. Compare the column percentages and gammas for each category of the control variable (for example, male and female) with each other and with the entire sample. Use the output to complete Research Report 7.4.

NAME

INSTRUCTOR

DATE

1. Complete the summary table showing the effect of controlling for SEX. Construct a similar summary table showing the effect of your control variable, using as many lines as necessary.

FEAR by INCOME by SEX

	Lower Income	Middle Income	Higher Income	Gamma
All	54%	44%	45%	.14
Males	——	——	——	——
Females	——	——	——	——

FEAR by INCOME by _____

	Lower Income	Middle Income	Higher Income	Gamma
All	54%	44%	45%	.14
_____	——	——	——	——
_____	——	——	——	——
_____	——	——	——	——

2. For the full sample, FEAR decreases as income increases. The gamma of .14 indicates a weak-to-moderate relationship. Describe the effect of controlling for SEX.

   a. *For males*: FEAR _____ (increases/decreases) as income increases. The gamma of ____ indicates a _____ (weak/moderate/strong) relationship.

   b. *For females*: FEAR _____ (increases/decreases) as income increases. The gamma of ____ indicates a _____ (weak/moderate/strong) relationship.

   c. Compare the pattern of FEAR for males, females, and the full sample. Is the pattern basically the same for all three? Are there any important differences in the relationship between FEAR and INCOME?

(Research Report continues)

3. Analyze the results of controlling for the variable you selected. Does FEAR still decrease as income increases for each category of your control variable?

   a. *For the first category of the control variable*: FEAR

      _____ (increases/decreases) as income increases. The

      gamma of _____ indicates a _____

      (weak/moderate/strong) relationship.

   b. *For the second category of the control variable*: FEAR

      _____ (increases/decreases) as income increases. The

      gamma of _____ indicates a _____

      (weak/moderate/strong) relationship.

   c. (If necessary) *For the third category of the control variable*: FEAR

      _____ (increases/decreases) as income increases. The

      gamma of _____ indicates a _____

      (weak/moderate/strong) relationship.

   d. Compare the pattern of FEAR and INCOME for all categories of your control variable. Is the pattern basically the same or does it change? Explain.

NAME _____

INSTRUCTOR _____

DATE _____

In Exercise 7.1, you tested the relationships between four independent variables and BURGLR. What other characteristics might affect a person's vulnerability to burglary? Select another potential independent variable from the GSS94TAB.SAV data set. State a hypothesis and use **Crosstabs**, following Command Block 7.1, to test for a relationship with BURGLR.

1. Name of your independent variable: _____ State and briefly explain your hypothesis.

2. *Summarize your results*: On line 1 of the following summary table, fill in the blank with the name of your independent variable. On line 2, write in the names of the categories of your independent variable, using as many blanks as necessary. On line 3, fill in the blanks with the percentage burglarized for each category of the independent variable.

   Lines

   1.   BURGLR by _____

   2.   _____ _____ _____ _____ _____

   3. % Burglarized   _____ _____ _____ _____ _____

   The column percentages _____ (do/do not) change, so there

   _____ (is/is not) a relationship between these variables. The

   significance of chi square is _____ (less than/more than) .05,

   so this relationship _____ (is/is not) statistically significant.

   If the independent variable is **not** *numerical*: The value of Cramer's *V*

   is _____ , so this is a _____ (weak/moderate/strong)

   relationship.

   If the independent variable **is** *numerical*: The value of gamma is _____,

   so this is a _____ (weak/moderate/strong) relationship. The

   sign of gamma indicates that this is a _____ (positive/negative) relationship. As _____ increases, victimization

   _____ (increases/decreases).

(Independent Project continues)

3. Was your hypothesis confirmed? Explain.

NAME _____

INSTRUCTOR _____

DATE _____

1. How much support is there in U.S. society for capital punishment? Run the **Frequencies** procedure for CAPPUN and describe the results. Are Americans generally for or against the death penalty?

2. What factors might account for the variations in support of the death penalty? Choose two potential independent variables and state hypotheses linking each variable to CAPPUN. You can develop hypotheses in any of three ways: (1) consult your textbook or other course materials, if relevant; (2) consider BURGLR and FEAR as independent variables; or (3) choose your own independent variables from the GSS94TAB.SAV data set. Would people who have been victimized by crime or those who are most fearful of crime be more in favor of the death penalty?

   a. State and briefly explain a hypothesis for your first independent variable.

   b. State and briefly explain a hypothesis for your second independent variable.

3. Using Command Block 7.1 as a guide, run **Crosstabs** with CAPPUN in the rows and your independent variables in the columns. Get column percentages, chi square, and Cramer's *V* or gamma. Summarize the results.

   a. *For your first independent variable*: On line 1 of the following summary table, fill in the blank with the name of your independent variable. On line 2, write in the names of the categories of your independent variable, using as many blanks as necessary. On line 3, fill in the blanks with the percentage who said "yes" on CAPPUN for each category of the independent variable.

   Lines

   1.   CAPPUN by _____

   2.   _____ _____ _____ _____ _____

   3. % Yes   _____ _____ _____ _____ _____

(Independent Project continues)

The column percentages——————— (do/do not) change, so there——————— (is/is not) a relationship between these variables. The significance of chi square is ———————(less than/more than) .05, so this relationship———————(is/is not) statistically significant.

If the independent variable is **not** *numerical*: The value of Cramer's *V* is ——— , so this is a———————(weak/moderate/strong) relationship.

If the independent variable **is** *numerical*: The value of gamma is ——— , so this is a———————(weak/moderate/strong) relationship. The sign of gamma indicates that this is a——————— (positive/negative) relationship. As———————increases, support for capital punishment——————— (increases/decreases).

b. *For your second independent variable*: On line 1 of the following summary table, fill in the blank with the name of your independent variable. On line 2, write in the names of the categories of your independent variable, using as many blanks as necessary. On line 3, fill in the blanks with the percentage who said "yes" on CAPPUN for each category of the independent variable.

Lines

1.   CAPPUN by———————

2.   ———— ———— ———— ———— ————

3. % Yes   ———— ———— ———— ———— ————

The column percentages———————(do/do not) change, so there———————(is/is not) a relationship between these variables. The significance of chi square is———————(less than/more than) .05, so this relationship——————— (is/is not) statistically significant.

If the independent variable is **not** *numerical*: The value of Cramer's *V* is ———, so this is a——————— (weak/moderate/strong) relationship.

If the independent variable **is** *numerical*: The value of gamma is ——— , so this is a——————— (weak/moderate/strong) relationship. The sign of gamma indicates that this is a——————— (positive/negative) relationship. As——————— increases, support for capital punishment——————— (increases/decreases).

4. Were your hypotheses confirmed? Explain.

NAME _____

INSTRUCTOR _____

DATE _____

Choose one of the independent variables from Independent Project 7.2 for further testing. Next, choose a control variable that has only two or three values (preferably two). RACE and SEX might be good choices for a control variable.

Run the **Crosstabs** procedure with CAPPUN as the dependent variable (in the rows) and your independent variable in the columns. Your control variable should be in the box at the bottom of the **Crosstabs** dialog window. Use Command Block 7.2 as a guide, substituting CAPPUN for BURGLR, your independent variable for INCOME, and your control variable for RACE.

1. Using Table 7.2 as a guide, complete a summary table to display the results of your multivariate analysis. On line 1, fill in the names of your independent and control variables. On line 2, write in the names of the categories of your independent variable, using as many blanks as necessary. On line 3, fill in the percentage of each category of the independent variable who said "yes" on CAPPUN for the whole sample. You generated this information for Independent Project 7.2. On line 4, fill in the percentage of each category of the independent variable who said "yes" on CAPPUN for the first category of the control variable. On line 5 and (if necessary) line 6, fill in the percentage of each category of the independent variable who said "yes" on CAPPUN for the second (and third) category of the control variable.

Lines

1.   CAPPUN by _____ by _____

                                                                    Cramer's *V*
2.   _____ _____ _____ _____   or Gamma

3. All   ____   ____   ____   ____   ____

4. _____ ____   ____   ____   ____   ____

5 _____   ____   ____   ____   ____   ____

6. _____ ____   ____   ____   ____   ____

2. Analyze these results as you did in Research Reports 7.2 and 7.4. Did the relationship between your independent variable and CAPPUN change over the categories of the control variable? How? Which subgroup is most in favor of the death penalty? Which is most opposed?

NAME _____

INSTRUCTOR _____

DATE _____

1. Load the GSS72.SAV data set and get a frequency distribution of CAPPUN. Compare this table with the frequency distribution you created in Independent Project 7.2 (item 1). In 1972, _____% of the respondents supported the death penalty. In 1994, support had _____ (risen/fallen) to _____%.

2. Have the causes of support for the death penalty changed? Select one of the independent variables you used in Independent Project 7.2 and use the **Crosstabs** procedure to test its relationship with CAPPUN in 1972. Use Command Block 7.1 as a guide. Use the output to complete the following summary table. On line 1, fill in the blank with the name of your independent variable. On line 2, write in the names of the categories of your independent variable, using as many blanks as necessary. On line 3, fill in the blanks with the percentage who said "yes" on CAPPUN for each category of the independent variable.

   Lines

   1.   CAPPUN by _____

   2.   _____ _____ _____ _____ _____

   3. % Yes   _____ _____ _____ _____ _____

   The column percentages _____ (do/do not) change, so there _____ (is/is not) a relationship between these variables.

   The significance of chi square is _____ (less than/more than) .05, so this relationship _____ (is/is not) statistically significant.

   If the independent variable is **not** *numerical*: The value of Cramer's *V* is _____ , so this is a _____ (weak/moderate/strong) relationship.

   If the independent variable **is** *numerical*: The value of gamma is _____ , so this is a _____ (weak/moderate/strong) relationship. The sign of gamma indicates that this is a _____ (positive/negative) relationship. As _____ increases, support for capital punishment _____ (increases/decreases).

(Comparative Analysis continues)

3. Compare results with those you obtained for the 1994 GSS data set in Independent Project 7.2. Has the relationship between your independent variable and CAPPUN changed over the years? Explain.

Main Points

■ This chapter investigated criminal victimization and fear of crime.

■ Multivariate analysis investigates relationships between more than two variables. A multivariate technique called elaboration was used to examine burglary victimization and fear.

SPSS Commands Introduced in This Chapter

COMMAND BLOCK 7.2   *Running Crosstabs with a Control Variable**

Click **Statistics** → **Summarize** → **Crosstabs** →
Highlight the name of the dependent variable →
Click the arrow pointing to the **Row(s):** box →
Highlight the name of the independent variable →
Click the arrow pointing to the **Column(s):** box →
Highlight the name of the control variable →
Click arrow pointing to the box at the bottom of the window →
Click **Cells** →
Click **Columns** in the **Percentages** box →
Click **Continue** →
In the Crosstabs dialog box, click **Statistics** →
Select **Chi square** and **Cramer's V** or **Gamma** →
Click **Continue** →
Click **OK**

*(*Note*: This is a generalized statement of SPSS commands. Substitute actual variable names where appropriate.)

Chapter 8 Inequality and Social Class in the United States

In the next three chapters we explore a central feature of U.S. society: **inequality**, or the uneven distribution of valued goods and services (for example, money, health care, education, or material possessions) across the population. This chapter focuses on **social class**; in the following chapters we will explore patterns of inequality associated with gender and race. Several new SPSS procedures and statistical techniques are introduced to aid us in our inquiry.

The Dimensions of Inequality

With the possible exception of small hunting and gathering bands, inequality seems to be a universal trait of human society. That is, in virtually every society, some people get more of whatever is valued and some get less. However, the extent of the inequality (that is, *how much more* the privileged get) varies dramatically. In smaller, simpler societies, the difference between the highest and lowest ranked person can be very slight, so subtle that it is imperceptible to an outsider. In other societies, life at the top may be so far removed from life at the bottom that the privileged groups may think of the lower classes as subhuman.

Social inequality can be conceptualized in a variety of ways but most sociologists agree that it is a complex phenomenon that involves several different dimensions or systems. In this chapter, we will explore two of the dimensions of inequality in U.S. society.[1] The first involves inequalities in income, wealth, and control of property. Differences between people on this dimension can be measured in terms of the size of their paychecks, bank accounts, stock portfolios, real estate holdings, or other tangible assets.

The second dimension is less materialistic and involves the differences in prestige, respect, or honor between people. The criteria by which prestige is allocated vary from society to society. In some societies, the highest prestige may be accorded to the greatest hunter, singer, or healer, whereas in other societies prestige may depend on a person's physical characteristics or family lineage.

In the United States, the two dimensions of inequality are related and prestige tends to increase as wealth and affluence increase. However, the dimensions are not synonymous and a particular person's rank on one dimension may bear no relationship to his or her rank on the other dimension. A person whose wealth was the

---

1. Sociologists often distinguish a third dimension of inequality: *power*, or a person's ability to affect the decision-making process in society. Although obviously important, the GSS contains no variable that could be used as a measure of power, so we must ignore this dimension in the analysis.

result of illegal or disreputable activities (for example, through the illegal drug trade, prostitution, or pornography) might be very affluent but otherwise command little respect. Likewise, some people who have few material possessions may be highly regarded in their communities or societies (Mother Teresa comes to mind).

<table>
<tr><td>EXERCISE 8.1</td><td>**Exploring Inequality**</td></tr>
</table>

The first exercise in exploring inequality will be to measure the extent to which material wealth and prestige are related in our sample and, thus, in U.S. society. For this analysis, we will use the GSS94COR.SAV data set—the other version of the 1994 General Social Survey supplied with this text and introduced in Chapter 3. This database includes several variables that can be used to measure affluence and prestige. Specifically, we will use the variable RINCOME91 (respondent's income) as a measure of the materialistic dimension of inequality and PRESTG80 as a measure of prestige. Follow the instructions in Command Block 8.1 and load the **GSS94COR.SAV** data set now:

COMMAND BLOCK 8.1   Loading GSS94COR.SAV

> Click **File → Open → Data. . . →**
> Click **GSS94COR.SAV →**
> Click **OK**

Information on the RINCOME91 variable can be found in Appendix A, or by clicking the **Utilities** command. This variable measures the respondent's own income (unlike the variable INCOME in the GSS94TAB.SAV data set, which measures total family income) and has scores ranging from 1 (an income of less than $1000) to 21 (incomes of $75,000 and up). Familiarize yourself with these categories. Note especially that RINCOME91 does *not* record income in actual dollar values but in scores that indicate the category into which a respondent's income falls. For example, an income of "13" does *not* mean that a respondent earned $13 but, rather, that he or she falls into category 13; his or her income was between $20,000 and $22,499.

Now find the variable PRESTG80 in Appendix A, or use the **Utilities** command. The scores on this variable reflect the amount of respect or esteem accorded by the general public to the respondent's *occupation* (not to the respondent per se). These scores were determined by asking large samples of Americans to rank occupations in terms of prestige. Highly ranked occupations include Supreme Court justice, physicians, and airline pilots. Occupations that rank low in prestige include janitor, bill collector, and shoe shiner.

Note that RINCOME91 and PRESTG80 are not perfect matches with their related concept. Income is not the same thing as wealth or affluence; a person's total economic assets (houses, stocks, bonds, and so on) may be completely unrelated to mere take-home pay. Thus, as a measure of affluence, RINCOME91 will misclassify people who have modest salaries but considerable wealth (that is, such people will seem "moderate" in terms of affluence when they should be ranked "high"). Similarly, someone who holds a prestigious occupation will be ranked "high" on PRESTG80 even if he or she is personally held in low regard by peers or in the community (for example, a medical doctor with a reputation for incompetence). These kinds of dissimilarities between our concrete variables and abstract concepts are common in social research and are not a particular cause for alarm. Even imperfect measures can be used to examine relations between concepts as long as we are careful to qualify our conclusions appropriately.

Scatterplots

To explore the association between numerical variables with many scores, it is useful to construct a graph called a **scatterplot**. Scatterplots have two dimensions, which form right angles with each other. The horizontal axis (or X axis) is marked off in scores of one variable (usually the independent variable), and the vertical axis (or Y axis) is calibrated in scores of the other variable (usually the dependent variable).

Like bivariate tables, scatterplots display the scores of each case on both variables. Each case is represented by a dot placed at the point where that case's scores intersect. The pattern or "scatter" of the dots will give us information about the strength and direction of the relationship between the variables.

Producing Scatterplots

We can illustrate the interpretation of these graphs with a scatterplot for RINCOME91 and PRESTG80. From the menu bar, click **Graphs** and then **Scatter...**; the Scatterplot dialog box appears:

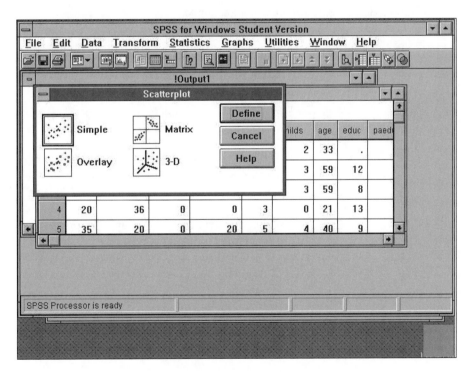

We want to do a Simple scatterplot and this option is already highlighted. Click **Define** and the Simple Scatterplot dialog box appears:

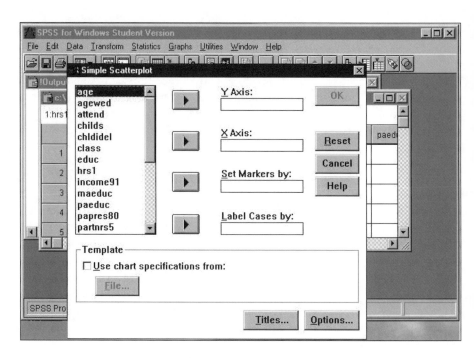

Let's make PRESTG80 the independent variable and array it along the *X*, or horizontal, axis. RINCOME91 is the dependent variable and goes along the *Y*, or vertical, axis. Command Block 8.2 summarizes the necessary commands:

COMMAND BLOCK 8.2   Producing a Scatterplot

> Click **Graphs** → **Scatter. . .** →
> Click **Simple** → **Define** →
> Highlight **RINCOME91** →
> Click the arrow pointing to the **Y Axis:** box —>
> Highlight **PRESTG80** →
> Click the arrow pointing to the **X Axis:** box →
> Click **OK**

The following scatterplot soon appears on the screen. Click **Edit** to move the chart to a Chart window, as depicted:

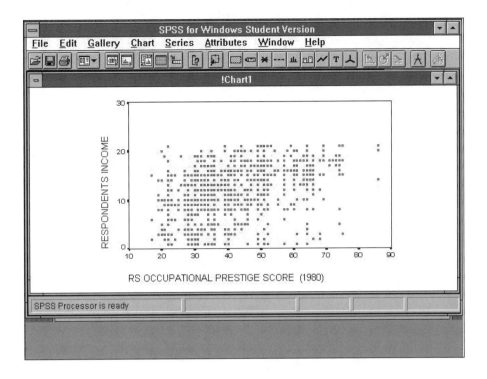

Adding the Regression Line

Scatterplots are easier to read if we draw a straight line through the dots to sum-marize their overall pattern. For this purpose, researchers use the **regression line**, the single straight line that touches all of the data points or comes as close as pos-sible to doing so. To add the regression line to the scatterplot (after the chart has been moved to a Chart window), click the **Edit** button. Then, from the menu bar, click **Chart** and **Options. . .** The Scatterplot Options dialog box appears:

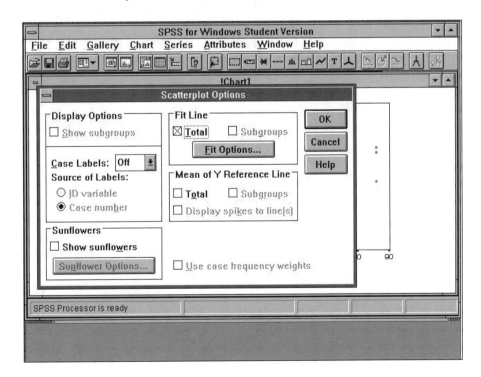

In the Fit Line box at the upper right, click **Total** and then click **OK**. These commands are presented in Command Block 8.3:

COMMAND BLOCK 8.3   Adding the Regression Line to a Scatterplot

> Click **Edit** →
> Click **Chart** → **Options. . .** →
> From the Scatterplot Options dialog box, click **Total** in the **Fit Line** box →
> Click **OK**

The scatterplot with the regression line added is presented in Figure 8.1.

FIGURE 8.1   **Output of Scatterplot for RINCOME91 and PRESTG80** (1994 GSS)

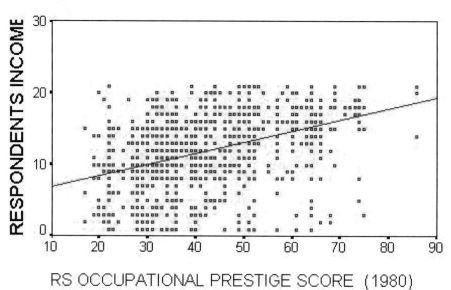

You may want to save or print the scatterplots at this point. This can be done by making the usual selections from the File menu. When you are finished with the scatterplot (wait until the end of this section), click the button in the upper-left corner of the Chart window and select **Close**. SPSS will ask if you want to save the chart before closing, and you may want to do so if you haven't already.

Reading Scatterplots

Remember that each dot in the graph represents a case. The placement of a case is determined by its scores on each of the two variables. Thus, cases in the lower-left portion of the graph are low on both income and prestige, cases in the upper-left portion are high on income but low in prestige, cases in the lower-right portion have high prestige but low incomes, and cases in the upper-right portion of the scatterplot are high on both income and prestige.

The regression line and the scattering of the dots indicates the direction and strength of the relationship. When, as in the preceding scatterplot, the regression line rises from the lower-left part of the graph to the upper right, the variables have a generally positive relationship. That is, as one variable increases (as prestige increases) the other does as well (income tends to rise). In negative relationships, the regression line will run from upper left to lower right, indicating that as one variable increases in value the other decreases.

The strength of the relationship can be estimated from the extent to which the dots are scattered around the regression line: the tighter the clustering, the stronger the relationship. In perfect (the strongest possible) relationships, all of the dots lie exactly on the regression line.

What does our scatterplot tell us about the relationship between prestige and income? The variables are positively related and people with greater prestige tend to have higher incomes. In terms of the strength of the relationship, we can see that the dots are quite scattered around the regression line, so the relationship is far from perfect. Beyond this, it's difficult to characterize the strength of the relationship (weak, moderate, or strong) other than impressionistically. A more satisfactory way of describing strength is presented in the next section.

A Measure of Association: Pearson's *r*

To aid in the interpretation of relationships between numerical variables, a statistic called **Pearson's *r*** is usually calculated. This measure of association, like gamma, ranges from 0.00 (no relationship) to plus or minus 1.00 (perfect positive and negative relationships).

Pearson's *r* is a sophisticated and powerful statistic and has a precise interpretation. If we square the value of *r* (multiply *r* by itself) and multiply by 100, we produce a statistic that tells us what percentage of the variation in one variable is explained by the other variable. For example, suppose a Pearson's *r* of .50 had been calculated between a test of mathematical aptitude and grades in a college math courses. This result would mean that 25% ($.50 \times .50 = .25$ and $.25 \times 100 = 25\%$) of the variation in math grades (or the differences in grades from student to student) was due to, or explained by, their ability or "talent" for math.

This would be strong evidence that ability is an important cause of success in math courses. Note, however, that this result would also mean that 75% of the variation in GPA is *not* due to ability or aptitude. The variation in math grades that is not accounted for by ability would be due, presumably, to such factors as motivation, effort, amount of study time, and even random chance. Thus, Pearson's *r* tells us exactly how much of the variation in one variable is accounted for by the other variable, and how much is due to the effects of other factors.

Producing and Interpreting Pearson's *r*

Pearson's *r* is one of three measures of association available in the **Bivariate Correlations** dialog window. To activate this window, click **Statistics**, and, from the menu bar, click **Correlate** and then **Bivariate**. The Bivariate Correlations dialog window appears:

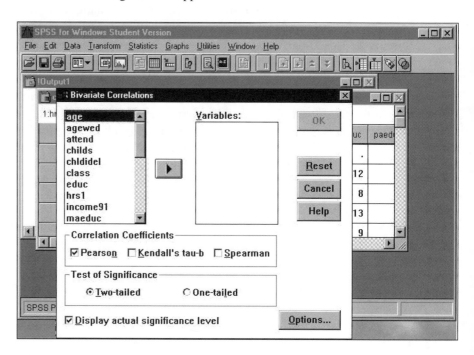

Transfer the names of our variables (RINCOME91 and PRESTG80) to the Variables: box and click **OK**. See Command Block 8.4 for a summary of these commands:

COMMAND BLOCK 8.4   Producing Pearson's *r*

Click **Statistics** → **Correlate** → **Bivariate** →
Highlight **RINCOME91** →
Click the arrow to transfer **RINCOME91** to the **Variables:** box →
Highlight **PRESTG80** →
Click the arrow to transfer **PRESTG80** to the **Variables:** box →
Click **OK**

The output is presented here as Figure 8.2. This procedure produces a **correlation matrix**, a table that shows the correlations between all possible combinations of variables—including correlations of each variable with itself. The relationship between each pair of variables is presented in a cell with the value of Pearson's r in the top row, the number of cases on which the calculations were based in parentheses in the middle row, and the results of a test for the statistical significance of the correlation in the bottom row. This last value is the probability that the variables are not correlated in the population. As always, we will take values of less than .05 as indicating a significant (or nonrandom) relationship. Remember that, when working with random samples like the GSS, we must always deal with the possibility that our results are produced by random chance and do not reflect actual relationships in the population.

FIGURE 8.2   **A Correlation Matrix for PRESTG80 and RINCOME91**

```
                    - -  Correlation Coefficients  - -

             RINCOM91    PRESTG80

RINCOM91      1.0000       .4121
             (  970)     (  970)
             P= .        P= .000

PRESTG80       .4121      1.0000
             (  970)     ( 1411)
             P= .000     P= .


(Coefficient / (Cases) / 2-tailed Significance)

" . " is printed if a coefficient cannot be computed
```

For PRESTG80 and RINCOME91, Pearson's r is .41, indicating a strong, positive relationship between the variables. Pearson's r confirms what we saw in the scatterplot but in a compact and convenient form.

Recall that our original purpose was to ascertain if income and prestige are different dimensions of inequality. What can be concluded? Both the scatterplot and Pearson's r support the idea that, although these variables are positively and closely related, they also measure separate dimensions or systems of inequality. If both variables measured exactly the same dimension, all cases in the scatterplot would fall on the regression line and Pearson's r would be 1.00. By observing the scatterplot, we can see that there are many cases that were high on one of the variables but low on the other (for example, the cases in the lower-right portion of the scatterplot were high on prestige but low on income).

On the other hand, if RINCOME91 and PRESTG80 were completely unrelated (if prestige had no relationship with income), the regression line would be parallel to the horizontal axis and Pearson's r would be 0.00. Thus, we may conclude that these results show that people tend to occupy similar but not exactly the same ranks on the two dimensions of inequality.

EXERCISE 8.2   **The Correlates of Inequality**

Now we are ready to use these new procedures to test some ideas about inequality in the United States. We'll start with an old argument about how people "get ahead" in our society. One position is that education is the key to opportunity and upward mobility. People with more years of schooling will be in occupations with greater prestige and have higher incomes.

An opposed position holds that what really matters is not your education or talent but the family into which you are born. People born into higher-status families have an advantage in the pursuit of success and will fare better in the social class system than people born to lower-status families.

We (actually, you) can test these two theories with scatterplots and Pearson's *r*. Use RINCOME91 as a measure of success or the dependent variable, EDUC (years of schooling) to measure education, and PAPRES80 (the prestige of the respondent's *father's* occupation) as an indicator of social class background. If income has a stronger relationship with years of education than with father's prestige, the first theory of social mobility will be supported. If, on the other hand, father's prestige has the stronger relationship with income, the argument that "it's not what you know, it's who you know" will be supported.

Follow Command Blocks 8.2 and 8.3 to get a scatterplot with a regression line for RINCOME91 and EDUC. RINCOME91 will be the dependent variable and should be placed on the vertical, or *Y*, axis and EDUC, as the independent variable, should be placed on the horizontal, or *X*, axis. Print and/or save the scatterplot.

Now, repeat this procedure for RINCOME91 and PAPRES80. The latter is the independent variable and, like EDUC in the previous scatterplot, it should be arrayed along the *X*, or horizontal, axis. Remember to print and/or save the scatterplot.

Use Command Block 8.5 to get Pearson's *r* for all three variables. Use the two scatterplots and the output of Pearson's *r* to complete Research Report 8.1.

COMMAND BLOCK 8.5   Producing Pearson's *r* for Three Variables

> Click **Statistics** → **Correlate** → **Bivariate** →
> Highlight **RINCOME91** →
> Click the arrow pointing to the **Variables:** box →
> Highlight **EDUC** →
> Click the arrow pointing to the **Variables:** box →
> Highlight **PAPRES80** →
> Click the arrow pointing to the **Variables:** box →
> Click **OK**

NAME _____

INSTRUCTOR _____

DATE _____

1. For the relationship between EDUC and RINCOME91:

   a. Observe the scatterplot. The direction of the relationship is _____ (positive/negative). As years of education increase, income _____ (increases/decreases). Judging from the spread of the dots (cases) around the regression line, the relationship seems to be _____ (weak/moderate/strong).

   b. Pearson's *r* for EDUC and RINCOME91 is _____. This indicates a _____ (weak/moderate/strong) relationship that is _____ (negative/positive) in direction. The relationship _____ (is/is not) statistically significant. (See the value for "*p* = " in the correlation matrix. If less than .05, the relationship is significant.)

2. For the relationship between PAPRES80 and RINCOME91:

   a. Observe the scatterplot. The direction of the relationship is _____ (positive/negative). As father's prestige increases, income _____ (increases/decreases). Judging from the spread of the dots (cases) around the regression line, the relationship seems to be _____ (weak/moderate/strong).

   b. Pearson's *r* for PAPRES80 and RINCOME91 is _____. This indicates a _____ (weak/moderate/strong) relationship that is _____ (negative/positive) in direction. The relationship _____ (is/is not) statistically significant. (See the value for "*p* = " in the correlation matrix. If less than .05, the relationship is significant.)

3. Which explanation of mobility and success in the United States is supported by these results? Is education the key to upward mobility? Does the status of the family into which a person is born make any difference? Explain.

EXERCISE 8.3   **The Consequences of Class**

In this exercise, you will explore the notion that a person's position in the class structure can have a strong effect on his or her opinions and behaviors. We have already shown that social class is related to religiosity (Chapter 4), socialization values and practices (Chapter 6), and criminal victimization (Chapter 7). In coming chapters, we will document the effects of class on political behavior, the institution of marriage and the family, and other areas of social life.

If social class is such an important independent variable, it should be correlated with a wide variety of other variables. To test this idea, begin by choosing either RINCOME91 or PRESTG80 as an independent variable. Now, look through the GSS94COR.SAV data set and choose two *numerical* dependent variables that, in your view, might be related to social class. Don't use any of the variables we have already used in this chapter and try to find dependent variables that are very different from each other. Use your textbook or other course materials, if relevant, to help develop hypotheses linking your dependent variables to class; use scatterplots and Pearson's *r* to test your ideas. See Command Blocks 8.2, 8.3, and 8.4 for the necessary instructions. In the scatterplots, the variable on the *X* axis should be your independent variable (your measure of social class). Summarize your results in Research Report 8.2.

Main Points

- Inequality is multidimensional. In this chapter, we examined two of these dimensions: income and prestige.

- Scatterplots give information about the strength and direction of relationships between two numerical variables. Pearson's *r* is a measure of association for relationships involving two numerical variables.

- We examined hypotheses about the correlates of success and the ancient aphorism that there is no association between money and happiness.

SPSS Commands Introduced in This Chapter

COMMAND BLOCK 8.2   *Producing a Scatterplot*

Click **Graphs** → **Scatter. . .** →
Click **Simple** → **Define** →
Highlight **RINCOME91** →
Click the arrow pointing to the **Y Axis:** box →
Highlight **PRESTG80** →
Click the arrow pointing to the **X Axis:** box →
Click **OK**

8.3   *Adding the Regression Line to a Scatterplot*

Click **Edit** →
Click **Chart** → **Options. . .** →
From the Scatterplot Options dialog box, Click **Total** in the **Fit Line** box →
Click **OK**

8.4   *Producing Pearson's r*

Click **Statistics** → **Correlate** → **Bivariate** →
Highlight **RINCOME91** →
Click the arrow to transfer **RINCOME91** to the **Variables:** box →
Highlight **PRESTG80** →
Click the arrow to transfer **PRESTG80** to the **Variables:** box →
Click **OK**

NAME _____

INSTRUCTOR _____

DATE _____

Name of your measure of inequality: _____
(RINCOME91/PRESTG80).

1. a. Name of your first dependent variable: _____ . State and
      briefly explain your hypotheses for this variable.

   b. Name of your second dependent variable: _____ . State
      and briefly explain your hypotheses for this variable.

2. State your results.
   For the first dependent variable:

   a. Observe the scatterplot. The direction of the relationship is
      _____ (positive/negative). As your measure of social
      class increases, your dependent variable _____
      (increases/decreases). Judging from the spread of the dots (cases)
      around the regression line, the relationship seems to be
      _____ (weak/moderate/strong).

   b. Pearson's *r* for these two variables is _____. This indicates a
      _____ (weak/moderate/strong) relationship that is
      _____ (negative/positive) in direction. The relationship
      _____ (is/is not) statistically significant. (See the value
      for "*p* = " in the correlation matrix. If less than .05, the relationship
      is significant.)

(Research Report continues)

For the second dependent variable:

a. Observe the scatterplot. The direction of the relationship is
    _____ (positive/negative). As years of education
    increase, income _____ (increases/decreases). Judging
    from the spread of the dots (cases) around the regression line, the
    relationship seems to be _____ (weak/moderate/strong).

b. Pearson's *r* for EDUC and RINCOME91 is _____. This indicates a
    _____ (weak/moderate/strong) relationship that is
    _____ (negative/positive) in direction. The relationship
    _____ (is/is not) statistically significant. (See the value
    for "*p* = " in the correlation matrix. If less than .05, the relationship
    is significant.)

3. Were your hypotheses confirmed? Explain in terms of the strength and
   direction of these relationships.

EXERCISE 8.4   **Can Money Buy Happiness?**

Any number of aphorisms and clichés assert that there is little relationship between material success and happiness ("Money isn't everything"; "Money can't buy love"). Other folk wisdom asserts that the less affluent are actually happier than the more affluent because they have fewer worries. Without being too cynical, one suspects that these thoughts are kept alive by people who have never experienced hunger or want or, perhaps, by poor people attempting to console themselves.

In this exercise, you will actually test the veracity of these sentiments. The dependent variable will be level of happiness and it will be measured by people's response to the question: "Taken all together, how would you say things are these days—would you say that you are very happy, pretty happy, or not too happy?" Because this variable, called HAPPY, has only three response categories, it was placed in the GSS94TAB.SAV data set. To access this data set, follow Command Block 8.6:

COMMAND BLOCK 8.6   Loading GSS94TAB.SAV

> Click **File → Open → Data. . . →**
> Click **GSS94TAB.SAV →**
> Click **OK**

Use CLASS, which has four categories or scores, as an independent variable. Because both HAPPY and CLASS have a limited number of scores, scatterplots and Pearson's r are not appropriate. To analyze this relationship, use the **Crosstabs** procedure (see Command Block 8.7) to produce a bivariate table with column percentages, chi square, and gamma. If it is true that "money can't buy happiness," the column percentages will not change much, chi square will not be significant, and gamma will approach zero. Use the output from this procedure to complete Research Report 8.3.

COMMAND BLOCK 8.7   Producing a Crosstab Table for HAPPY and CLASS

> Click **Statistics → Summarize → Crosstabs →**
> Highlight **HAPPY →**
> Click the arrow pointing to the **Row(s):** box →
> Highlight **CLASS →**
> Click the arrow pointing to the **Column(s):** box →
> Click **Cells →**
> Click **Columns** in the **Percentages** box →
> Click **Continue →**
> In the Crosstabs dialog box, click **Statistics →**
> Select **Chi square** and **Gamma →**
> Click **Continue →**
> Click **OK**

NAME _____

INSTRUCTOR _____

DATE _____

1. Complete the following summary table. For percentages, fill in the blanks with the percentage of people from each social class who said that they were "very happy."

	CLASS			
HAPPY	**Lower**	**Working**	**Middle**	**Upper**
% Very happy	_____	_____	_____	_____

The column percentages _____ (do/do not) change, so there _____ (is/is not) a relationship between happiness and class. The significance of chi square is _____ (less than/more than) .05, so this relationship _____ (is/is not) statistically significant. The value of gamma is _____ , so this is a _____ (weak/moderate/strong) relationship. The sign of gamma indicates that this is a _____ (positive/negative) relationship. As the CLASS increases, happiness _____ (increases/decreases). (Be careful about direction; remember that gamma shows the direction of the relationship between the *scores* of the variables.)

3. Are these results consistent with the idea that there is no relationship between money and happiness? Explain.

NAME _____

INSTRUCTOR _____

DATE _____

In Research Report 8.1, you tested two views of social mobility. One view was that a person's success in life is a matter of personal qualifications (measured by level of education). The opposing view was that success is determined by family background (measured by father's prestige). An individual's success was measured by his or her income level (RINCOME91).

Replicate this analysis with the GSS94COR.SAV data set but substitute PRESTG80 for RINCOME91 as the measure of success and father's education (PAEDUC) instead of father's prestige as the indicator of family background. Use both scatterplots and Pearson's r (see Command Blocks 8.2, 8.3, and 8.4 for the necessary commands) to examine relationships between PRESTG80 and EDUC and PRESTG80 and PAEDUC.

1. For the relationship between EDUC and PRESTG80:

    a. Observe the scatterplot. The direction of the relationship is _____ (positive/negative). As years of education increase, occupational prestige _____ (increases/decreases). The relationship seems to be _____ (weak/moderate/strong).

    b. Pearson's r for EDUC and PRESTG80 is _____. This indicates a _____ (weak/moderate/strong) relationship that is _____ (negative/positive) in direction. The relationship _____ (is/is not) statistically significant.

2. For the relationship between PAEDUC and PRESTG80:

    a. Observe the scatterplot. The direction of the relationship is _____ (positive/negative). As father's years of education increase, prestige _____ (increases/decreases). The relationship seems to be _____ (weak/moderate/strong).

    b. Pearson's r for PAEDUC and PRESTG80 is _____. This indicates a _____ (weak/moderate/strong) relationship that is _____ (negative/positive) in direction. The relationship _____ (is/is not) statistically significant.

(*Independent Project continues*)

3. Which explanation of mobility and success in the United States is more supported by these results? Are a person's qualifications (education) the key? Does the status of a person's family make any difference? Is PRESTG80 more closely related to PAEDUC or to EDUC? Explain.

NAME _____

INSTRUCTOR _____

DATE _____

In Research Report 8.3, you tested the idea that "money can't buy happiness" using CLASS as a measure of affluence. Choose a different independent variable to measure a person's wealth or social status and replicate that study with the GSS94TAB.SAV data set. Use the **Crosstabs** procedure with column percentages, chi square, and gamma. (See Command Block 8.7.)

1. On line 1 of the following summary table, fill in the blank with the name of your independent variable. On line 2, write in the names of the categories of your independent variable, using as many blanks as necessary. On line 3, fill in the blanks with the percentage who were "very happy" for each category of the independent variable.

   Lines

   1. HAPPY by _____

   2. _____ _____ _____ _____ _____

   3. % Very
      Happy _____ _____ _____ _____ _____

   The column percentages _____ (do/do not) change so there _____ (is/is not) a relationship between these variables.

   The significance of chi square is _____ (less than/more than) .05 so this relationship _____ (is/is not) statistically significant. The value of gamma is _____ , so this is a _____ (weak/moderate/strong) relationship. The sign of gamma indicates that this is a _____ (positive/negative) relationship. As _____ increases, the score on HAPPY_____ (increases/decreases). (Be careful about direction; remember that gamma shows the direction of the relationship between the *scores* of the variables.)

3. Are these results consistent with the idea that there is no relationship between money and happiness? Explain.

NAME   _____

INSTRUCTOR   _____

DATE   _____

In Research Report 8.1 and Independent Project 8.1, you compared two different explanations of social mobility. Was education any more or less important as a cause of personal success in 1972? What about the effects of one's family? To find out, load the 1972 General Social Survey data set (GSS72.SAV) and replicate Research Report 8.1. Use INCOME72 as a measure of success, EDUC as a measure of a person's credentials, and PAPRES16 as an indicator of the status of a person's family of origin. Get both scatterplots and Pearson's r to help evaluate the theories.

1. For the relationship between EDUC and INCOME72:

   a. Observe the scatterplot. The direction of the relationship is

      _____ (positive/negative). As years of education

      increase, income _____ (increases/decreases). Judging

      from the spread of the dots (cases) around the regression line, the

      relationship seems to be _____ (weak/moderate/strong).

   b. Pearson's r for EDUC and INCOME72 is _____. This indicates a

      _____ (weak/moderate/strong) relationship that is

      _____ (negative/positive) in direction. The relationship

      _____ (is/is not) statistically significant.

2. For the relationship between PAPRES16 and INCOME72:

   a. Observe the scatterplot. The direction of the relationship is

      _____ (positive/negative). As father's prestige

      increases, income_____ (increases/decreases). Judging

      from the spread of the dots (cases) around the regression line, the

      relationship seems to be _____ (weak/moderate/strong).

   b. Pearson's r for PAPRES16 and INCOME72 is _____ . This indicates a

      _____ (weak/moderate/strong) relationship that is

      _____ (negative/positive) in direction. The relationship

      _____ (is/is not) statistically significant.

3. Which explanation of mobility and success in the United States is supported by these results? Were the relationships between the variables any different in 1972 from those in 1994? Explain.

NAME _____

INSTRUCTOR _____

DATE _____

With the 1972 GSS, replicate the study of the relationship between affluence and happiness. Following Command Block 8.7, use the **Crosstabs** procedure with CLASS as the independent variable and HAPPY as the dependent variable.

1. Complete the following summary table. For percentages, fill in the blanks with the percentage of people from each social class who said that they were "very happy."

	CLASS			
HAPPY	Lower	Working	Middle	Upper
% Very happy	____	____	____	____

The column percentages _____ (do/do not) change, so there _____ (is/is not) a relationship between happiness and class. The significance of chi square is _____ (less than/more than) .05, so this relationship _____ (is/is not) statistically significant. The value of gamma is _____, so this is a _____ (weak/moderate/strong) relationship. The sign of gamma indicates that this is a _____ (positive/negative) relationship. As the CLASS increases, happiness _____ (increases/decreases). (Be careful about direction; remember that gamma shows the direction of the relationship between the *scores* of the variables.)

2. Are these results consistent with the idea that there is no relationship between money and happiness? Explain.

(Comparative Analysis continues)

3. Does the relationship between CLASS and HAPPY change between 1972 and 1994? Explain.

Chapter 9   Inequality and Gender

Sexism in the United States

Do women have a lower place in the U.S. class system than men? Is there inequality in education? Jobs? Income? How about sexist attitudes and opinions? To what extent do Americans believe that women should be only wives and mothers and not work outside the home or take leadership positions in society? Who is most likely to subscribe to these beliefs about "a woman's proper place"?

EXERCISE 9.1   **Charting the Inequalities of Gender**

In virtually all societies, men control larger shares of wealth, property, power, and prestige than women. Is the United States an exception to this generalization? We'll begin to answer this question in this exercise and, at the same time, further explore the graphing capabilities of SPSS. We will use **multiple line charts** to display the amount of inequality between men and women on three variables in the GSS94COR.SAV data set: years of education (EDUC), occupational prestige (PRESTG80), and income (RINCOME91). The chart for each of these variables will display two lines: one for females and one for males. The differences between the lines will give us a visual indication of the degree of gender inequality: the greater the differences between the lines, the greater the inequality. We will present the graph for EDUC and SEX and leave the others to you.

After loading the GSS94COR.SAV data set, click **Graphs** from the menu bar and then **Line. . . .** The Define Line Chart dialog box appears. When we graphed variables one at a time (see Chapter 3), we selected the Simple line chart, the option highlighted now. We now want to include a second variable (SEX) in the analysis, so we need to select (click on) the **Multiple** box. Do this and then click **Define**. The Define Multiple Line box appears.

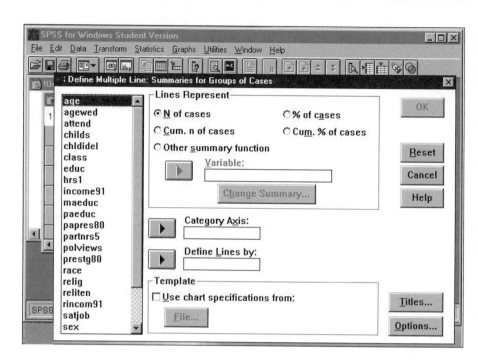

Select (move the cursor over) EDUC in the list of variables, and click the arrow pointing to the **Category Axis:** box. Then, select and transfer SEX to the **Define Lines by:** box. Also, have SPSS display the percentage of cases rather than the number of cases by clicking the radio button next to **% of cases.** Women outnumber men in the sample and the use of percentages will assure us that any differences between the lines in the chart will reflect differences in the proportional distribution of the sexes on the variable and not differences in their relative sizes.

Your version of SPSS may include "missing values" (responses such as "Don't Know" or "No Answer") in charts. To be sure that these cases are eliminated, click the **Options. . .** button in the lower-right corner of the Define Multiple Lines dialog box. If the box next to **Display groups defined by missing values** is checked, click it so that it is blank. Click **Continue** and then **OK** on the Define Multiple Lines dialog box. These commands are presented in Command Block 9.1.

COMMAND BLOCK 9.1   Producing a Multiple Line Chart for EDUC and SEX

Click **Graphs** → **Line. . .** →
Click **Multiple** on the **Define Line Chart** dialog box → Click **Define** →
In the **Define Multiple Line Chart** dialog box, highlight **EDUC** →
Click the arrow pointing to the **Category Axis:** box →
Highlight **SEX** →
Click the arrow pointing to the **Define Lines by:** box →
Click the radio button next to % of cases in the **Lines Represent** box →
Click the **Options. . .** button →
Make sure the box next to **Display groups defined by missing values** is *not* checked →
Click **Continue** →
Click **OK**

The line chart, with missing values eliminated, is presented in Figure 9.1.

FIGURE 9.1   **Multiple Line Chart for EDUC and SEX**
(1994 GSS)

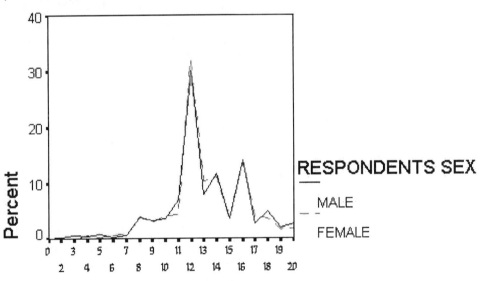

HIGHEST YEAR OF SCHOOL COMPLETED

Editing and Printing Charts

In Figure 9.1, note that the line for males is solid black, whereas the line for females is a series of dashes. If you are using a color monitor and a color printer, these lines will both be solid and different in color. On noncolor printers, however, both of the lines will be solid black and it will be difficult to distinguish males from females. To enhance clarity, we changed the format and style of the line for females and, if you are not using a color printer, you should too.

To change the appearance of (or edit) a chart, click the **Edit** button and the chart will move to a Chart window. Do this now and follow the commands in Command Block 9.2 to change line styles, even if you are using a color printer:

COMMAND BLOCK 9.2   Changing the Style of a Line in a Chart

Click **Edit** →

Click anywhere on one of the lines in the chart →

Click **Attributes** → **Line Style** →

In the **Line Style** dialog box → select a style from the box on the left →

Select a weight from the box on the right →

Click **Apply**

Now, print the chart by selecting **Print** from the **File** menu. If you are using a noncolor printer and the two lines are still not easily distinguishable, repeat the steps in Command Block 9.2 and experiment with different line styles or weights until you are satisfied. You might also explore the other options available.

Once you have a good, clear chart for EDUC and SEX, close the Chart window by clicking the button in the upper-left corner of the Chart window and clicking **Close** from the menu. SPSS will ask if you want to save the chart before closing and you may want to do so if you haven't already.

Next, follow Command Block 9.1 to construct a multiple line chart for PRESTG80 and SEX. This time, when you click **Graphs** and **Line. . .** , the Multiple option will already be highlighted and EDUC and SEX will already be selected. Click on the Category Axis: box and move EDUC back to the variable list by clicking the left-pointing arrow. Then, select PRESTG80, move it to the Category Axis: box, click **OK**, and save or print the chart. If necessary, follow the commands in Command Block 9.2 to change line styles or weights. Repeat these operations, placing RINCOME91 in the Category Axis: box.[1]

Examine each of the three charts carefully. Compare the lines across the graph (from the lower to the higher scores) to see if one line is noticeably higher or lower than the other. Which line (males or females) is higher for low scores? Scores in the middle? High scores? Use the charts to complete Research Report 9.1.

---

1. The actual amount of gender inequality on income is obscured in the GSS. Recall that scores on RINCOME91 represent categories rather than dollar values and that the top category includes incomes that range from $75,000 to untold millions. Aggregating data in this way diminishes the actual size of differences between groups. For example, the U.S. Census Bureau, using dollar values, estimates that women earn less than 70% of what men earn (U.S. Bureau of the Census, 1993, p. 467). In contrast, RINCOME91 shows that women earn about 85% of what men earn, a much narrower gap.

NAME _____

INSTRUCTOR _____

DATE _____

1. On years of education (EDUC), men are generally _____ (higher than/lower than/the same as) women. This chart indicates that the genders _____ (are/are not) equal in level of education.

2. For occupational prestige (PRESTG80), men are generally _____ (higher than/lower than/the same as) women. This chart indicates that the genders _____ (are/are not) equal in prestige.

3. For income (RINCOME91), men are generally _____ (higher than/lower than/the same as) women. This chart supports the conclusion that there _____ (is/is not) gender equality in the United States.

EXERCISE 9.2

Testing the Inequalities of Gender for Statistical Significance

The line charts produced for Research Report 9.1 are useful visual representations of gender inequality in the United States, but there are two important questions they cannot answer. First, the charts do not indicate the exact size of gender differences. Second, remember that the men and women of the 1994 GSS sample are a random sample, and we need to know if the gender differences could have been produced by random chance or if they reflect actual differences between men and women in the population.

In previous chapters, we used the Crosstabs procedure and chi square to test for statistical significance and the effects of random chance. Can we use the Crosstabs procedure in our present situation? Because all three of our measures of inequality (EDUC, PRESTG80, and RINCOME91) have many scores, Crosstabs would produce tables with many rows (one for each value of the dependent variable) and two columns (one for males, one for females). These tables would be very large, too bulky for easy analysis.

We need a new technique to analyze these numerical variables and, not surprisingly, SPSS includes a procedure called **T Test** that fits this research situation quite well. T Test computes averages for each numerical variable for each group (men and women, in our case) separately and then tests the difference between the averages for statistical significance. In our case, if there is no gender inequality on a specific variable, the averages for men and women will be equal (or nearly so). The greater the difference between the male and female average scores, the greater the likelihood that they reflect gender differences in the population on the variables in question.

We will continue to use the value of .05 to identify a statistically significant result. In the present situation, this will mean that if it is unlikely (with a probability less than .05) that the differences in average scores for men and women were produced by random chance, we will conclude that a difference exists between all adult U.S. men and women.

Instructions for the T Test procedure are given in Command Block 9.3. In the terms of this procedure, EDUC, PRESTG80, and RINCOME91 will be our Test Variables and SEX will be our Grouping Variable. For each test variable, SPSS will calculate an average score for each category of the grouping variable (males and females in this case) and then test the differences in the means for statistical significance.

COMMAND BLOCK 9.3   Running T Test for EDUC, PRESTG80, and RINCOME91 by SEX

> Click **Statistics** → **Compare Means** → **Independent Samples T Test** →
>
> Scroll through the variable names and highlight **EDUC** →
>
> Click the arrow pointing to the **Test Variable(s):** box →
>
> Highlight **PRESTG80** →
>
> Click the arrow pointing to the **Test Variable(s):** box →
>
> Highlight **RINCOME91** →
>
> Click the arrow pointing to the **Test Variable(s):** box →
>
> Highlight **SEX** →
>
> Click the arrow pointing to the **Grouping Variable:** box →
>
> Click the **Define Groups** button →
>
> Click on the **Group 1** box and type **1** →
>
> Click on the **Group 2** box and type **2** →
>
> Click **Continue** → Click **OK**

When completed, the dialog box looks like this:

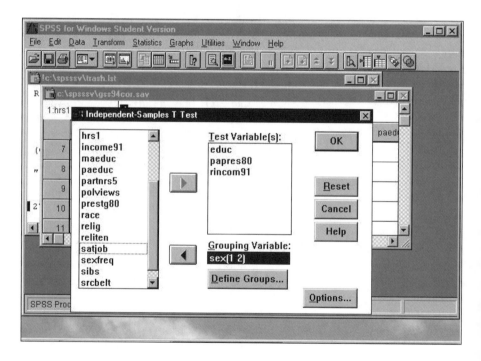

The results of the T Test for EDUC and SEX are presented in Figure 9.2.

FIGURE 9.2   **Output from T Test Procedure for EDUC and SEX**
(1994 GSS)

```
t-tests for Independent Samples of SEX      RESPONDENTS SEX


                              Number
    Variable                  of Cases      Mean         SD     SE of Mean

    EDUC   HIGHEST YEAR OF SCHOOL COMPLETED

    MALE                        639       13.1111      3.169       .125
    FEMALE                      840       13.1214      2.903       .100


           Mean Difference = -.0103

           Levene's Test for Equality of Variances: F= 3.418  P= .065


         t-test for Equality of Means                              95%
    Variances   t-value      df    2-Tail Sig    SE of Diff     CI for Diff

    Equal         -.07     1477       .948          .159       (-.321,  .301)
    Unequal       -.06   1307.35      .949          .160       (-.325,  .304)
```

Reading the Output from T Test

Along with other information, SPSS displays the average years of education for males (13.11) and females (13.12) at the top of the output under the heading of "Mean." On the average, men and women had almost exactly the same number of years of education in 1994. The results of the test for significance are reported in a box labeled "t-test for Equality of Means." Look at the middle column labeled "2-Tail Sig," which reports the probability we are seeking (.948) in the top row. This value is much greater than our standard criteria for a significant result ($p < .05$) and indicates that the very small difference in average years of education between men and women is *not* statistically significant. In other words, the average number of years of education in the population (all adult U.S. men and women) is roughly equal. This should confirm our impression from the multiple line chart.

Observe the results of the T Test for PRESTG80 and RINCOME91 and use this information to complete Research Report 9.2. Remember to look in the top row of the column labeled "2-Tail Sig" for the probability that the differences between men and women occurred by random chance and do not reflect actual differences in the population.

NAME   _____

INSTRUCTOR   _____

DATE   _____

Complete the following summary tables for the results of the T Test.

	Mean on EDUC	2-Tail Sig		Mean on PRESTG80	2-Tail Sig
Men	13.11		Men	_____	_____
Women	13.12	.948	Women	_____	_____

	Mean on RINCOME91[2]	2-Tail Sig
Men	_____	_____
Women	_____	_____

1. Men's average occupational prestige was _____ (higher than/lower than/the same as) women's and the difference _____ (is/is not) significant.

2. Men's average income was _____ (higher than/lower than/the same as) women's average income and the difference (is/is not) significant.

3. Compare these results with the line charts produced in Exercise 9.1. What information does T Test add that you didn't have before?

4. Looking at both the line charts and the T Test, what conclusions can be made about gender inequality in the United States? How much inequality is there? Where does it exist? In educational achievement? In the work world? In both areas?

_____

2. Remember that RINCOME91 groups incomes into broad categories. The values for the sample means represent these categories, not dollar values. Use **Utilities** → **Variables:**, or refer to Appendix A for the coding scheme.

(Research Report continues)

5. Think a little more about the relationships between these three measures of inequality. Do you see a pattern? Is there a time order between them? Which usually comes first in a person's life: schooling or a job? Which is usually dependent on the other? If there is gender equality on some of these variables, why not others? What can you conclude about gender inequality in the United States? See the section at the end of the chapter for our conclusions (don't cheat—write your own conclusions first).

EXERCISE 9.3   **The Correlates of Sexism**

One barrier to equality women face is **sexism**, the belief that women are inferior to men and should occupy subordinate positions in society. How widespread is this belief system? What type of person is most likely to agree with sexist statements?

We have included two possible measures of sexism in the GSS94TAB.SAV data set. One item (FEWORK) asked respondents if they "approve or disapprove of a married woman earning money in business or industry if she has a husband capable of supporting her." The second item (FEPOL) asked respondents if they agreed or disagreed that "most men are better suited emotionally for politics than are most women." What percent of the U.S. population do you think would disapprove of women working outside the home (FEWORK) or agree that women are less suited for politics (FEPOL)? To find out, load the GSS94TAB.SAV data set and get frequency distributions for FEWORK and FEPOL. Record the results in item 1 of Research Report 9.3.

What are the correlates of sexism? Pick either FEWORK or FEPOL as a measure of sexism (the dependent variable). Which of the two seems like a more valid (see Chapter 2) indicator of whether or not the respondent thinks that women are inferior to men? Explain your selection in item 2 of Research Report 9.3.

Next, find two potential causes of sexism from among the variables in the GSS94TAB.SAV data set. Do you suppose that sexism is linked to level of education? Social class? Gender? Race? Political or religious beliefs? What other factors might be causes of sexism? Use your textbook or other course materials, if relevant, to help identify the correlates of sexism. In item 3 of Research Report 9.3, state hypotheses linking your independent variables to sexism. Use **Crosstabs**, column percentages, chi square, and either Cramer's *V* (for non-numerical variables) or gamma (for numerical variables) to evaluate the relationships. Use the output from this procedure to complete Research Report 9.3. If you need a reminder on the commands for Crosstabs, see Command Block 8.7 in Chapter 8, or Appendix B.

NAME _____

INSTRUCTOR _____

DATE _____

1. Summarize the frequency distributions for the two measures of sexism by noting the percentage of the sample that supports the more sexist response.

   % Disapprove on FEWORK _____

   % Agree on FEPOL _____

   Based on these percentages, would you describe the level of sexism in the United States as high, moderate, or low? Explain.

2. Which variable (FEWORK or FEPOL) seems to be a more valid measure of sexism (defined as the belief that women are inferior to men and should occupy subordinate positions)?_____ . Explain your choice.

3. State the names of the independent variables you selected:

   _____ and _____ . State a hypothesis about the relationship between each independent variable and sexism.

   a.

   b.

4. Summarize the results of the Crosstab analysis for each independent variable.
   a. *For your first independent variable*: On line 1 of the following summary table, fill in the blanks with the names of your variables. On line 2, write in the names of the categories of your independent variable, using as many blanks as necessary. On line 3, fill in the blanks with the percentage of respondents who gave the more sexist response ("disapprove" for FEWORK and "agree" for FEPOL).

(Research Report continues)

Lines

1.   ———————— (FEWORK/FEPOL) by ————————

2.   ————— ————— ————— ————— —————

3. % Sexist———— ————— ————— ————— —————

The column percentages ————————————(do/do not) change, so

there ————————————(is/is not) a relationship between these

variables. The significance of chi square is ————————————

(less than/more than) .05, so this relationship ————————————

(is/is not) statistically significant.

If the independent variable is **not** *numerical*: The value of Cramer's

V is ———— , so this is a ———————————— (weak/moderate/strong)

relationship.

If the independent variable **is** *numerical*: The value of gamma is

———— , so this is a ————————————(weak/moderate/strong)

relationship. The sign of gamma indicates that this is a

———————————— (positive/negative) relationship. As

———————————— (name of your independent variable) increases,

sexism ———————————— (increases/decreases). (Be careful when

interpreting direction; remember that the sign of gamma refers to the

direction of the relationship between the *scores* of the variables.)

b. *For your second independent variable*: On line 1 of the following
summary table, fill in the blanks with the names of your variables.
On line 2, write in the names of the categories of your independent
variable, using as many blanks as necessary. On line 3, fill in the
blanks with the percentage of respondents who gave the more sexist response ("disapprove" for FEWORK and "agree" for FEPOL).

Lines

1.   ————————(FEWORK/FEPOL) by ————————

2.   ————— ————— ————— ————— —————

3. % Sexist ———— ————— ————— ————— —————

(Research Report continues)

The column percentages_____ (do/do not) change, so
there_____(is/is not) a relationship between these
variables. The significance of chi square is _____
(less than/more than) .05, so this relationship
_____ (is/is not) statistically significant.

If the independent variable is **not** *numerical*: The value of Cramer's
V is _____ , so this is a _____ (weak/moderate/strong)
relationship.

If the independent variable **is** *numerical*: The value of gamma is
_____ , so this is a _____(weak/moderate/strong)
relationship. The sign of gamma indicates that this is a
_____ (positive/negative) relationship. As
_____ (name of your independent variable)
increases, sexism_____(increases/decreases). (Be
careful when interpreting direction; remember that the sign of
gamma refers to the direction of the relationship between the *scores*
of the variables.)

5. Were your hypotheses confirmed? Explain.

EXERCISE 9.4   **Multivariate Analysis of Sexism**

The elaboration technique for multivariate analysis was introduced in Chapter 7. This technique involves controlling for a third variable or observing what happens to a bivariate relationship for each category of a control variable. In this exercise, the results of a multivariate analysis of sexism while controlling for SEX will be summarized. Then, you will select control variables and conduct a similar analysis of sexism. Your results will be reported in Research Report 9.4.

What is the relationship between education and sexism? Are more educated people more or less sexist? To deal with these questions, we used DEGREE as an indicator of level of education and FEWORK as a measure of sexism. You may have analyzed this relationship as part of Research Report 9.3 but, if not, we will simply tell you that the relationship between these variables is statistically significant (at the .05 level) and strong (gamma = –.35). Respondents with less than a high school education were almost three times more likely to disapprove of women working than respondents with at least some college (31% vs. 11%). The negative sign of the gamma indicates that as scores increased on DEGREE (as level of education rose), scores on FEWORK decreased (people were more likely to approve—a score of 1—than disapprove—a score of 2).

At this point, we know that more educated people are less sexist. Will sexism decline with education regardless of the gender of the respondent? Will more educated men be just as nonsexist as more educated women? These are the kinds of questions that can be answered with the elaboration technique of multivariate analysis. To control for a third variable, we re-ran the bivariate relationship (with the dependent variable in the rows and the independent variable in the columns) and transferred the name of the control variable (SEX, in this case) to the bottom window or "layer box" of the Crosstabs dialog box. See Command Block 7.2 or Appendix B for further instructions on using a control variable in Crosstabs. A summary of the effect of controlling for SEX is presented in Table 9.1.

TABLE 9.1   **Disapproval of Women Working, by Degree and Sex** (Percentages)

	Less Than High School	High School	At Least Some College	Gamma
All	31	18	11	–.35
Men	30	20	15	–.26
Women	32	17	9	–.42

Source: 1994 GSS

First, note that for both men and women disapproval of women working is highest for the least educated and declines as education increases. Second, women at the lowest level of education have the highest percentage of disapprovers, and the relationship between education and FEWORK is stronger for women than for men. What other differences can you spot between men and women? How might these differences be explained?

Now it's your turn. Choose one of your bivariate relationships from Research Report 9.3 for further analysis. Choose the relationship that is the most interesting to you or, all other things being equal, choose the strongest relationship (use

Cramer's *V* or gamma to measure strength). Do not choose a relationship in which SEX or DEGREE was an independent (column) variable. Now, choose SEX and one other variable as control variables. Choose a variable with only two or three categories or scores as a control variable (preferably two). Follow Command Block 9.4 to produce multivariate tables (you already have the bivariate tables) with SEX as the control variable:

COMMAND BLOCK 9.4   Producing Multivariate Tables Controlling for SEX

Click **Statistics** → **Summarize** → **Crosstabs** →
Highlight **FEWORK** or **FEPOL** →
Click the arrow pointing to the **Row(s):** box →
Highlight your independent variable →
Click the arrow pointing to the **Column(s):** box →
Highlight **SEX** →
Click the arrow pointing to the "layer" box at the bottom of the window →
Click **Cells** →
Click **Columns** in the **Percentages** box →
Click **Continue** →
In the Crosstabs dialog box, click **Statistics** →
Select **Chi Square** and **Cramer's V** or **Gamma** →
Click **Continue** →
Click **OK**

Repeat these commands with the name of your other control variable substituted for SEX and use the output to complete Research Report 9.4.

NAME   _____

INSTRUCTOR   _____

DATE   _____

1. *For the first control variable (SEX)*: Using Table 9.1 as a guide, complete a summary table to display the results of your multivariate analysis. In line 1, fill in the blank with the name of your dependent and independent variables. In line 2, write in the names of the categories of your independent variable, using as many blanks as necessary. In line 3, fill in the percentage of each category of the independent variable who gave the more sexist response ("disapprove" for FEWORK and "agree" for FEPOL). This information can be copied from Research Report 9.3.

   In line 4, fill in the percentage of each category of the independent variable who gave the more sexist response for men. In line 5, do the same for women.

   Lines

   1.   _____ (FEWORK/FEPOL) by _____

   2.   _____ _____ _____ _____   Cramer's *V* or Gamma

   3. All   _____ _____ _____ _____ _____

   4. Men   _____ _____ _____ _____ _____

   5. Women   _____ _____ _____ _____ _____

   Use the column percentages and the measure of association to analyze these results. Were sexism and your independent variable related in the same way for both men and women? What differences and similarities can you identify? Which subgroup is most sexist? Which is least sexist? Explain.

2. *For the second control variable*: Using Table 9.1 as a guide, complete a summary table to display the results of your multivariate analysis. In line 1, fill in the blank with the name of your dependent, independent, and control variables. In line 2, write in the names of the categories of your independent variable, using as many blanks as necessary. In line 3, fill in the percentage of each category of the independent variable who gave the more sexist response ("disapprove" for FEWORK and "agree" for FEPOL). This information can be copied from item 1 of this research report.

(Research Report continues)

In line 4, fill in the percentage of each category of the independent variable who gave the more sexist response for the first category of your control variable. In line 5 and, if necessary, line 6, do the same for the other categories of your control variable.

Lines

1.   _____ (FEWORK/FEPOL) by _____

       (independent variable) by_____ (control variable)

					Cramer's *V* or Gamma
2.	_____	_____	_____	_____	_____
3. All	_____	_____	_____	_____	_____
4. _____	_____	_____	_____	_____	_____
5. _____	_____	_____	_____	_____	_____
6. _____	_____	_____	_____	_____	_____

Use the column percentages and the measure of association to analyze these results. Were sexism and your independent variable related in the same way for all categories of the control variable? What differences and similarities can you identify? Which subgroup is most sexist? Which is least sexist? Explain.

Our Analysis of Gender Inequality for Research Reports 9.1 and 9.2

Both the line charts and the T tests showed that there was no significant difference between men and women in terms of educational achievements (EDUC) and occupational prestige (PRESTG80). Significant gender inequality was evident only on income (RINCOME91). How can we account for this pattern? Specifically, if men and women are roughly equal in their qualifications for the job market (average years of education), shouldn't they also be equal in income?

One possible explanation is that these patterns are caused by continuing gender inequality. Studies have shown that, compared with men, women are less likely to work outside the home, more likely to work part-time rather than full-time, and less likely to occupy top management positions and/or to pursue the most prestigious professions. Women who work outside the home tend to be concentrated in such relatively low paid occupations as retail clerk, nurse, schoolteacher, secretary, and waitress.

The pattern of gender differences in the 1994 GSS sample may reflect the fact that the movement toward gender equality in the larger society has been only partially successful. Women have achieved near parity in some areas of social life (education) but not in others (work); society has some distance to go before gender equality is fully realized.

Main Points

■ Line charts and T tests were used to explore gender inequality in 1994 for three variables: educational attainment, occupational prestige, and income.

■ Crosstab tables and elaboration were used to measure the levels of sexism in the United States and to seek the causes of sexist attitudes.

SPSS Commands Introduced in This Chapter

COMMAND BLOCK 9.1   *Producing Multiple Line Charts*

Click **Graphs** → **Line. . .** →

Click **Multiple** on the Define Line Chart dialog box → Click **Define** →

In the **Define Multiple Line Chart** dialog box, highlight the name of the dependent variable (this variable should be numerical)→

Click the arrow pointing to the **Category Axis:** box →

Highlight the name of the independent variable →

Click the arrow pointing to the **Define Lines by:** box →

If you wish, click the radio button next to % of cases in the **Lines Represent** box →

Click the **Options. . .** button →

Make sure the box next to **Display groups defined by missing values** is *not* checked →

Click **Continue** →

Click **OK**

9.2   *Changing the Style of a Line in a Chart*

> Click **EDIT**
> Click anywhere on one of the lines in the chart →
> Click **Attributes** → **Line Style** →
> In the **Line Style** dialog box, select a style from the box on the left →
> Select a weight from the box on the right →
> Click **Apply**

9.3   *Running T Test (for independent variables with only two categories)*

> Click **Statistics** → **Compare Means** → **Independent Samples T Test** →
> Highlight the names of each dependent variable →
> Click the arrow pointing to the **Test Variable(s):** box →
> Highlight the name of the independent variable →
> Click the arrow pointing to the **Grouping Variable:** box →
> Click the **Define Groups** button →
> Click on the **Group 1** box and type **1** →
> Click on the **Group 2** box and type **2** →
> Click **Continue** → Click **OK**

NAME _____

INSTRUCTOR _____

DATE _____

Continue the analysis of the causes of sexism you started in Research Report 9.3, with two new independent variables from the **GSS94TAB.SAV** data set. (Do not use SEX.)

1. Name your independent variables: _____ and _____.

   State hypotheses linking each variable with your measure of sexism.

   a.

   b.

2. Use the **Crosstabs** procedure (with column percentages, chi square, and either Cramer's *V* or gamma) to analyze the relationship between your independent variables and either FEWORK or FEPOL. Summarize your results for each independent variable.

   a. *For your first independent variable*: On line 1 of the following summary table, fill in the blanks with the names of your variables. On line 2, write in the names of the categories of your independent variable, using as many blanks as necessary. On line 3, fill in the blanks with the percentage of respondents who gave the more sexist response ("disapprove" for FEWORK and "agree" for FEPOL).

      Lines

      1. _____ (FEWORK/FEPOL) by _____

      2. _____ _____ _____ _____ _____

      3. % Sexist _____ _____ _____ _____ _____

      The column percentages _____ (do/do not) change, so there _____ (is/is not) a relationship between these variables. The significance of chi square is _____ (less than/more than) .05, so this relationship _____ (is/is not) statistically significant.

      *If the independent variable is **not** numerical*: The value of Cramer's *V* is _____, so this is a _____ (weak/moderate/strong) relationship.

(Independent Project continues)

If the independent variable **is** *numerical*: The value of gamma is
_____, so this is a _____(weak/moderate/strong) rela-
tionship. The sign of gamma indicates that this is a_____
(positive/negative) relationship. As _____(name of your
independent variable) increases, sexism _____
(increases/decreases).

b. *For your second independent variable*: On line 1 of the following
summary table, fill in the blanks with the names of your variables.
On line 2, write in the names of the categories of your independent
variable, using as many blanks as necessary. On line 3, fill in the
blanks with the percentage of respondents who gave the more sexist response ("disapprove" for FEWORK and "agree" for FEPOL).

Lines

1.   _____(FEWORK/FEPOL) by _____

2.   _____ _____ _____ _____ _____

3.   % Sexist _____   _____   _____   _____   _____

The column percentages_____(do/do not) change, so
there_____(is/is not) a relationship between these variables. The significance of chi square is _____(less
than/more than) .05, so this relationship _____(is/is not)
statistically significant.

If the independent variable is **not** *numerical*: The value of Cramer's
V is_____, so this is a_____ (weak/moderate/strong)
relationship.

If the independent variable **is** *numerical*: The value of gamma is
_____ , so this is a_____(weak/moderate/strong) relationship. The sign of gamma indicates that this is a
(positive/negative) relationship. As _____(name of your
independent variable) increases, sexism _____
(increases/decreases).

3. Were your hypotheses confirmed? Explain.

NAME _____

INSTRUCTOR _____

DATE _____

1. Pick one of the relationships you examined in Independent Project 9.1. What happens to this bivariate relationship when you control for SEX? Use the **Crosstabs** procedure to analyze the relationship while controlling for SEX. Name your dependent variable (either FEWORK or FEPOL) as the row variable, your independent variable as the column variable, and SEX as the control variable (move SEX to the bottom box of the **Crosstabs** dialog box). See Command Block 9.4 for the necessary commands.

2. Complete the following summary table to display your results for the full sample and for men and women separately. In line 1, fill in the blank with the name of your dependent and independent variables. In line 2, write in the names of the categories of your independent variable, using as many blanks as necessary. In line 3, fill in the percentage of each category of the independent variable who gave the more sexist response ("disapprove" for FEWORK and "agree" for FEPOL). The information for this line can be copied from Independent Project 9.1. In line 4, fill in the percentage of each category of the independent variable who gave the more sexist response for men. In line 5, do the same for women.

Lines

1. _____ (FEWORK/FEPOL) by _____ by SEX

2. _____ _____ _____ _____   Cramer's *V* or Gamma _____

3. All _____ _____ _____ _____   _____

4. Men _____ _____ _____ _____   _____

5. Women _____ _____ _____ _____   _____

3. Use the column percentages and the measure of association to analyze these results. Were sexism and your independent variable related in the same way for both men and women? What differences and similarities can you identify? Which subgroup is most sexist? Which is least sexist? Explain.

NAME _____

INSTRUCTOR _____

DATE _____

Repeat the analysis done in Research Report 9.1, using the 1972 General Social Survey (**GSS72**). Get multiple line charts for EDUC, PRESTIGE, and INCOME72 by SEX. Use the charts to complete the following statements.

1. On years of education (EDUC), men were generally _____ (higher than/lower than/the same as) women. This chart indicates that men and women _____ (were/were not) equal in level of education in 1972.

2. For occupational prestige (PRESTIGE), men are generally _____ (higher than/lower than/the same as) women. This chart indicates that men and women _____(were/were not) equal in prestige in 1972.

3. For income (INCOME72), men are generally _____(higher than/lower than/the same as) women. This chart supports the conclusion that there _____(was/was not) gender equality in the United States in 1972.

4. Compare these results with those presented in Research Report 9.1. Has the amount of gender inequality declined or increased since 1972? For which variables? Do these patterns support our explanation of 1994 gender inequality presented at the end of the chapter? Explain.

NAME _____

INSTRUCTOR _____

DATE _____

Repeat the analysis done in Research Report 9.2, using the 1972 General Social Survey (**GSS72**). Run the T Test procedure with EDUC, PRESTIGE, and INCOME72 as the test variables and SEX as the grouping variable. Complete the following summary tables to display the results.

	Mean on EDUC	2-Tail Sig
Men	_____	
Women	_____	_____

	Mean on PRESTIGE	2-Tail Sig
Men	_____	
Women	_____	_____

	Mean on INCOME72	2-Tail Sig
Men	_____	
Women	_____	_____

1. In 1972, men averaged _____ (more/fewer) years of education than women and the difference _____ (is/is not) significant.

2. In 1972, men's average occupational prestige was _____ (higher/lower) than women's and the difference _____ (is/is not) significant.

3. In 1972, men had a _____ (higher/lower) average income than women and the difference _____ (is/is not) significant.

4. Summarize these results. How much gender inequality existed in 1972? On which variables? Was there more or less gender inequality in 1972 than in 1994? Explain.

NAME _____

INSTRUCTOR _____

DATE _____

1. Was sexism stronger in 1972 than in 1994? Use FEWORK from the GSS72 database as a measure of sexism. Get a frequency distribution (use the **Frequencies** procedure) for this variable. In Research Report 9.3, we saw that about 18% of the sample disapproved of women working. What percentage of the sample disapproved in 1972? _____ . Between 1972 and 1994, sexism _____ (decreased/increased/stayed the same).

2. Test the relationship between one of the independent variables you used in this chapter and FEWORK for 1972. Use **Crosstabs**, with column percentages, chi square, and Cramer's V or gamma to analyze the relationship. Summarize your results in the following table. On line 1, fill in the blank with the name of your independent variable. On line 2, write in the names of the categories of your independent variable, using as many blanks as necessary. On line 3, fill in the blanks with the percentage of respondents who gave the more sexist response ("disapprove").

    Lines

    1.   FEWORK by_____

    2.   _____ _____ _____ _____ _____

    3.   % Sexist _____ _____ _____ _____ _____

    The column percentages _____ (do/do not) change, so there _____ (is/is not) a relationship between these variables. The significance of chi square is _____ (less than/more than) .05, so this relationship _____ (is/is not) statistically significant.

    *If the independent variable is **not** numerical*: The value of Cramer's V is _____ , so this is a _____ (weak/moderate/strong) relationship.

If the independent variable **is** *numerical*: The value of gamma is

_____ , so this is a _____ (weak/moderate/strong) rela-

tionship. The sign of gamma indicates that this is a _____

(positive/negative) relationship. As _____ (name of your

independent variable) increases, sexism _____

(increases/decreases).

3. Compare the 1972 relationship with your 1994 results. Have the correlates of sexism changed over the years? Explain.

Chapter 10 Inequality and Race

Chapter 9 explored gender inequality and sexism in the United States. This chapter conducts a parallel investigation of racial inequality and racial prejudice. How much inequality between black and white Americans exists in education, jobs, and income? How strong is racial prejudice? Who is most likely to support racist beliefs?

The Legacy of Racial Inequality

Inequality between the races began at the birth of U.S. society. American slavery was created in the 1660s, just decades after the founding of Jamestown, and this oppressive system institutionalized powerlessness and low status for blacks. Following the Civil War, the Southern states replaced slavery with a new form of inequality called segregation. Under this system, a series of laws forced African Americans into inferior positions in virtually every aspect of society: schools, jobs, neighborhoods, the political system, and in the courts. Legalized, state-supported segregation ended in the 1960s, just three decades ago. What is the legacy of these three centuries of racial inequality? How much inequality between the races remains in the 1990s? Have African Americans achieved parity with white Americans in schooling, employment, or income?

EXERCISE 10.1   **Charting the Inequalities of Race**

We will answer these questions by using line graphs (as in Chapter 9) to display the degree of inequality between the races on three variables: years of education (EDUC), occupational prestige (PRESTG80), and income (RINCOME91). To refresh your memory, these charts will display two lines, one for whites and one for blacks, for each of the three variables. The greater the racial inequality in the United States, the greater the differences between the two lines. As in Chapter 9, we will present the graph for EDUC and leave most of the work to you. The instructions that follow are an abbreviated version of those in Chapter 9 (see especially Command Blocks 9.1 and 9.2), with RACE substituted for SEX.

First, load the **GSS94COR.SAV** data set and request a line chart by clicking **Graphs** from the menu bar and then **Line. . . .** The Define Line Chart dialog box appears. Select the Multiple box and then click **Define**. The Define Multiple Line box appears. In the Define Multiple Line box, select and transfer EDUC to the Category Axis: window and RACE to the Define Lines by: window. Also, because the numbers of whites and blacks in the sample is so different, have SPSS display the percentage of cases by clicking the appropriate box.

These procedures are summarized in Command Block 10.1, and the chart for EDUC and RACE is presented in Figure 10.1.

COMMAND BLOCK 10.1   Producing a Multiple Line Chart for EDUC and RACE

> Click **Graphs** → **Line. . .** →
> Click **Multiple** → Click **Define** →
> Highlight **EDUC** and click the arrow pointing to the **Category Axis:** box →
> Highlight **RACE** and click the arrow pointing to the **Define Lines by:** box →
> Click the radio button next to **% of cases** in the **Lines Represent** box →
> Click **Options** and make sure that **Display groups defined by missing values** is *not* checked →
> Click **Continue** →
> Click **OK**

FIGURE 10.1   **Output of Line Chart for RACE and EDUC**
(1994 GSS)

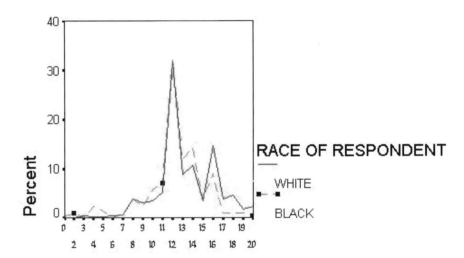

Printing and Editing Charts

The chart in Figure 10.1 was printed on a noncolor printer and, originally, both lines were solid black. The style of the line representing black Americans was changed to enhance clarity. If you are not using a color printer, you can change line styles by following the instructions in Command Block 9.2. Once you are satisfied with the appearance of your chart, print it by selecting **Print** from the **File** menu. You may also wish to **Save** the chart at this time. You can close this window by clicking the button in the upper-left corner and choosing **Close**.

Now, follow Command Block 10.1 to get multiple line charts for PRESTG80 and RACE and for RINCOME91 and RACE. This time, when you click **Graphs** and **Line. . .** , the Multiple option will already be highlighted and EDUC and RACE will already be selected. Click on the Category Axis: box and move EDUC back to the variable list by clicking the left-pointing arrow. Then, select PRESTG80, move it to the Category Axis: box, click **OK**, and **Edit**, **Save**, and **Print** the chart. Finally, repeat these operations, placing RINCOME91 in the Category Axis: box.

Examine each chart carefully. Compare the lines across the graph from left to right (or from lower to higher scores) to see how the lines change in relationship to each other. Remember that higher lines indicate more common scores. Use the three charts to complete Research Report 10.1.

NAME _____

INSTRUCTOR _____

DATE _____

1. On years of education (EDUC), blacks are generally _____ (higher than/lower than/the same as) whites. This chart indicates that the races _____ (are/are not) equal in level of education.

2. For occupational prestige (PRESTG80), blacks are generally _____ (higher than/lower than/the same as) whites. This chart indicates that the races _____ (are/are not) equal in prestige.

3. For income (RINCOME91), blacks are generally _____ (higher than/lower than/the same as) whites. This chart supports the conclusion that there _____ (is/is not) racial equality in the United States.

EXERCISE 10.2   **Testing Racial Inequalities for Statistical Significance**

Because we are working with a random sample, we need to know if the differences between the races on the three measures of inequality (EDUC, PRESTG80, and RINCOME91) could have been produced by random chance. Because all three variables are numerical and have many scores, the T Test procedure is appropriate (see Chapter 9). This procedure computes an average score for each group (race) and then tests the difference between the averages for statistical significance. If there is no racial inequality on the variable, the averages will be equal (or nearly so). The more dissimilar the averages, the greater the likelihood that the difference did not occur by random chance and that it reflects patterns in the population (that is, differences between *all* black Americans and *all* white Americans). We will continue to use the value of .05 to identify a statistically significant result.

To run the T Test procedure, follow the instructions in Command Block 10.2. EDUC, PRESTG80, and RINCOME91 are the Test Variables, and RACE is the Grouping Variable. This procedure is explained in detail in Chapter 9 (p. 211) with SEX instead of RACE as the grouping variable. The output for this procedure for EDUC and RACE is presented in Figure 10.2.

COMMAND BLOCK 10.2   Running T Test for EDUC, PRESTG80, and RINCOME91 by RACE

> Click **Statistics** → **Compare Means** → **Independent Samples T Test** →
>
> The **Independent Samples T Test** dialog box appears →
>
> Highlight **EDUC** and click the arrow pointing to the **Test Variable(s):** box →
>
> Highlight **PRESTG80** and click the arrow pointing to the **Test Variable(s):** box →
>
> Highlight **RINCOME91** and click the arrow pointing to the **Test Variable(s):** box →
>
> Highlight **RACE** and click the arrow pointing to the **Grouping Variable:** box →
>
> Click the **Define Groups** button →
>
> Click on the **Group 1** box and type **1** →
>
> Click on the **Group 2** box and type **2** →
>
> Click **Continue** → Click **OK**

FIGURE 10.2   **Output from T Test for RACE and EDUC**
(1994 GSS)

```
t-tests for Independent Samples of RACE     RACE OF RESPONDENT


                              Number
Variable                      of Cases       Mean        SD    SE of Mean

EDUC   HIGHEST YEAR OF SCHOOL COMPLETED

WHITE                          1213        13.2630      2.962      .085
BLACK                           209        12.1914      3.018      .209


           Mean Difference = 1.0716

           Levene's Test for Equality of Variances: F= 4.726  P= .030


        t-test for Equality of Means                               95%
_Variances  t-value     df    2-Tail Sig    SE of Diff       CI for Diff

Equal        4.82     1420      .000          .222        (.635, 1.508)
Unequal      4.75    281.45     .000          .225        (.628, 1.515)
```

Reading the Output from T Test

SPSS displays the average years of education for whites (13.26) and blacks (12.19) under the heading of "Mean" at the top of the output. On the average, white Americans have about one year more schooling than black Americans. The statistical significance of this difference is reported in the box labeled "t-test for Equality of Means." Look at the middle column labeled "2-Tail Sig," which reports the probability we are seeking in the top row. This value (.000) is less than our standard criteria for a significant result (.05) and indicates that the difference in average years of education *is* statistically significant. In other words, it is unlikely that the difference in average scores between blacks and whites was caused by random chance. On the average, black Americans have significantly fewer years of education than white Americans.

Use the results of the T Test for PRESTG80 and RINCOME91 to complete Research Report 10.2. Remember to look in the top row of the column labeled "2-Tail Sig" for the probability that the differences occurred by random chance and do not reflect actual differences in the population. Values of less than .05 indicate a significant difference.

NAME _____

INSTRUCTOR _____

DATE _____

Complete the following summary tables for the results of the T Test.

	Mean on EDUC	2-Tail Sig		Mean on PRESTG80	2-Tail Sig
Whites	_____		Whites	_____	
Blacks	_____	_____	Blacks	_____	_____

	Mean on RINCOME91[1]	2-Tail Sig
Whites	_____	
Blacks	_____	_____

1. Whites are _____ (higher than/lower than/the same as) blacks on occupational prestige, and the difference _____ (is/is not) statistically significant.

2. Average income for whites is _____ (higher than/lower than/the same as) average income for blacks, and the difference _____ (is/is not) significant.

3. Looking at both the line charts and the T Test, what conclusions can be made about racial inequality in the United States? How much inequality is there? Where does it exist? In educational achievement? In work? In both areas?

4. Compare these results with Research Report 9.2. Which is greater: racial inequality or sexual inequality? (You can determine this by comparing the amount and the significance of the differences between group means.)

1. Remember that RINCOME91 groups incomes into categories. The values of the sample means represent these categories, not dollar values. Use **Utilities → Variables. . .** or Appendix A to see the coding scheme.

EXERCISE 10.3   **The Extent and Causes of Racial Prejudice in the United States**

Prejudice may be defined as an attitude toward other groups that combines negative feelings or emotions (such as contempt or dislike) and negative ideas or stereotypes (such as the perception that Jews are stingy, Irish are drunks, Italians are hot-tempered, or that African Americans are irresponsible). How extensive is racial prejudice in the United States? We can explore this issue with the GSS94TAB.SAV data set. Load this data set now.

Selecting Respondents Before analyzing anti-black racial prejudice, it makes sense to eliminate black respondents from the sample and focus on whites only. We can do this by choosing the **Select Cases: If** command. This command is appropriate when we are interested only in cases with certain characteristics or qualities. After the **Select Cases: If** command is executed, SPSS procedures (like Frequencies) will be performed only on cases that have the characteristics we specify. For example, we could confine the sample to older respondents, people who reside on the East Coast, Democrats, and so forth. In this case, we will limit the sample to white respondents only.

Begin by selecting **Data** from the menu bar and then click on **Select Cases** in the drop-down menu. The Select Cases dialog box appears.

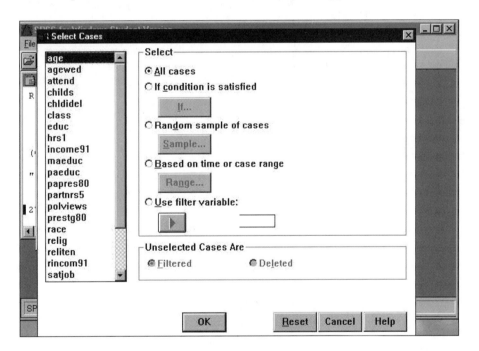

As you can see, there are several options for limiting or refining the sample. In our case, we want to select cases if they are white, or have a score of "1" on RACE. Click the **If condition is satisfied** radio button and then click the **If** button. The Select Cases: If dialog box appears:

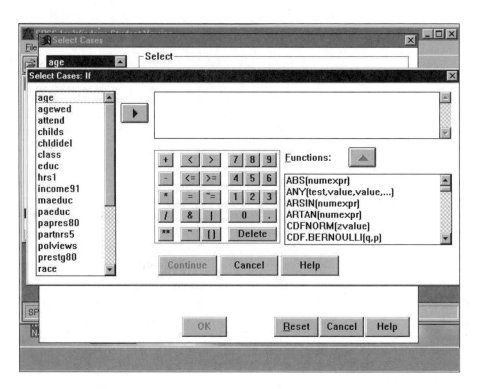

Find RACE in the variable list to the left of the box and move it to the rectangle at the top of the dialog box by clicking the right-pointing arrow. Now, select the equals (=) sign from the calculator pad and the number **1**. The expression in the rectangle should read

> race = 1

Click **Continue** to return to the Select Cases: If box and then click **OK**. These commands are summarized in Command Block 10.3:

COMMAND BLOCK 10.3   Selecting White Respondents Only

> Click **Data** → **Select Cases** →
> From the **Select Cases** dialog box, click **If condition is satisfied** →
> Click **IF** →
> In the **Select Cases: If** dialog box, highlight **RACE** and click
> the right-pointing arrow →
> Click the = sign and the number **1** from the calculator pad →
> Click **Continue** →
> Click **OK**

Depending on how your version of SPSS is installed, the selection process may be performed when you click **OK** or when you request a procedure. Once you have run the necessary procedures with the refined sample, turn off the **Select Cases: If** command by clicking **Reset** in the Select Cases dialog box. This will restore the sample to its original composition.

Measuring Prejudice

Social scientists have developed numerous ways of measuring racial prejudice, and the General Social Survey includes a number of items that operationalize these feelings and stereotypes. One measure of prejudice asked respondents to accept or reject each of four explanations for racial inequality in the United States, one of which (RACDIF2) attributed racial inequality to the *inborn* lack of ability of black Americans. Respondents who agreed with this explanation presumably see blacks as inferior to whites. Thus, we will operationalize racial prejudice as agreement with (or a response of "yes" to) this explanation of racial inequality.

We can use the Frequency procedure to determine the percentage of white respondents who are prejudiced (that is, who agree with the "inborn ability" explanation of racial inequality). This will give an indication of the extent of prejudice in the United States.

Click **Statistics** → **Summarize** → **Frequencies** from the menu bar. Select RACDIF2 from the variable list and click **OK**. Print and/or save the table and use it to complete item 1 in Research Report 10.3.

What Causes Prejudice?

Beyond measuring the extent of prejudice, social scientists would naturally want to know something about the causes of this attitude. What types of Americans would subscribe to the belief that black Americans are innately inferior? Use your textbook or other course materials, if relevant, to identify two possible causes of racial prejudice. Could education be a causal factor? Social class? Age? Political ideology? Develop hypotheses linking your independent variables to RACDIF2 and use the **Crosstabs** procedure, with column percentages, chi square, and Cramer's *V* (for non-numerical independent variables) or gamma (for numerical independent variables) to evaluate the strength and significance of the relationships. Use the output to complete Research Report 10.3. Instructions for Crosstabs can be found in Command Block 8.7 and Appendix B.

NAME _____

INSTRUCTOR _____

DATE _____

1. *Measuring the extent of racial prejudice*: _____% of the sample agreed
   ("yes" on RACDIF2) that racial inequality is caused by the lack of
   ability of black Americans. Based on this result, the degree of prejudice in the United States is _____ (high/moderate/low).
   (You may want to reserve judgment on the extent of prejudice in the
   United States until you complete Exercise 10.4.)

2. State the names of the independent variables you selected: _____
   and _____. State and briefly explain a hypothesis about the
   relationship between each independent variable and prejudice.

   a.

   b.

3. Summarize the results of the Crosstab analysis for each independent
   variable.

   a. *For your first independent variable*: On line 1 of the following
      summary table, fill in the blank with the name of your independent
      variable. On line 2, write in the names of the categories of your
      independent variable, using as many blanks as necessary. On line
      3, fill in the blanks with the percentage of respondents who were
      prejudiced ("yes" on RACDIF2).

      Lines

      1.   RACDIF2 by _____

      2.   _____ _____ _____ _____ _____

      3. % Prejudiced _____ _____ _____ _____ _____

      The column percentages _____ (do/do not) change, so

      there _____ (is/is not) a relationship between these

      variables. The significance of chi square is _____ (less

      than/more than) .05, so this relationship _____ (is/is

      not) statistically significant.

(Research Report continues)

If the independent variable is **not** *numerical*: The value of Cramer's *V* is ____, so this is a _____ (weak/moderate/strong) relationship.

If the independent variable **is** *numerical*: The value of gamma is ____, so this is a _____ (weak/moderate/strong) relationship. The sign of gamma indicates that this is a _____ (positive/negative) relationship. As _____ (name of your independent variable) increases, prejudice _____ (increases/decreases).

b. *For your second independent variable*: On line 1 of the following summary table, fill in the blank with the name of your independent variable. On line 2, write in the names of the categories of your independent variable, using as many blanks as necessary. On line 3, fill in the blanks with the percentage of respondents who were prejudiced ("yes" on RACDIF2).

Lines

1.   RACDIF2 by _____

2.   _____ _____ _____ _____ _____

3. % Prejudiced _____ _____ _____ _____ _____

The column percentages _____ (do/do not) change, so there _____ (is/is not) a relationship between these variables. The significance of chi square is _____ (less than/more than) .05, so this relationship _____ (is/is not) statistically significant.

If the independent variable is **not** *numerical*: The value of Cramer's *V* is ____, so this is a _____ (weak/moderate/strong) relationship.

If the independent variable **is** *numerical*: The value of gamma is ____, so this is a _____ (weak/moderate/strong) relationship. The sign of gamma indicates that this is a _____ (positive/negative) relationship. As _____ (name of your independent variable) increases, prejudice _____ (increases/decreases).

4. Were your hypotheses confirmed? Explain.

| EXERCISE 10.4 | **Another Look at Prejudice in the United States: Modern Racism** |

The frequency distribution for RACDIF2 indicates that only a small minority of white Americans believe that black Americans are innately inferior. This result is consistent with public opinion surveys over the past 50 years, which show that blatant racial prejudice has declined and that the United States has become a more tolerant society.

Before congratulating ourselves too heartily on our greater tolerance, however, we need to pay heed to another, less rosy view of America's racial attitudes. A number of scholars have been investigating the possibility that blatant racial prejudice hasn't so much declined as it has changed form and become more subtle and indirect (Sears, 1988; Bobo & Kluegal, 1993). According to this line of research, prejudice has grown softer and less overt but it remains an important feature of American race relations.

This new form of prejudice is called symbolic or **modern racism**; a measure of it is included in the list of explanations for racial inequality presented to respondents in the GSS. For this exercise, modern racism can be operationalized as agreement with the statement that "Most blacks just don't have the motivation or willpower to pull themselves out of poverty" (RACDIF4). Presumably, those who agree with this explanation believe that black Americans have the ability to close the racial gap but choose not to do so.

Is agreement with this explanation really an expression of prejudice? The researchers who have been studying modern racism would point out that, first, this explanation of racial inequality stereotypes black Americans and ascribes a single characteristic (lack of willpower) to the entire community. Second, it places the blame for racial inequality on the victims rather than on the overall society. That is, those who agree with RACDIF4 see the problem as residing in African Americans, not in the structure or history of the United States.

Ultimately, however, the question of whether or not modern racism is a disguised version of traditional American racial prejudice can be decided by research. If modern racism and traditional prejudice are different versions of the same underlying attitude, then RACDIF4 should "behave" like RACDIF2. If *both* variables measure prejudice, they should have similar causes, patterns, and consequences. There are at least three ways to explore the relationship between RACDIF2 and RACDIF4.

First, use the **Crosstabs** procedure. Run the procedure with RACDIF2 as the column variable and RACDIF4 as the row variable. Request column percentages, chi square, and gamma. If these variables are different measures of the same underlying attitude, they should have a strong, significant relationship. Use the results of this procedure to complete item 1 of Research Report 10.4.

Second, re-run one of the crosstab tables you produced for Research Report 10.3 with RACDIF4 in place of RACDIF2. If RACDIF4 (modern racism) is a disguised version of RACDIF2 (traditional racial prejudice), the variables should have the same correlates and should display similar (but not exactly the same) relationships with independent variables. In other words, the crosstab table with RACDIF4 as the dependent variable should closely resemble the table from Research Report 10.3 in which RACDIF2 was the dependent variable. Use the results of this procedure to complete item 2 of Research Report 10.4.

Third, if both RACDIF2 and RACDIF4 are measures of prejudice, they should be related in similar ways to measures of support for policies and programs for racial change. One such variable is BUSING, which measures support for school busing for the purpose of racial integration. Run the **Crosstabs** procedure with BUSING as the row variable and RACDIF2 and then RACDIF4 as the column variables. As usual, get column percentages, chi square, and gamma. If RACDIF4 and RACDIF2 both measure prejudice, they should have similar relationships (significance, strength, and direction) with BUSING. Use this output to complete item 3 of Research Report 10.4.

NAME _____

INSTRUCTOR _____

DATE _____

1. For the bivariate table of RACDIF2 and RACDIF4, summarize results by completing the following table. Fill in the blanks with the percentage of traditionally prejudiced people ("yes" on RACDIF2) who are also "modern racists" ("yes" on RACDIF4) and the percentage of non-traditionally prejudiced people ("no" on RACDIF2) who are "modern racists" ("yes" on RACDIF4).

Modern Racism (RACDIF4) and Traditional Prejudice (RACDIF2)

	RACDIF2	
RACDIF4:	**Yes**	**No**
% Yes	_____	_____

The significance of chi square is_____, so the relationship between these variables(is/is not) significant at the .05 level. Gamma is _____, which indicates a _____ (weak/moderate/ strong) relationship in the _____ (negative/positive) direction. Does it seem likely that RACDIF2 and RACDIF4 are different measures of the same underlying attitude? Explain.

2. a. Summarize results for the crosstab table you re-did from Research Report 10.3. On line 1 of the following table, fill in the blank with the name of your independent variable. On line 2, write in the names of the categories of your independent variable, using as many blanks as necessary. On line 3, fill in the blanks with the percentage of respondents who were modern racists ("yes" on RACDIF4).

   Lines

   1. RACDIF4 by _____

   2. _____ _____ _____ _____ _____

   3. % Racist _____ _____ _____ _____ _____

(Research Report continues)

The column percentages _____ (do/do not) change, so there _____ (is/is not) a relationship between these variables. The significance of chi square is _____ (less than/more than) .05, so this relationship _____ (is/is not) statistically significant.

*If the independent variable is **not** numerical*: The value of Cramer's *V* is _____, so this is a _____ (weak/moderate/strong) relationship.

*If the independent variable **is** numerical*: The value of gamma is _____, so this is a _____ (weak/moderate/strong) relationship. The sign of gamma indicates that this is a _____ (positive/negative) relationship. As _____ (name of your independent variable) increases, modern racism _____ (increases/decreases).

b. Compare this table with the one you created for Research Report 10.3. Were the relationships between your independent variable and RACDIF4 generally the same as the relationships between your independent variable and RACDIF2? Use column percentages, the significance of chi square, and your measure of association to make the comparisons. Do these results support the view that RACDIF2 and RACDIF4 are closely related? Explain.

3. For the analysis with BUSING, complete the summary tables and related statements.
   a. *Support for busing and traditional prejudice*:

BUSING by RACDIF2

	RACDIF2	
BUSING:	**Yes**	**No**
Opposed	_____	_____

The column percentages _____ (do/do not) change so there _____ (is/is not) a relationship between these variables. The significance of chi square is _____ (less than/more than) .05, so this relationship _____ (is/is not) statistically significant. The value of gamma is _____, so this is a _____ (weak/moderate/strong) relationship. The sign of gamma indicates that this is a _____ (positive/negative) relationship. As prejudice increases, opposition to busing _____ (increases/decreases).

b. *Support for busing and modern racism*

BUSING by RACDIF4

	RACDIF4	
BUSING:	**Yes**	**No**
Opposed	_____	_____

The column percentages_____ (do/do not) change, so there_____ (is/is not) a relationship between these variables. The significance of chi square is_____ (less than/more than) .05, so this relationship _____ (is/is not) statistically significant. The value of gamma is _____ , so this is a _____ (weak/moderate/strong) relationship. The sign of gamma indicates that this is a _____ (positive/negative) relationship. As modern racism increases, opposition to busing _____ (increases/decreases).

c. RACDIF2 and RACDIF4 have _____ (similar/dissimilar) relationships with support for busing. These results _____ (support/do not support) the idea that RACDIF2 and RACDIF4 both measure prejudice. Explain.

(Research Report Continues)

4. Looking over the results for items 1 through 3, what conclusions can be made with regard to the idea that prejudice has not declined but has changed to a less blatant form? Are these results consistent with the notion that prejudice, even in disguised form, is still an important factor in American race relations? Explain.

EXERCISE 10.5 A   **A Multivariate Analysis of Prejudice and Social Class**

Prejudice is a complex phenomenon with a variety of forms and causes. One independent variable frequently linked to prejudice is competition between groups over scarce resources such as jobs, housing, or land. As intergroup competition increases, prejudice intensifies and group members who feel the most threatened tend to be the most prejudiced (see Noel, 1968; Sherif, 1961; and Bonacich, 1976).

Given the historical patterns of racial inequality in the United States, it can be hypothesized that, for white Americans, racial prejudice will be strongest in the lowest income groups—those most likely to fear displacement by changes in black-white relationships. Test this idea on the GSS94TAB.SAV data set by running the **Crosstabs** procedure with INCOME as the independent variable (in the columns) and RACDIF2 as the dependent variable. Don't forget column percentages, chi square, and gamma. Use the results to complete item 1 in Research Report 10.5. (You may have already explored the relationship between RACDIF2 and INCOME for Research Report 10.3. If so, simply copy your results to Research Report 10.5.)

Would the relationship between RACDIF2 and INCOME be the same for females as for males? Would the difference in income levels of men and women (see Chapter 9) lead to differences in levels of threat? Would low-income white women feel particularly threatened by racial change? We can answer these questions by observing the effect of SEX on the relationship between prejudice and income level. Run the **Crosstabs** procedure again and name SEX as the control variable by moving it to the bottom box in the Crosstabs dialog box. Use the output to complete item 2 in Research Report 10.5.

What other control variables might affect the relationship between social class and prejudice? Would age be relevant? Would older, lower-income whites feel more or less threatened than younger, lower-income whites? How about political ideology (POLVIEWS)? Education (DEGREE)? Pick another control variable and run the **Crosstabs** procedure again, placing your control variable in the bottom or "layer" box of the Crosstabs dialog box. Remember that control variables should have only two or three categories or scores. Use the output to complete item 3 in Research Report 10.5.

Main Points

- This chapter conducted an investigation of racial inequality and prejudice, which paralleled the investigation of gender inequality and sexism in Chapter 9.

- Line charts and T tests were used to explore racial inequality in 1994 for level of educational attainment, occupational prestige, and income.

- Crosstab tables and the elaboration technique were used to measure levels of prejudice and to seek the causes of these attitudes.

- The distinction between traditional, overt prejudice and modern, more subtle forms of prejudice was explored and we tried to ascertain if racial prejudice is truly declining or merely changing forms.

SPSS Commands Introduced in This Chapter

COMMAND BLOCK 10.3   *Selecting White Respondents Only*

> Click **Data** → **Select Cases** →
> The **Select Cases** dialog box appears →
> Click **If condition is satisfied** →
> Click **IF** →
> The **Select Cases: If** dialog box appears →
> Highlight **RACE** and click the right-pointing arrow →
> Click the **=** sign and the number **1** from the calculator pad →
> Click **Continue** →
> Click **OK**

NAME _____

INSTRUCTOR _____

DATE _____

1. a. Summarize results for RACDIF2 and INCOME by completing the following table. On line 3, fill in the blanks with the percentage of respondents who were prejudiced ("yes" on RACDIF2) for each income category.

   Lines

   1.   RACDIF2 by INCOME

   2.   Low   Moderate   High

   3.   % Prejudiced _____ _____   _____

   The column percentages _____ (do/do not) change, so

   there _____ (is/is not) a relationship between these vari-

   ables. The significance of chi square is _____ (less

   than/more than) .05, so this relationship _____ (is/is

   not) statistically significant. The value of gamma is _____, so this is

   a _____ (weak/moderate/strong) relationship. The sign

   of gamma indicates that this is a _____ (positive/nega-

   tive) relationship. As income increases, prejudice _____

   (increases/decreases).

   b. Do these results support the idea that competition and sense of threat are a cause of prejudice? Explain.

2. a. Complete the following summary table to display the results of the multivariate analysis of RACDIF2 and INCOME while controlling for SEX. In line 3, copy from item 1 the percentage of prejudiced respondents ("yes" on RACDIF2) for each category of income and the value of gamma for the bivariate relationship. In line 4, fill in the percentage of prejudiced males for each income category; do the same for prejudiced women in line 5.

Lines

1.   RACDIF2 by INCOME by SEX

2.   Low   Moderate   High   <u>Gamma</u>

3.   % Prejudiced
     All   ____   ____   ____   ____

4.   Men   ____   ____   ____   ____

5.   Women   ____   ____   ____   ____

b. Use the column percentages and gamma to analyze these results. Were prejudice and income related in the same way for both men and women? What differences and similarities can you identify? Which subgroup is most prejudiced? Which is least prejudiced? Explain.

3. a. Complete the following summary table to display the results of the multivariate analysis of RACDIF2 and INCOME while controlling for the variable you selected. In line 1, fill in the blank with the name of your control variable. In line 3, copy from item 1 the percentage of prejudiced respondents ("yes" on RACDIF2) for each category of income and the value of gamma for the bivariate relationship. In line 4, fill in the percentage of prejudiced respondents for the first category of your control variable. In line 5, do the same for the second category of your control variable. If necessary, use line 6 to fill in the percentage of prejudiced respondents for the third category of your control variable.

    ____   ____   ____   ____

Lines

1.   RACDIF2 by INCOME by _____

2.   Low   Moderate   High   Gamma

3.   % Prejudiced
     All   ____   ____   ____   ____

4.   _____   ____   ____   ____   ____

5.   _____   ____   ____   ____   ____

6.   _____   ____   ____   ____   ____

b. Use the column percentages and gamma to analyze these results. Were prejudice and income related in the same way for the different categories of the control variable? What differences and similarities can you identify? Which subgroup is most prejudiced? Which is least prejudiced? Explain.

NAME _____

INSTRUCTOR _____

DATE _____

Is opposition to gender equality related to racial prejudice? Do people who disapprove of the entry of women into politics (FEPOL) also see black Americans as innately inferior? Use RACDIF2 as a measure of racial prejudice and run the **Crosstabs** procedure—with column percentages, chi square, and gamma—with RACDIF2 as the column variable and FEPOL as the row variable. If sexism and prejudice are related, the relationship between these variables will be significant and substantial. Use the output to complete item 1.

Is there a relationship between sexism or prejudice and political ideology? Run the **Crosstabs** procedure again with POLVIEWS as the column variable and first RACDIF2 and then FEPOL as row variables. Don't forget column percentages, chi square, and gamma. Use the output to complete items 2 and 3.

1. a. Summarize results for RACDIF2 and FEPOL by completing the following table. On line 3, fill in the blanks with the percentage of respondents who were sexist ("agree" on FEPOL) for each category of RACDIF2.

   Lines

   1.   FEPOL by RACDIF2

                            RACDIF2
   2.   Yes   No

   3. % Sexist   _____   _____

   The column percentages _____ (do/do not) change, so

   there _____ (is/is not) a relationship between these vari-

   ables. The significance of chi square is _____ (less

   than/more than) .05, so this relationship _____ (is/is

   not) statistically significant. The value of gamma is _____, so this is

   a _____ (weak/moderate/strong) relationship. The sign

   of gamma indicates that this is a _____ (positive/nega-

   tive) relationship. As prejudice increases, sexism _____

   (increases/decreases).

   b. Are sexism and prejudice related? How? Describe the relationship.

(Independent Project continues)

2. a. Summarize results for RACDIF2 and POLVIEWS by completing the following table. On line 3, fill in the blanks with the percentage of respondents who were prejudiced ("yes" on RACDIF2) for each category of POLVIEWS.

Lines

1.   RACDIF2 by POLVIEWS

2.   Liberal   Moderate   Conservative

3.   % Prejudiced   ____   ____   ____

The column percentages _____ (do/do not) change, so there _____ (is/is not) a relationship between these variables. The significance of chi square is _____ (less than/more than) .05, so this relationship _____ (is/is not) statistically significant. The value of gamma is ____ , so this is a _____ (weak/moderate/strong) relationship. The sign of gamma indicates that this is a _____ (positive/negative) relationship. As political ideology becomes more conservative, prejudice _____ (increases/decreases).

b. Are prejudice and political ideology related? How? Describe the relationship.

3. a. Summarize results for FEPOL and POLVIEWS by completing the following table. On line 3, fill in the blanks with the percentage of respondents who were sexist ("agree" on FEPOL) for each category of POLVIEWS.

Lines

1.   FEPOL by POLVIEWS

2.   Liberal   Moderate   Conservative

3.   % Prejudiced   ____   ____   ____

(*Independent Project continues*)

The column percentages _____ (do/do not) change, so there _____ (is/is not) a relationship between these variables. The significance of chi square is _____ (less than/more than) .05, so this relationship _____ (is/is not) statistically significant. The value of gamma is _____, so this is a _____ (weak/moderate/strong) relationship. The sign of gamma indicates that this is a _____ (positive/negative) relationship. As political ideology becomes more conservative, sexism _____ (increases/decreases).

b. Are sexism and political ideology related? How? Describe the relationship.

NAME _____

INSTRUCTOR _____

DATE _____

Repeat the analysis of the causes of prejudice you did in Research Report 10.3 with two new independent variables (Do not use SEX.)

1. State hypotheses linking each variable with RACDIF2:

   a.

   b.

2. Summarize the results of the Crosstab analysis for each independent variable.
   a. *For your first independent variable*: On line 1 of the following summary table, fill in the blank with the name of your independent variable. On line 2, write in the names of the categories of your independent variable, using as many blanks as necessary. On line 3, fill in the blanks with the percentage of respondents who were prejudiced ("yes" on RACDIF2).

   Lines

   1.   RACDIF2 by _____

   2.   _____ _____ _____ _____ _____

   3. % Prejudiced _____ _____ _____ _____ _____

   The column percentages _____ (do/do not) change, so there _____ (is/is not) a relationship between these variables. The significance of chi square is _____ (less than/more than) .05, so this relationship _____ (is/is not) statistically significant.

   If the independent variable is **not** *numerical*: The value of Cramer's *V* is ____ , so this is a _____ (weak/moderate/strong) relationship.

   If the independent variable **is** *numerical*: The value of gamma is _____ , so this is a _____ (weak/moderate/strong) relationship. The sign of gamma indicates that this is a_____ (positive/negative) relationship. As _____ (name of your independent variable) increases, prejudice _____ (increases/decreases).

b. *For your second independent variable*: On line 1 of the following summary table, fill in the blank with the name of your independent variable. On line 2, write in the names of the categories of your independent variable, using as many blanks as necessary. On line 3, fill in the blanks with the percentage of respondents who were prejudiced (said "yes" on RACDIF2).

Lines

1.   RACDIF2 by _____

2.   _____ _____ _____ _____ _____

3.   % Prejudiced_____ _____ _____ _____ _____

The column percentages _____ (do/do not) change, so there _____ (is/is not) a relationship between these variables. The significance of chi square is _____ (less than/more than) .05, so this relationship _____ (is/is not) statistically significant.

*If the independent variable is **not** numerical*: The value of Cramer's *V* is ____, so this is a _____ (weak/moderate/strong) relationship.

*If the independent variable **is** numerical*: The value of gamma is ____ , so this is a _____ (weak/moderate/strong) relationship. The sign of gamma indicates that this is a _____ (positive/negative) relationship. As _____ (name of your independent variable) increases, prejudice _____ (increases/decreases).

3. Were your hypotheses confirmed? Explain.

NAME

INSTRUCTOR

DATE

1. Pick one of the bivariate relationships you examined in either Research Report 10.3 or Independent Project 10.2. What happens to this bivariate relationship when you control for SEX? Run the **Crosstabs** procedure with RACDIF2 in the rows, your independent variable in the columns, and SEX as the control variable. Get column percentages, chi square, and either Cramer's *V* (if your independent variable is not numerical) or gamma (if your independent variable is numerical) as your measure of association.

2. Complete the following summary table to display your results for the full sample and for men and women separately. In line 1, fill in the blank with the name of your independent variable. In line 2, write in the names of the categories of your independent variable, using as many blanks as necessary. In line 3, fill in the percentage of prejudiced respondents ("yes" on RACDIF2) for each category of the independent variable. The information for this line can be copied from Research Report 10.3 or Independent Project 10.2. In line 4, fill in the percentage of prejudiced men for each category of the independent variable. In line 5, do the same for women.

   Lines

   1.   RACDIF2 by ——————— by SEX

   2.   ____ ____ ____ ____   Cramer's *V* or Gamma

   3. All   ____ ____ ____ ____   ____

   4. Men   ____ ____ ____ ____   ____

   5. Women   ____ ____ ____ ____   ____

3. Use the column percentages and the measure of association to analyze these results. Were prejudice and your independent variable related in the same way for both men and women? What differences and similarities can you identify? Which subgroup is most prejudiced? Which is least prejudiced? Explain.

NAME _____

INSTRUCTOR _____

DATE _____

Repeat the analysis done in Research Report 10.1, using the 1972 General Social Survey (**GSS72**). Construct multiple line charts for EDUC, PRESTIGE, and INCOME72 by RACE and complete the following statements.

1. On years of education (EDUC), whites were generally _____ (higher than/lower than/equal to) blacks. This chart indicates that the races _____ (were/were not) equal in level of education in 1972.

2. For occupational prestige (PRESTIGE), whites were generally _____ (higher than/lower than/equal to) blacks. This chart indicates that the races _____ (were/ were not) equal in prestige in 1972.

3. For income (INCOME72), whites were generally _____ (higher than/lower than/equal to) blacks. This chart supports the conclusion that there _____ (was/was not) racial equality in the United States in 1972.

4. Compare these results with Research Report 10.1. Can you tell if the amount of racial inequality declined or increased between 1972 and 1994? Explain.

NAME   _____

INSTRUCTOR   _____

DATE   _____

Repeat the analysis done in Research Report 10.2, this time using the 1972 General Social Survey. Run **T Test** with EDUC, PRESTIGE, and INCOME72 as the testing variables and RACE as the grouping variable. Complete the following summary tables to display the results.

	Mean on EDUC	2-Tail Sig		Mean on PRESTIGE	2-Tail Sig
Whites	_____		Whites	_____	
Blacks	_____	_____	Blacks	_____	_____

	Mean on INCOME72	2-Tail Sig
Whites	_____	
Blacks	_____	_____

1. In 1972, whites averaged _____ (more/fewer) years of education than blacks, and the difference _____ (was/was not) significant.

2. In 1972, whites' average occupational prestige was _____ (higher/lower) than blacks, and the difference _____ (was/was not) significant.

3. In 1972, whites had _____ a (higher/lower) average income than blacks, and the difference _____ (was/was not) significant.

4. Summarize these results. How much racial inequality existed in 1972? Was inequality greater in 1972 or in 1994? Explain.

Unfortunately, because RACDIF2 and RACDIF4 were not included in the 1972 GSS, the levels of prejudice cannot be directly compared with 1994. (Other measures of prejudice were asked in both years but, because of space limitations, none of these are included in the data set supplied with this text.) Instead, you can conduct a test to see if the causes of prejudice were the same in both years.

Using the GSS72.SAV data set, measure prejudice with the variable RACPRES, which asked respondents if they would vote for a black candidate for president who was nominated by their party and otherwise qualified. Assume that those who answered "no" are prejudiced. Choose an independent variable from the 1972 data set that matches one of the independent variables you used for Research Report 10.3 or Independent Project 10.2 and run the **Crosstabs** procedure (with column percentages, chi square, and Cramer's *V* or gamma) to analyze the relationship.

Compare your 1972 results for RACPRES with the 1994 results for RACDIF2. If prejudice is shaped by similar causal processes in both years, the bivariate relationships should be similar in spite of the substantial differences in dependent variables. What can you conclude? Have the correlates of prejudice changed over the years?

Chapter 11   The Family Institution: Forms and Functions

The Basic Building Block of Society

The family institution has often been called the basic building block of society, a characterization supported by a great deal of sociological and anthropological research. The family is universal (every known society has some form of family institution) and universally important. It is charged with primary responsibility for many tasks that are crucial to the survival of society, including reproduction, socialization, production and consumption of goods and services, and emotional support.

Although the family is universally important, it is highly variable in its structure. From society to society (and from time to time), considerable variation can be found in rules of marriage (for example, how many spouses are allowed at one time), authority and decision-making patterns, child-rearing customs, rules of kinship, rules regulating divorce, and along scores of other dimensions.

Over the last century, the family institution in the United States has undergone notable change, and new forms of family life have emerged along with new understandings and attitudes about marriage, sex, child rearing, and divorce. In this chapter, we will identify some of these new family forms and measure how common they are. The traditional American family is usually thought to consist of two married adults (of opposite sex) and their minor children. What percentage of the population actually lives in such a family arrangement? Do the nontraditional family forms exist only in certain social locations? How well do they function?

This chapter also examines a crucial and controversial area of human life: sex. The regulation of sex has been a primary responsibility of the family, and changes in values and behaviors in this area have been a matter of great concern in the United States for many decades. We will measure both what people say about sex and what they do.

EXERCISE 11.1   **Forms of the Family**

You are probably aware that the nuclear family (parents and children living together in a single household) has become less common over the past several decades. A high rate of divorce combined with a high rate of remarriage, a willingness to experiment with nontraditional family structures, and the increased participation of women in the labor force have resulted in a variety of new family forms: single-parent families, dual-career families, step-families, and cohabitants to name a few.

How common are these new family forms? Has the nuclear family disappeared? In what kind of family relationship do most Americans live? You partially answered these questions in Research Report 3.1 when you produced a bar graph for MARITAL, showing the percentage of the GSS sample who are married, divorced, widowed, and so forth. If you no longer have this report or the output, don't worry. It can easily be produced while completing this exercise.

The response categories for MARITAL are sometimes inadequate to describe the actual family situations in which people were living in 1994. The GSS94TAB.SAV data set supplied with this text includes another variable called FAMTYPE, which records people's living arrangements in somewhat different terms. The information from these two variables can be combined to form a more complete picture of the types of family structures currently in existence in the United States.

Run the **Frequencies** procedure for FAMTYPE (and MARITAL if necessary). Some of the response categories for FAMTYPE may need a little clarification. "Childless couples" are legally married but have no children, whereas people living in **nuclear families** are legally married and have at least one child. "Single parents" are single adults of any marital status living with a child, whereas "single adults" live alone. Finally, "cohabitants" are living with a member of the opposite sex but are not legally married. The GSS does not contain further information about this last category and we do not know if the cohabiting couples are merely "roommates" or if they have a more intimate, sexual relationship (of course, the same point could be made about people who are legally married). Use the output from the **Frequencies** procedure to complete items 1 and 2 of Research Report 11.1.

Next, run the **Crosstabs** procedure with FAMTYPE as the row variable and MARITAL as the column variable. Get column percentages but don't bother with other statistics. Take a moment to observe the table and note that it is very large— much larger than other tables we have examined. Both FAMTYPE and MARITAL have five categories, so the table has (5 × 5 or) 25 distinct cells. In tabular analysis, such large tables are usually avoided because the sheer number of separate cells makes it difficult to see patterns and relationships. In the case at hand, the analytical task can be simplified by ignoring the cells that have very few cases—say, cells that include less than 5% of all cases in a column. Use the output from the **Crosstabs** procedure to complete item 3 in Research Report 11.1

NAME _____

INSTRUCTOR _____

DATE _____

1. Summarize the frequency distribution for MARITAL: The most common family status for these respondents is _____ . The second most common status is _____ and the least common status is _____ . Note any other interesting features of this table.

2. Summarize the frequency distribution for FAMTYPE: The most common living arrangement for respondents is _____ . The second most common is _____ and the least common arrangement is _____ . Note any other interesting features of this table.

3. Now analyze the crosstabulation of MARITAL and FAMTYPE.

   a. For "married" respondents, _____ % are childless couples, whereas _____ % are nuclear families.

   b. The household arrangement for the great majority of the "widowed" respondents is _____ .

   c. Most "divorced" respondents are living as _____, but _____ % are single parents and _____ % are cohabiting.

   d. Most "separated" respondents are living as _____, but _____ % are single adults and _____ % are cohabiting.

   e. Most people who have "never married" are living as _____, but some (_____%) are cohabiting and others (_____%) are single parents.

4. What patterns do you see in these results? What common types of family relationships exist in the United States besides the nuclear family?

EXERCISE 11.2   **The Correlates of Types of Living Arrangements**

Are the various living arrangements included in FAMTYPE more likely to be found among certain groups or are they evenly distributed across the population? For example, are younger people more likely to cohabit and, if so, would this tendency be reflected in a relationship between AGE and FAMTYPE? Would nuclear families be more common in a particular social class? Could there be a relationship between religion or religiosity and type of living arrangement? Use your textbook or other course materials, if relevant, to identify other possible causal factors. Select two potential independent variables and state hypotheses linking each to FAMTYPE. State and explain your hypotheses in item 1 of Research Report 11.2. Run the **Crosstabs** procedure on the GSS94TAB.SAV data set with FAMTYPE in the rows and your independent variables in the columns. This time, get chi square and Cramer's *V* as well as column percentages and use this information to complete Research Report 11.2.

As was the case in Exercise 11.1, the bivariate tables you create for this exercise may be quite large and, thus, difficult to analyze. In the previous exercise, we were looking for common family types and suggested that cells with few cases and/or rare or unusual combinations of scores could be ignored. That advice should *not* transfer to the present exercise. Now, we are looking for causal relationships between variables and our goal will be to understand all aspects and nuances of those relationships, not just the most common.

NAME _____

INSTRUCTOR _____

DATE _____

1. State the names of the independent variables you selected:

   _____ and _____. State and briefly explain a

   hypothesis about the relationship between each independent variable

   and FAMTYPE.

   a.

   b.

2. a. *For your first independent variable*: Summarize the output from
      the Crosstabs procedure by filling in the name of the category of
      your independent variable that had the highest column percentage
      for each category of FAMTYPE. In the case of ties, list all cate-
      gories.

	Name of Category	*Percentage*
Childless couple	_____	____
Single parent	_____	____
Single adult	_____	____
Cohabitants	_____	____
Nuclear family	_____	____

   b. The significance of chi square for this relationship was ____ ,

      which is _____ (less than/more than) .05, so this

      _____ (is/is not) a significant relationship. The value of

      Cramer's V was ____ , so this is a _____ (weak/moder-

      ate/strong) relationship.

3. a. *For your second independent variable*: Summarize the output from the Crosstabs procedure by filling in the name of the category of your independent variable that had the highest column percentage for each category of FAMTYPE. In the case of ties, list all categories.

	Name of Category	*Percentage*
Childless couple	_____	____
Single parent	_____	____
Single adult	_____	____
Cohabitants	_____	____
Nuclear family	_____	____

b. The significance of chi square for this relationship was _____ , which is _____(less than/more than) .05, so this _____ (is/is not) a significant relationship. The value of Cramer's *V* was _____, so this is a _____(weak/moderate/strong) relationship.

4. Were your hypotheses confirmed? Explain.

EXERCISE 11.3   **Type of Family and Happiness**

In Exercise 11.2, FAMTYPE was a dependent variable and you tested for causal relationships with two independent variables. In this exercise, FAMTYPE will become an independent variable and you will assess how well the various living arrangements function. Specifically, the research question will be: Is personal happiness (as measured by the variable HAPPY) related to type of living arrangement? Are people who live in some settings happier than those living in other settings? Are people living alone (single adults) more or less happy than those living in nuclear families? Are childless couples more or less happy than people who are cohabiting?

Develop a hypothesis about the relationship between FAMTYPE and HAPPY, using your textbook and other course materials, if relevant. State and explain the hypothesis in item 1 of Research Report 11.3. Run the **Crosstabs** procedure on the GSS94TAB.SAV data set with FAMTYPE as the column (independent) variable and HAPPY in the rows. Get chi square, Cramer's *V*, and column percentages and use this information to complete Research Report 11.3.

NAME _____

INSTRUCTOR _____

DATE _____

1. State and briefly explain your hypothesis linking FAMTYPE and HAPPY.

2. Present the results of the Crosstabs procedure by completing the following summary table. On line 3, fill in the blanks with the percentage of respondents who were "very happy" for each type of living arrangement.

   Lines

   1. HAPPY by FAMTYPE

	Childless Couple	Single Parent	Single Adult	Cohabitants	Nuclear Family
2.					
3. % Very Happy	_____	_____	_____	_____	_____

   The column percentages _____ (do/do not) change, so

   there _____ (is/is not) a relationship between these vari-

   ables. The type of living arrangement with the highest level of happi-

   ness (highest percentage of cases "very happy") was _____.

   The type of living arrangement with the lowest level of happiness was

   _____ . The significance of chi square is _____

   (less than/more than) .05, so this relationship _____ (is/is

   not) statistically significant. The value of Cramer's V is_____, so this

   is a _____ (weak/moderate/strong) relationship.

3. Was your hypothesis confirmed? Explain.

EXERCISE 11.4 | **Multivariate Analysis of Happiness and Living Arrangement**

What will happen to the relationship between FAMTYPE and HAPPY when a control variable is introduced into the analysis? Are males and females equally happy in the various living arrangements? What about people from different income levels? People from different age groups? We will analyze the result of controlling for SEX, and then you will have the opportunity to analyze the relationship between FAMTYPE and HAPPY for a different control variable.

HAPPY and FAMTYPE, Controlling for SEX We used the Crosstabs procedure to examine the relationship between HAPPY and FAMTYPE, while controlling for SEX. Our results are summarized in Table 11.1. The percentages of "very happy" respondents are presented for the full sample and for males and females separately.

TABLE 11.1   **Happiness by Living Arrangement by Sex**

	Living Arrangement					
	Childless Couple	**Single Parent**	**Single Adult**	**Cohabitant**	**Nuclear Family**	**Cramer's V**
% Very Happy						
All	40	11	21	19	34	.18
Males	38	21	19	19	36	.14
Females	42	9	22	19	33	.20

With one exception, the percentage of males and females in each living arrangement who report that they are "very happy" is quite similar to the full sample. Also, the Cramer's V's for males and females are comparable in value to the Cramer's V for the full sample. These patterns strongly suggest that, for the most part, gender does not affect the relationship between FAMTYPE and HAPPY.

The exception, of course, is for female single parents who are much lower in level of happiness than male single parents. In fact, the percentage of "very happy" people for this subgroup is dramatically lower than for any other subgroup in the table.

What would explain this single sharp difference between the sexes? Why would single-parent females be so much less happy then single-parent males? One possible explanation is economic. Because females earn less than males (see Chapter 9), female-headed households tend to operate at a lower quality of life than those headed by males. The difference in happiness between the genders could be a direct reflection of the difficulties created when single parent status is compounded with poverty.

How could this explanation be tested? One possibility would be to examine the relationship between living arrangement and happiness while controlling for both gender and income at the same time. In other words, additional tables could be generated, one showing the relationship between living arrangement and happiness for low-income females, another for low-income males, a third for middle-income females, and so forth. Using this technique, we would be able to isolate female single parents who are also low in income and systematically compare their levels of happiness with all other combinations of living arrangement, income, and gender.

Unfortunately, using the Crosstabs procedure to control for more than one variable at a time quickly becomes impractical. Many different tables, each with many cells, would have to be generated and the researcher could become lost in a mountain of details. More important, unless we are working with a huge sample, many of the cells in these tables would have few or no cases and, for reasons we need not get into here, cells with few or no cases create many statistical problems and should be avoided.

If it is impractical to test the economic explanation for the unhappiness of single-parent females, what can be done? One possibility is to control for income by itself (without controlling for gender simultaneously). If we found that low-income single parents report less happiness than more affluent single parents, this would provide at least some support for the economic explanation. If this sounds like a reasonable course of action, you may want to pursue it in connection with Research Report 11.4.

Additional Multivariate Analysis of HAPPY and FAMTYPE Select an additional control variable that might affect the relationship between happiness and family type. To pursue the economic hypothesis advanced in the previous section, choose INCOME as a control variable. Whichever variable you select, remember that control variables should have only two or three categories or scores. Follow Command Block 11.1 to produce multivariate tables (you produced the bivariate table for Research Report 11.3), with your variable as the control. Use this output to complete Research Report 11.4.

COMMAND BLOCK 11.1   Producing Multivariate Tables

Click **Statistics** → **Summarize** → **Crosstabs** →
Highlight **HAPPY** →
Click the arrow pointing to the **Row(s):** box →
Highlight **FAMTYPE** →
Click the arrow pointing to the **Column(s):** box →
Highlight your control variable →
Click the arrow pointing to the "layer" box at the bottom of the window →
Click **Cells** →
Click **Columns** in the **Percentages** box →
Click **Continue** →
In the Crosstabs dialog box, click **Statistics** →
Select **Cramer's V** →
Click **Continue** →
Click **OK**

NAME ⎯⎯⎯⎯⎯⎯⎯⎯⎯⎯⎯⎯⎯⎯⎯⎯⎯⎯⎯⎯⎯⎯

INSTRUCTOR ⎯⎯⎯⎯⎯⎯⎯⎯⎯⎯⎯⎯⎯⎯⎯⎯⎯⎯⎯⎯⎯⎯

DATE ⎯⎯⎯⎯⎯⎯⎯⎯⎯⎯⎯⎯⎯⎯⎯⎯⎯⎯⎯⎯⎯⎯

1. Complete the following summary table to display the results of the multivariate analysis of HAPPY and FAMTYPE. On line 1, fill in the blank with the name of your control variable. On line 3, fill in the percentages of respondents in each living arrangement who were "very happy" for the full sample. On line 4, fill in the percentage of respondents who were "very happy" for each living arrangement for the first value of the control variable. On line 5 do the same for the second value of the control variable. If necessary, use line 6 to report the percentage of respondents who were "very happy" for each living arrangement for the third value of the control variable.

Lines

1.   Happy by FAMTYPE by ⎯⎯⎯⎯⎯⎯⎯⎯⎯⎯

2.	Childless Couple	Single Parent	Single Adult	Cohabi-tants	Nuclear Family	Cramer's *V*
3. All	⎯⎯	⎯⎯	⎯⎯	⎯⎯	⎯⎯	⎯⎯
4. ⎯⎯	⎯⎯	⎯⎯	⎯⎯	⎯⎯	⎯⎯	⎯⎯
5. ⎯⎯	⎯⎯	⎯⎯	⎯⎯	⎯⎯	⎯⎯	⎯⎯
6. ⎯⎯	⎯⎯	⎯⎯	⎯⎯	⎯⎯	⎯⎯	⎯⎯

2. Use the column percentages and Cramer's *V* to analyze these results. Were happiness and living arrangement related in the same way for each category of the control variable? Which subgroup is happiest? Which is least happy? Explain.

EXERCISE 11.5 | **Attitudes about Sex**

To this point in this chapter, we have focused on the forms of the American family. Now, we turn our attention to one of the most important areas for which the family has responsibility: sex. In this exercise, we will examine attitudes about sex before marriage and, in the next exercise, we will analyze sexual behavior.

Respondents to the General Social Survey were asked if they thought premarital sex was "always wrong," "almost always wrong," "wrong only sometimes," or "not wrong at all." What percentage of the American public would condemn or condone sex before marriage? To find out, run the **Frequencies** procedure for PREMARSX. Use the information to complete item 1 of Research Report 11.5.

What variables would be likely causes of attitudes about premarital sex? Would attitudes about sex be related to gender? Race? Religion or religiosity? Social class? Political ideology? Use your textbook and other course materials, if relevant, to help identify two potential independent variables. For each variable, state a hypothesis about its relationship to PREMARSX in item 2 of Research Report 11.5. Run the **Crosstabs** procedure with PREMARSX as the row variable and your choices for independent variables in the columns. Get column percentages and the usual statistics (chi square and Cramer's *V* for non-numerical independent variables or gamma for numerical independent variables). Use the output to complete Research Report 11.5.

NAME   _____

INSTRUCTOR   _____

_____

1. Summarize the frequency distribution for PREMARSX. Did the sample generally disapprove of or condone premarital sex? What patterns did you expect to find?

2. State the names of the independent variables you selected:

   _____ and _____ . State hypotheses about the relationship between each independent variable and PREMARSX. Specify the category of each independent variable that you expect to be most disapproving (have the highest percentage of respondents who felt that premarital sex was "always wrong").

   a.

   b.

3. Summarize the results of the Crosstab analysis for each independent variable.
   a. *For your first independent variable*: On line 1 of the following summary table, fill in the blank with the name of your independent variable. On line 2, write in the names of the categories of your independent variable, using as many blanks as necessary. On line 3, fill in the blanks with the percentage of respondents who most disapproved of premarital sex (said it was "always wrong").

   Lines

   1.   PREMARSX by _____

   2.   _____ _____ _____ _____ _____

   3. % Always
         Wrong   _____ _____ _____ _____ _____

The column percentages _____ (do/do not) change, so
there _____ (is/is not) a relationship between these
variables. The significance of chi square is _____ (less
than/more than) .05, so this relationship _____ (is/is
not) statistically significant.

*If the independent variable is **not** numerical*: The value of Cramer's
V is _____ , so this is a _____ (weak/moderate/strong)
relationship.

*If the independent variable **is** numerical*: The value of gamma
is _____ , so this is a _____ (weak/moderate/strong)
relationship. The sign of gamma indicates that this is a
_____ (positive/negative) relationship. As
_____ (name of your independent variable) increases,
disapproval of premarital sex _____ (increases/
decreases). (Be careful when interpreting the direction of relationships; remember that the sign of gamma indicates the direction of
the relationship between the *scores* of the variables.)

b. *For your second independent variable*: On line 1 of the following
summary table, fill in the blank with the name of your independent
variable. On line 2, write in the names of the categories of your
independent variable, using as many blanks as necessary. On line
3, fill in the blanks with the percentage of respondents who most
disapproved of premarital sex (said it was "always wrong").

Lines

1.   PREMARSX by_____

2.   _____ _____ _____ _____ _____

3. % Always
   Wrong   _____ _____ _____ _____ _____

The column percentages _____ (do/do not) change, so
there _____ (is/is not) a relationship between these
variables. The significance of chi square is _____ (less
than/more than) .05, so this relationship _____ (is/is
not) statistically significant.

(Research Report continues)

If the independent variable is **not** *numerical*: The value of Cramer's *V* is _____ , so this is a _____ (weak/moderate/strong) relationship.

If the independent variable **is** *numerical*: The value of gamma is _____, so this is a _____ (weak/moderate/strong) relationship. The sign of gamma indicates that this is a _____ (positive/negative) relationship. As _____ (name of your independent variable) increases, prejudice _____ (increases/decreases). (Be careful when interpreting the direction of relationships; remember that the sign of gamma indicates the direction of the relationship between the *scores* of the variables.)

4. Were your hypotheses confirmed? Explain.

EXERCISE 11.6   **Sexual Behavior**

How often do Americans have sex? Is it common for people to have more than one sexual partner? Does U.S. society bear any resemblance to the wide-open, sexually permissive society sometimes portrayed in the media and in popular culture? We can get some answers to these questions with the GSS94COR.SAV data set. Respondents were asked about the frequency of their sexual activity over the past year (SEXFREQ) and were also asked how many different sex partners they have had during the past five years (PARTNRS5). We can begin our investigation into American sexuality with simple frequency distributions (use the **Frequencies** procedure) for each of these two variables. Run these now and use the output to complete item 1 of Research Report 11.6

The frequency distributions will show you that there is a good deal of variety in people's activity level. What might account for this diversity? Might social class factors such as income or prestige be involved? What about level of education? Could age be a factor? Do levels of sexual activity decline as age increases? We will present an analysis of the relationship between SEXFREQ and AGE, and then it will be your turn to select and analyze some potential causes of SEXFREQ and PARTNRS5.

Analyzing SEXFREQ and AGE For this exercise we used scatterplots and Pearson's *r*, both of which were introduced in Chapter 8. These techniques are appropriate for numerical variables, such as age or income, that have many scores. As you recall, scatterplots are similar to bivariate tables and show the pattern of scores for all cases on both variables. In conjunction with the regression line, scatterplots present a visual indication of the linearity, strength, and direction of a bivariate relationship. Pearson's *r* is a measure of association, like Cramer's *V* and gamma, which indicates the strength and direction of the linear relationship between two variables. Instructions for producing scatterplots are given in Command Block 11.2, and instructions for Pearson's *r* are listed in Command Block 11.3. In both cases, the relationship between SEXFREQ and AGE is used as an example. The output from these procedures is presented in Figures 11.1 and 11.2.

COMMAND BLOCK 11.2   Producing a Scatterplot for SEXFREQ and AGE

> Click **Graphs** → **Scatter. . .** →
> Click **Simple** → **Define** →
> Highlight **SEXFREQ** →
> Click the arrow pointing to the **Y Axis:** box →
> Highlight **AGE** →
> Click the arrow pointing to the **X Axis:** box →
> Click **OK**
> Click **Edit** →
> Click **Chart** → **Options. . .** →
> From the **Scatterplot Options** dialog box, click **Total** in the **Fit Line** box →
> Click **OK**
> **Save** and/or **Print** the scatterplot

COMMAND BLOCK 11.3   Running a Bivariate Correlation for SEXFREQ and AGE

Click **Statistics** → **Correlate** → **Bivariate** →
Highlight **SEXFREQ** →
Click the arrow to transfer **SEXFREQ** to the **Variables:** box →
Highlight **AGE** →
Click the arrow to transfer A**GE** to the **Variables:** box →
Click **OK**

FIGURE 11.1   **Output of Scatterplot for SEXFREQ and AGE**

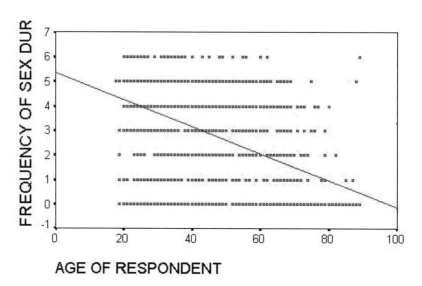

FIGURE 11.2   **Output of Bivariate Correlation for SEXFREQ and AGE**
(1994 GSS)

```
                        - -  Correlation Coefficients  - -

               AGE          SEXFREQ

AGE           1.0000        -.4747
             ( 1483)       ( 1311)
             P= .          P= .000

SEXFREQ       -.4747        1.0000
             ( 1311)       ( 1312)
             P= .000       P= .


(Coefficient / (Cases) / 2-tailed Significance)

" . " is printed if a coefficient cannot be computed
```

In Figure 11.1, note that the scores are strung out in discrete horizontal lines rather than "scattered." This is because, although numerical, SEXFREQ has been collapsed into seven scores (see Appendix A or use the **Utilities** procedure to examine the scores for this variable) and each of the lines corresponds to one of those scores. Also, note that the regression line slopes down from left to right, indicating a negative relationship. The Pearson's r (Figure 11.2) is –.48, indicating a strong, negative relationship. The output also tells us that this relationship is statistically significant (or, that the variables are almost certainly related in the population). These results suggest that AGE and SEXFREQ have an important relationship that may be causal: as people get older, their level of sexual activity decreases.

Further Analysis of SEXFREQ Now it's your turn. Pick a numerical variable that seems like a possible cause of SEXFREQ from the GSS94COR.SAV data set. If relevant, consult your textbook or other course materials for some ideas about causal relationships. State and briefly explain a hypothesis linking your independent variable to SEXFREQ in item 2a of Research Report 11.6. Use Command Blocks 11.2 and 11.3 to construct scatterplots and Pearson's r for SEXFREQ and your independent variable.

Next, pick a potential independent variable for PARTNRS5. Make sure that your independent variable is numerical. What causal factors might help explain the number of different sexual partners a person would have? Once again, consult your textbook or other course materials, if relevant, for some ideas about possible causes. State and briefly explain a hypothesis linking your independent variable to PARTNRS5 in item 2b of Research Report 11.6. Construct a scatterplot and get Pearson's r, and use the information to complete Research Report 11.6.

Main Points

- Some new family forms were identified, and the possible causes of different types of living arrangements were investigated. We also assessed the various household arrangements in terms of personal happiness.

- Attitudes about premarital sex were analyzed with crosstab tables.

- Some sexual behaviors (frequency of sex and number of different sex partners) in the United States were analyzed with scatterplots and Pearson's *r*.

SPSS Commands Introduced in This Chapter

No new commands were introduced in this chapter.

NAME _____

INSTRUCTOR _____

DATE _____

1. Describe the frequency distributions for SEXFREQ and PARTNRS5. Which is the most common score on these variables? Are high or low scores more common? What do these data suggest about sexuality in the United States? Based on these results, would you describe U.S. society as permissive and sexually open or as sexually conservative?

2. a. Name your independent variable for SEXFREQ: _____ .

    State and briefly explain your hypothesis linking these two variables.

    b. Name your independent variable for PARTNRS5: _____ .

    State and briefly explain your hypothesis linking these two variables.

3. For SEXFREQ: Taking account of both the scatterplot and Pearson's r:

   This is a _____ (weak/moderate/strong) relationship that is

   _____ (negative/positive) in direction. The relationship

   _____ (is/is not) statistically significant. (See the value for

   p. If less than .05, the relationship is significant.)

4. For PARTNRS5: Taking account of both the scatterplot and Pearson's r:

   This is a _____ (weak/moderate/strong) relationship that is

   _____ (negative/positive) in direction. The relationship

   _____ (is/is not) statistically significant. (See the value for

   p. If less than .05, the relationship is significant.)

(Research Report continues)

5. Evaluate your hypotheses. Were they supported by these results? Explain:

NAME _____

INSTRUCTOR _____

DATE _____

In Research Report 11.2, you analyzed two possible causes of FAMTYPE. Continue that investigation and select another potential independent variable, develop a hypothesis about its relationship with type of living arrangement, and run the **Crosstab** procedure, with column percentages, chi square, and Cramer's *V* to test your idea.

1. State the name of your independent variable: _____. State your hypothesis about the relationship between the independent variable and FAMTYPE.

2. Summarize the results of the Crosstab analysis.
   a. Which category of your independent variable was most likely to be associated with (or, have the highest column percentage for) each category of FAMTYPE? In the case of ties, list all categories or scores.

	Name of Category	*Percentage*
Childless couple	_____	_____
Single parent	_____	_____
Single adult	_____	_____
Cohabitants	_____	_____
Nuclear family	_____	_____

   b. The significance of chi square for this relationship was _____, which is _____ (less than/more than) .05, so this _____ (is/is not) a significant relationship. The value of Cramer's *V* was _____, so this is a _____ (weak/moderate/strong) relationship.

3. Was your hypothesis confirmed? Explain.

NAME _____

INSTRUCTOR _____

DATE _____

In Research Report 11.5, you analyzed relationships between two potential independent variables and attitudes about premarital sex. Continue that investigation by selecting another possible independent variable. State a hypothesis about its relationship with PREMARSX in the space below. Run the **Crosstabs** procedure to assess the relationship with PREMARSX. Get column percentages, chi square, and either Cramer's V (if your independent variable is not numerical) or gamma (if your independent variable is numerical).

1. State the name of your independent variable: _____. State your hypothesis about the relationship between the independent variable and PREMARSX. Specify the category of the independent variable that you expect to have the highest percentage of respondents who felt that premarital sex was "always wrong."

2. Summarize the results of the Crosstab analysis. On line 1 of the following summary table, fill in the blank with the name of your independent variable. On line 2, write in the names of the categories of your independent variable, using as many blanks as necessary. On line 3, fill in the blanks with the percentage of respondents who most disapproved of premarital sex (said it was "always wrong").

Lines

1.   PREMARSX by _____

2.   _____ _____ _____ _____ _____

3. % Always
    Wrong   _____ _____ _____ _____ _____

The column percentages _____ (do/do not) change, so there _____ (is/is not) a relationship between these variables.

The significance of chi square is _____ (less than/more than) .05, so this relationship _____ (is/is not) statistically significant.

(Independent Project continues)

If the independent variable is **not** *numerical*: The value of Cramer's *V* is_____, so this is a _____(weak/moderate/strong) relationship.

If the independent variable **is** *numerical*: The value of gamma is _____, so this is a _____(weak/moderate/strong) relationship. The sign of gamma indicates that this is a _____(positive/negative) relationship. As _____(name of your independent variable) increases, disapproval of premarital sex _____ (increases/decreases). (Be careful when interpreting the direction of relationships; remember that the sign of gamma indicates the direction of the relationship between the *scores* of the variables.)

3. Was your hypothesis confirmed? Explain.

NAME _____

INSTRUCTOR _____

DATE _____

Pick one of the bivariate relationships you examined in Research Report 11.5 or Independent Project 11.2. (Do not select a relationship in which SEX was an independent variable.) What happens to this bivariate relationship when you control for SEX? Run the **Crosstabs** procedure with PREMARSX in the rows, your independent variable in the columns, and SEX as the control variable. Get column percentages, chi square, and either Cramer's *V* (if your independent variable is not numerical) or gamma (if your independent variable is numerical) as your measure of association.

1. Complete the summary table. On line 1, fill in the blank with the name of your independent variable. On line 2, fill in the blanks with the names of the categories of your independent variable, using as many blanks as necessary. On line 3, fill in the percentages of respondents for each category of the independent variable who were most disapproving of premarital sex ("always wrong") for the full sample, using as many blanks as necessary. On line 4, fill in the percentage of male respondents who said "always wrong" for each category of the independent variable. On line 5 do the same for females.

    Lines

    PREMARSX by _____ by SEX

    1.   (Percentage "Always Wrong")

    2. _____ _____ _____ _____   Measure of Association

    3. All   _____ _____ _____ _____   _____

    4. Males _____ _____ _____ _____   _____

    5. Females _____ _____ _____ _____   _____

2. Use the column percentages and the measure of association to analyze these results. Which subgroup was most disapproving of premarital sex (had the highest percentage of "always wrong")? _____ . Which subgroup was least disapproving of premarital sex (had the lowest percentage of "always wrong")? _____ . Is there a difference in the relationship between your independent variable and attitude about premarital sex for males and females? Explain.

NAME   _____

INSTRUCTOR   _____

DATE   _____

In Chapters 9 and 10, multiple line charts were used to display differences in education, prestige, and income by sex and race. In this independent project, those same techniques will be used to see if levels or patterns of sexual activity vary by gender. Do men and women vary in frequency of
    311   311
sex (SEXFREQ) or in number of different partners (PARTNRS5)?

Using Command Block 9.1 or 10.1 as a guide, construct multiple line charts with SEXFREQ in the **Category Axis:** box and SEX in the **Define Lines by:** box. Select **% of cases** in the **Lines Represent** box and eliminate missing values if necessary (see Command Block 9.2). Edit the lines on the chart if necessary and print and/or save the charts. Once you have a good chart for SEXFREQ, repeat the procedure for PARTNRS5. Use the charts to answer the following questions.

1. Describe the overall pattern of sexual activity (SEXFREQ) for both sexes. How often do males and females have sex? Note the highest points (most common rates) on the graph and the lowest (least common rates).

               _____

In general, men report   (a higher/a lower/the same) frequency of sex (than/as) women. (*Optional*: If you picked an answer other than "the same," how would you explain the difference in rates, given the nature of sex?)

2. What were the most common numbers of sex partners for men and women? The least common?

(Independent Project continues)

Men generally report _____ (more/fewer/the same number of) sex partners (than/as) women. (*Optional*: If you picked an answer other than "the same number of," how would you explain the difference in rates, given the nature of sex?)

3. What can you conclude about sex in America from these charts? How would you characterize the society in terms of sexual activity?

NAME _____

INSTRUCTOR _____

DATE _____

Load the GSS72.SAV data set and run the **Frequencies** procedure for PREMARSX. Compare this table with the 1994 responses you generated for Research Report 11.5.

1. How have attitudes about sex changed since 1972? In 1994, people are

    _____(more/less) approving of premarital sex. The differ-

    ence between the two years is _____ (very large/large/

    small/very small).

    Select one of the independent variables you used in Research Report 11.5 or in Independent Project 11.1. Using the GSS72 data set, run the **Crosstabs** procedure and get column percentages, chi square, and select either Cramer's V (if your independent variable is not numerical) or gamma (if your independent variable is numerical) as your measure of association.

2. State the name of your independent variable: _____.

    Restate your hypothesis about the relationship between the independent variable and PREMARSX.

3. Summarize the results of the Crosstab analysis. On line 1 of the following summary table, fill in the blank with the name of your independent variable. On line 2, write in the names of the categories of your independent variable, using as many blanks as necessary. On line 3, fill in the blanks with the percentage of respondents who most disapproved of premarital sex (said it was "always wrong").

    Lines

    1.   PREMARSX by_____

    2.   _____ _____ _____ _____ _____

    3. % Always
       Wrong   _____ _____ _____ _____ _____

The column percentages _____ (do/do not) change, so there _____ (is/is not) a relationship between these variables. The significance of chi square is _____ (less than/more than) .05, so this relationship _____ (is/is not) statistically significant.

If the independent variable is **not** *numerical*: The value of Cramer's *V* is _____ , so this is a _____ (weak/moderate/strong) relationship.

If the independent variable **is** *numerical*: The value of gamma is _____ , so this is a _____ (weak/moderate/strong) relationship. The sign of gamma indicates that this is a _____ (positive/negative) relationship. As _____ (name of your independent variable) increases, disapproval of premarital sex _____ (increases/decreases). (Be careful when interpreting the direction of relationships; remember that the sign of gamma indicates the direction of the relationship between the *scores* of the variables.)

4. Compare the relationship between these variables for the two years. Were the variables related in substantially the same way? Were the results of the hypotheses tests the same? Explain.

The Political Institution in the United States: Voter Turnout, Presidential Choice, and the Gender Gap

Who participates in politics in the United States? Who votes? What factors shape a person's political preferences? Why do some people identify with the Democratic Party and others with the Republican Party? In the 1992 presidential election, who voted for Bill Clinton? George Bush? Ross Perot? To what extent do men and women have different political orientations? Why? In this chapter, we will use the General Social Survey to answer these and other questions.

Who Votes?

The citizens of the United States participate in the political process at a lower rate than most other democratic societies. Voter turnout is highest for presidential elections but, even for these contests, the percentage of eligible citizens who actually vote has fallen from nearly two-thirds to about 50% over the past three decades. Table 12.1 documents a steady decline in participation from the election of John F. Kennedy in 1960 to the election of George Bush in 1988.

TABLE 12.1 **Percentage of Those Eligible Who Voted in Presidential Elections (1960–1988)**

Year	Percentage Who Voted
1960	63
1964	62
1968	61
1972	55
1976	54
1980	53
1984	53
1988	50
1992	___

Source: U.S. Bureau of the Census, 1993, p. 284

EXERCISE 12.1 **Estimating Population Characteristics**

The turnout percentage for 1992 has deliberately been omitted from Table 12.1, so that you can estimate it from the 1994 General Social Survey sample. Recall from Chapter 2 that the GSS sample was randomly selected from the adult U.S.

population. A random sample will be representative of (that is, have about the same characteristics as) the population from which it was selected. Thus, the percentage of the GSS sample that voted in 1992 should be very close to the percentage of the entire population that voted.

A frequency distribution for VOTE92 will indicate the turnout for the 1994 GSS sample. Using the GSS94TAB.SAV data file, run the **Frequencies** procedure and record the percentage (use the Valid Percentage column) of people who said they voted in item 1 of Research Report 12.1.

Compare the reported turnout for the GSS sample with the 30-year trend in Table 12.1. If the sample percentage is an accurate estimate of the population turnout, it would appear that the decline in political participation was dramatically reversed in 1992. Can the sample percentage be accurate?

In most cases, because population characteristics are unknown, social scientists cannot assess the accuracy of their estimates from samples. In this particular case, the national voter turnout for the presidential election of 1992 is well documented: 56% of the adult U.S. citizens who were eligible to vote actually participated in that election. Note that the 30-year trend of declining participation *was* reversed but the actual turnout was some 15 percentage points lower than the rate claimed by our sample. How can we explain this huge discrepancy? Is the GSS sample unrepresentative of the U.S. electorate or were the respondents suffering from faulty memories?

First, because the sample was selected by a random process, it is unlikely to exactly duplicate the population. So, some of the discrepancy—about 3 percentage points—between the sample's voting percentage and the actual turnout could be due to random chance. What might account for the remainder of the difference?

Some (probably small) part of the difference could be due to the fact that the sample was drawn in a way that overrepresents people who are more likely to vote than the general population. Surveys usually do not draw respondents from institutions (such as colleges or hospitals), which include eligible voters but have very low turnout rates (Niemi & Weisberg, 1993, p. 15). Nor do interviewers contact people who have no addresses or telephones.

Statistical and sampling considerations aside, probably the most important reason for the discrepancy is the faulty or dishonest memory of some respondents. Those who neglected to take part in the 1992 election may be ashamed to admit it or they may be "misremembering" the occasion in a way that avoids embarrassment. At any rate, the discrepancy documented in this exercise brings us face to face with one important limitation of survey research: people do not always tell the truth or remember it accurately.

If the GSS information about voter turnout is suspect, can we still do research on voting behavior? The situation is not as difficult as it might seem at first glance. There has been a great deal of research on voting behavior over the years, and the correlates of participation are well established (Niemi & Weisberg, 1993, p. 15). If we find relationships between variables that are consistent with past research, we can assume that our conclusions will not be unduly compromised by the inaccurate memories of our respondents.

EXERCISE 12.2   **The Correlates of Voter Turnout in the United States**

Previous research has identified education, income, race, and age as important correlates of voting behavior. How would you expect these variables to be related to voter turnout? In item 2 of Research Report 12.1, state and briefly explain hypotheses linking each of these factors to voter turnout.

Test the effect of these potential independent variables on voter turnout using the GSS94TAB.SAV data set. Run the **Crosstabs** procedure with VOTE92 as the row variable and DEGREE, INCOME, RACE, and AGE as column variables. Get column percentages, chi square, and both Cramer's *V* and gamma. Use Cramer's *V* to measure the strength of the association with RACE and gamma for the other independent variables. Record your results in Research Report 12.1.

Following Research Report 12.1, the "well-established" correlates of voter turnout are briefly summarized so you can compare your thinking to what is known about these relationships. Read this section only after you have stated your own hypotheses!

NAME _____

INSTRUCTOR _____

DATE _____

1. In the 1992 presidential election, _____% of the 1994 GSS sample reported that they voted. The actual turnout for the 1992 election was 56%.

2. State and briefly explain your hypotheses.

   a. For DEGREE and VOTE92:

   b. For INCOME and VOTE92:

   c. For RACE and VOTE92:

   d. For AGE and VOTE92:

3. Summarize your results by completing the following table:

   a. For DEGREE: On line 3 of the following summary table, fill in the blanks with the percentage of respondents who said that they voted in 1992 for each educational level.

   Lines

   1.   VOTE92 by DEGREE

	Less Than High School	High School	College	Gamma
2.				
3. % Voted	_____	_____	_____	_____

   The column percentages _____ (do/do not) change, so there _____ (is/is not) a relationship between these variables. The significance of chi square is _____ (less than/more than) .05, so this relationship _____ (is/is not) statistically significant. The value of gamma is _____ , so this is a _____ (weak/moderate/strong) relationship. The sign of gamma indicates that this is a _____ (positive/negative) relationship. As education increases, voter turnout _____ (increases/decreases). (Be careful when interpreting the direction of relationships; remember that the sign of gamma indicates the direction of the relationship between the *scores* of the variables.)

b. For INCOME: On line 3 of the following summary table, fill in the blanks with the percentage of respondents who said that they voted in 1992 for each income level.

Lines

1.	VOTE92 by INCOME			
2.	Low	Moderate	High	Gamma
3. % Voted	___	___	___	___

The column percentages _____ (do/do not) change, so there _____ (is/is not) a relationship between these variables. The significance of chi square is _____ (less than/more than) .05, so this relationship _____ (is/is not) statistically significant. The value of gamma is ____, so this is a _____ (weak/moderate/strong) relationship. The sign of gamma indicates that this is a _____ (positive/negative) relationship. As income increases, voter turnout _____ (increases/decreases).

c. For RACE: On line 3 of the following summary table, fill in the blanks with the percentage of respondents who said that they voted in 1992 for each racial group.

Lines

1.	VOTE92 by RACE		
2.	Whites	Blacks	Cramer's *V*
3. % Voted	___	___	___

The column percentages _____ (do/do not) change, so there _____ (is/is not) a relationship between these variables. The significance of chi square is _____ (less than/more than) .05, so this relationship _____ (is/is not) statistically significant. The value of Cramer's *V* is ____, so this is a _____ (weak/moderate/strong) relationship.

(Research Report continues)

d. For AGE: On line 3 of the following summary table, fill in the blanks with the percentage of respondents who said that they voted in 1992 for each age group.

Lines

1.   VOTE92 by AGE

2.   Younger   Middle   Older   Gamma

3. % Voted   _____   _____   _____   _____

The column percentages _____ (do/do not) change, so there _____ (is/is not) a relationship between these variables. The significance of chi square is _____ (less than/more than) .05, so this relationship _____ (is/is not) statistically significant. The value of gamma is _____ , so this is a _____ (weak/moderate/strong) relationship. The sign of gamma indicates that this is a _____ (positive/negative) relationship. As age increases, voter turnout _____ (increases/decreases).

4. Were your hypotheses confirmed? Briefly describe each relationship in terms of who was more likely to vote and in terms of the significance, strength, and, if applicable, the direction of the relationship.

   a. For DEGREE and VOTE92:

   b. For INCOME and VOTE92:

   c. For RACE and VOTE92:

   d. For AGE and VOTE92:

Previous Research on Voter Turnout

Studies of voting behavior routinely show that higher rates of participation are associated with higher levels of education and income. Older people and whites are more likely to vote than younger people and blacks. Education usually has the single strongest relationship with turnout (Niemi and Weisberg, 1993, p. 15). Are these patterns consistent with those you analyzed in Research Report 12.1?

Some of these independent variables are highly correlated with each other. For example, income and education both measure the same underlying dimension of social class. Also, the lower turnout for black voters reported in the literature may reflect income and/or educational differences with white voters (see Chapter 10). How can we isolate the effects of these causal factors? Fortunately, multivariate analysis provides a technique.

EXERCISE 12.3   **Multivariate Analysis of Voter Turnout**

In Research Report 12.1, you found that more educated individuals voted at higher rates than the less educated and that this relationship was statistically significant and strong. Does this relationship between voting and education hold for both males and females? How about blacks and whites? Older and younger voters? We will analyze the combined effects of education and sex on voting behavior and leave the other possible relationships to you.

We used the **Crosstabs** procedure with VOTE92 as the row variable, DEGREE as the column variable, and SEX as the control variable. Our results are summarized in Table 12.2.

TABLE 12.2   **Voter Turnout by Education and Sex**
(Percentages)

% Who Voted	Less Than High School	High School	At Least Some College	Gamma
All	50	68	84	−.42
Males	54	65	85	−.44
Females	55	70	84	−.40

The percentage of voters is very similar for males and females at each level of education and the gammas for the bivariate table, the table for men, and the table for women have the same sign and are roughly the same value. These results suggest that education affects turnout in about the same way regardless of the sex of the respondent. Education is a factor in voter turnout, but sex is not.

Now it's your turn. Choose either RACE or AGE as a control variable and continue to analyze the relationship between education and voting. Run **Crosstabs** with VOTE92 as the row variable, DEGREE as the column variable, and your choice for a control variable. Summarize your results in Research Report 12.2.

NAME _____

INSTRUCTOR _____

DATE _____

1. Complete the summary table below to display the results of the multi-variate analysis of VOTE92. On line 1, fill in the blank with the name of your control variable. On line 3, fill in the percentages of respondents who voted for each category of the independent variable. On line 4, fill in the percentage of voters for the first value of your control variable; do the same on line 5 for the second category of your control variable. If you chose AGE as the control variable, fill in the percentage of voters for the oldest age group on line 6.

Lines

1.   VOTE92 by DEGREE by _____

	Less Than High School	High School	College	Gamma
2.				
3. % Voted All	____	____	____	____
4. _____	____	____	____	____
5. _____	____	____	____	____
6. _____	____	____	____	____

2. Compare and contrast the rate of turnout for the various categories of your control variable. Compare category percentages with each other and compare the strength and direction of the gammas. Which category (for example, older, well-educated people; black respondents with a high school education) had the highest turnout rate? _____. Which category had the lowest? _____. Does your control variable change the relationship between education and voting? Do the better educated still vote in higher numbers? Explain.

EXERCISE 12.4   **Presidential Preference in 1992: Who Voted for Whom?**

After analyzing who participated in the 1992 presidential election, it seems logical to move on to an examination of the choices people made in the voting booth. Are social factors (such as age, race, and education) correlated with presidential vote? How important is political ideology (how liberal or conservative a person is)?

Let's begin by examining how our sample voted. With the GSS94TAB.SAV data set loaded, run the **Frequencies** procedure for PRES92 and record the percentage voting for each candidate in item 1 of Research Report 12.3.

As you recall, the 1992 election had three candidates for president: Bill Clinton for the Democrats, George Bush for the Republicans, and Ross Perot running as an independent. Clinton was the victor with 43% of the vote, Bush had 38%, and 19% of the electorate cast their ballot for Perot. Note that there are discrepancies between how our sample said they voted and the actual results. The differences are small but note that the percentage of our respondents who claim to have voted for Clinton (the winner) is 6 points higher than the actual percentage. In contrast, the percentage of the sample who said they voted for the other two (losing) candidates is lower than the national percentage. This suggests that a few more respondents "remembered" that they voted for the winning candidate than actually did.

Next, let's explore *why* people voted as they did. One common idea is that U.S. politics can be partially understood in terms of social class. The Republican Party is said to represent the more affluent segments of society, whereas the Democrats are the party of the working class, labor union members, and minority groups. Test this idea by choosing a measure of social class position and RACE as independent variables. If support for presidential candidates does break down along social class and racial lines, we should see strong correlations between these variables and PRES92. Use the **Crosstabs** procedure, with column percentages, chi square, and Cramer's *V*. Also, to examine the role of ideology in the election, include POLVIEWS as an independent variable. Report your results in Research Report 12.3.

NAME _____

INSTRUCTOR _____

DATE _____

1. Complete the frequency distributions below with percentages (remember to use the "valid percentages" column).

Presidential Vote

Clinton	_____
Bush	_____
Perot	_____

2. a. *For social class*: On line 1 of the following summary table, fill in the blank with the name of the variable you choose to measure social class. On line 2, fill in the blanks with the names of the categories of your measure of social class, using as many blanks as necessary. On line 3, fill in the blanks with the percentage of respondents from each social class who voted for Clinton.

Lines

1.   PRES92 by RACE

2.   _____ _____ _____ _____   Cramer's *V*

3. % Voted for
   Clinton   _____ _____ _____ _____ _____

The column percentages _____ (do/do not) change, so there _____ (is/is not) a relationship between these variables. The significance of chi square is _____ (less than/more than) .05, so this relationship _____ (is/is not) statistically significant. The value of Cramer's *V* is _____ , so this is a _____ (weak/moderate/strong) relationship.

The social class most likely to vote for Clinton was _____ .

The social class most likely to vote for Bush was _____ .

The social class most likely to vote for Perot was _____ .

b. *For race*: On line 3, fill in the blanks with the percentage of respondents of each race who voted for Clinton.

Lines

1.   PRES92 by RACE

2.   White   Black   Cramer's *V*

3. % Voted for
   Clinton   _____   _____   _____

(Research Report continues)

The column percentages _____ (do/do not) change, so there _____ (is/is not) a relationship between these variables. The significance of chi square is _____ (less than/more than) .05, so this relationship _____ (is/is not) statistically significant. The value of Cramer's V is _____ , so this is a _____ (weak/moderate/strong) relationship.

Whites mostly voted for _____ .

Blacks mostly voted for _____ .

c. *For political ideology*: On line 3, fill in the blanks with the percentage of liberal, moderate, and conservative respondents who voted for Clinton.

Lines

	PRES92 by POLVIEWS			
1.				
2.	Liberal	Moderate	Conservative	Cramer's V
3. % Voted for Clinton	_____	_____	_____	_____

The column percentages _____ (do/do not) change, so there _____ (is/is not) a relationship between these variables. The significance of chi square is _____ (less than/more than) .05, so this relationship _____ (is/is not) statistically significant. The value of Cramer's V is _____, so this is a _____ (weak/moderate/strong) relationship.

Liberals mostly voted for _____ .

Moderates mostly voted for _____ .

Conservatives mostly voted for _____ .

4. Was the hypothesis that American politics can be understood in terms of race and social class confirmed? Explain.

5. How strong was the effect of political ideology? Was this election more a matter of social class, race, or political ideology? (Which of the three independent variables had the strongest relationship with PRES92 in terms of changes in column percentages and the value of Cramer's V?) Explain.

EXERCISE 12.5   **Multivariate Analysis of the 1992 Presidential Vote**

In Research Report 12.3, statistics were used to assess the importance of three independent variables (class, race, and political ideology) in explaining how respondents voted in 1992. Multivariate analysis provides another way to analyze these patterns. For example, we can get a sense of the relative importance of social class and race by observing how whites and blacks of each social class voted. If people of different races within the same social class voted the same way, we would be inclined to conclude that social class was a more important factor than race in shaping people's vote. On the other hand, if it was found that whites and blacks of the same social class had very different voting patterns, we would conclude that race was the more important factor.

Conduct this analysis now by running the **Crosstabs** procedure with PRES92 as the row variable, your measure of social class as the column variable, and RACE as the control variable. Don't forget column percentages and Cramer's *V*. Report your results in Research Report 12.4.

NAME _____

INSTRUCTOR _____

DATE _____

1. Complete the following summary table to display the results of the multivariate analysis of PRES92. On line 1, fill in the blank with the name of the variable you choose to measure social class. On line 2, fill in the blanks with the names of the categories of your independent variable, using as many blanks as necessary. On line 3, fill in the percentages of respondents from each social class who voted for Clinton. On line 4, fill in the percentage of white respondents from each social class who voted for Clinton and, on line 5, do the same for black respondents.

   Lines
   1.   PRES92 by _____ by RACE
              (Percentage Who Voted for Clinton)

   2.   _____ _____ _____ Gamma

   3. % Voted for
       Clinton
       All   _____   _____   _____   _____

   4. Whites   _____   _____   _____   _____

   5. Blacks   _____   _____   _____   _____

2. Compare and contrast the percentage of blacks and whites voting for Clinton for each class. Which category (for example, lower-class whites, middle-income blacks) had the highest percentage of support for Clinton? _____ . Which had the lowest? _____ . Do blacks and whites of the same social class have the same level of support for Clinton? Which was the more important factor in shaping the vote for president: social class or race? Explain.

EXERCISE 12.6 | **The Gender Gap**

In 1920, the 19th amendment to the Constitution extended the right to vote to women. Contrary to the predictions of some, men and women voted in about the same ways for decades and, until recently, sex was not found to be importantly related to choice of presidential candidate or to other political preferences. Then, in the 1980 presidential election, a perceptible difference between men and women voters appeared at the national level. A larger percentage of women voted for the Democratic candidate (Jimmy Carter) than for Republican (and winner of the election) Ronald Reagan. The **gender gap** was about 8 percentage points in 1980, and it reappeared in both the 1984 and 1988 presidential elections.

Did the gender gap affect the 1992 election? Run the **Crosstabs** procedure with PRES92 as the row variable and SEX as the column (independent) variable. Get column percentages, chi square, and Cramer's *V* and record the results in item 1 of Research Report 12.5. Was there a gender gap in 1992? How large was it?

What would cause men and women to vote differently? Two possible explanations can be tested, at least partially. One possibility is that a higher percentage of women are in economically precarious situations and are more likely to be unemployed, or underemployed, or to live in poverty. Because Democrats are typically seen as more sympathetic to the poor and more supportive of assistance programs for the disadvantaged, one source of the gender gap may be the greater economic distress of women. We can test this possible explanation using the INCOME variable from the GSS94TAB.SAV data set. If this explanation is true, support for Clinton will be higher among women who are lower in income. Run the **Crosstabs** procedure with PRES92 as the dependent variable, SEX as the independent variable, and INCOME as the control variable. Use the output to complete item 2 of Research Report 12.5.

A second possible explanation for the gender gap attributes the difference to a greater commitment to feminism and gender equality among women. The Democratic Party is more closely associated with these causes and, if this second explanation has merit, we should find higher levels of support for Clinton among women who also support feminist issues. Either FEPOL or FEWORK can be used to measure support for feminism. To test this explanation, run the **Crosstabs** procedure with PRES92 as the row variable, SEX as the column variable, and *either* FEPOL or FEWORK as the control variable. Don't forget column percentages and Cramer's *V*. Use these results to complete item 3 of Research Report 12.5.

NAME _____

INSTRUCTOR _____

DATE _____

1. For SEX and PRES92: _____% of the women voted for Clinton compared with _____% of the men. The gender gap in 1992 was _____ percentage points (subtract the % of men voting for Clinton from the % of women voting for Clinton to find the gap). The significance of chi square for the relationship between SEX and PRES92 was _____, which is _____ (less than/more than) .05, so this _____ (is/is not) a significant relationship. The value of Cramer's *V* was _____, so this is a _____ (weak/moderate/strong) relationship. Was there a similar gender difference for Bush or Perot? Explain.

2. For PRES92 and SEX, controlling for INCOME: Complete the summary table below to display the results of the multivariate analysis of PRES92 and SEX. On line 3, fill in the percentages of males and females who voted for Clinton. On line 4, fill in the percentage of low-income respondents from each gender who voted for Clinton and, on lines 5 and 6, do the same for middle- and high-income respondents.

Lines

		Males	Females	Cramer's *V*
1.	PRES92 by SEX by INCOME (Percentage Who Voted for Clinton)			
2.		Males	Females	Cramer's *V*
3.	% Voted for Clinton All	_____	_____	_____
4.	Low income	_____	_____	_____
5.	Middle income	_____	_____	_____
6.	High income	_____	_____	_____

Compare the size of the gender gap for each income group. These results _____ (do/do not) support the idea that the gender gap is due, in part, to the greater economic vulnerability of women. Explain.

3. For PRES92 and SEX, controlling for FEWORK or FEPOL: On line 1 of the following summary table, write in the name of the control variable you selected. On line 3, fill in the percentages of males and females who voted for Clinton. On line 4, fill in the percentage of the *more sexist* males and females ("disapprove" on FEWORK or "agree" on FEPOL) who voted for Clinton and, on line 5, do the same for the *less sexist* males and females ("approve" on FEWORK or "disagree" on FEPOL).

Lines

1.   PRES92 by SEX by ——————————

2.	Males	Females	Cramer's V
3. % Voted for Clinton All	____	____	____
4. More sexist	____	____	____
5. Less sexist	____	____	____

Compare the size of the gender gap for the "more sexist" and "less sexist" groups. These results _____ (do/do not) support the idea that the gender gap is due, in part, to the greater commitment of women to gender equality. Explain.

4. Which explanation of the gender gap (if either) is more supported by these results? Explain.

NAME _____

INSTRUCTOR _____

DATE _____

Continue the investigation of voter turnout begun in Research Report 12.1 by selecting another potential independent variable and using the **Crosstabs** procedure to assess its relationship with VOTE92. Get column percentages, chi square, and select either Cramer's *V* (if your independent variable is not numerical) or gamma (if your independent variable is numerical) as your measure of association.

1. State the name of your independent variable: _____. State and briefly explain a hypothesis about the relationship between your independent variable and VOTE92.

2. Summarize the results of the Crosstab analysis. On line 1 of the summary table, fill in the blank with the name of your independent variable. On line 2, write in the names of the categories of your independent variable, using as many blanks as necessary. On line 3, fill in the blanks with the percentage of respondents who voted in 1992.

   Lines

   1.   VOTE92 by _____

   2.   _____ _____ _____ _____ _____

   3. % Who Voted   _____ _____ _____ _____ _____

   The column percentages _____ (do/do not) change, so there _____ (is/is not) a relationship between these variables. The significance of chi square is _____ (less than/more than) .05, so this relationship _____ (is/is not) statistically significant. *If the independent variable is* **not** *numerical*: The value of Cramer's *V* is _____ , so this is a _____ (weak/moderate/strong) relationship.

If the independent variable **is** *numerical*: The value of gamma is _____, so this is a _____ (weak/moderate/strong) relationship. The sign of gamma indicates that this is a _____ (positive/negative) relationship. As _____ (name of your independent variable) increases, _____ voter turnout (increases/decreases).

3. Was your hypothesis confirmed? Explain.

NAME _____

INSTRUCTOR _____

DATE _____

What happens to the bivariate relationship you investigated in Independent Project 12.1 when you control for SEX? Run the **Crosstabs** procedure with VOTE92 in the rows, your independent variable in the columns, and SEX as the control variable. Get column percentages, chi square, and either Cramer's *V* (if your independent variable is not numerical) or gamma (if your independent variable is numerical) as your measure of association.

Complete the following summary table to display the results of the multivariate analysis of VOTE92. On line 1, fill in the blank with the name of your independent variable. On line 2, fill in the blanks with the names of the categories of your independent variable, using as many blanks as necessary. On line 3, fill in the blanks with the percentage of respondents who voted in 1992. On line 4, fill in the percentage of male respondents in each category of the independent variable who voted in 1992. On line 5, do the same for female respondents.

Lines

1.   VOTE92 by _____ by SEX

(Percentage Who Voted)

Cramer's *V*
or Gamma

2.   _____   _____   _____   _____   ‾‾‾‾‾‾

3. % Who Voted

All   ____   ____   ____   ____   ____

4. Males   ____   ____   ____   ____   ____

5. Females ____   ____   ____   ____   ____

Which subgroup had the highest turnout?_____. The lowest? _____. Compare the value (and sign, if applicable) of the measure of association (Cramer's *V* or gamma) for males and females. Is there a difference in the relationship between your independent variable and turnout for males and females? Explain.

NAME _____

INSTRUCTOR _____

DATE _____

Continue the investigation of candidate preference begun in Research Report 12.3 by selecting another potential independent variable and using the **Crosstabs** procedure to assess its relationship with PRES92. Get column percentages, chi square, and Cramer's *V*.

1. State the name of your independent variable: _____ .

   State a hypothesis about the relationship between your independent

   variable and PRES92:

2. Summarize the results of the Crosstab analysis. On line 1 of the following summary table, fill in the blank with the name of your independent variable. On line 2, fill in the blanks with the names of the categories of your independent variable, using as many blanks as necessary. On line 3, fill in the blanks with the percentage of respondents in each category of the independent variable who voted for Clinton.

   Lines

   1.　　　　　　　PRES92 by _____

   2.　　　　　　　_____ _____ _____ _____ Cramer's *V*

   3. % Voted for
      Clinton　　　_____ _____ _____ _____ _____

   The column percentages _____ (do/do not) change, so there

   _____ (is/is not) a relationship between these variables. The

   significance of chi square is _____ (less than/more than) .05,

   so this relationship _____ (is/is not) statistically significant.

   The value of Cramer's *V* is _____ , so this is a _____

   (weak/moderate/strong) relationship.

3. Was your hypothesis confirmed? Explain.

NAME _____

INSTRUCTOR _____

DATE _____

In Research Report 12.3, you conducted separate analyses of the effect of class, race, and political ideology on the presidential vote in 1992. In Research Report 12.4, you analyzed the combined effects of class and race on the presidential vote. In this project, you will investigate the joint effects of class and political ideology and race and political ideology on presidential vote. Combining the earlier reports and this project should give you a good indication of the relative importance of the three independent variables in shaping voting behavior.

1. Use the **Crosstabs** procedure to conduct a multivariate analysis of the relationship between PRES92 (dependent variable), social class (independent variable—use the same measure of social class you used in Research Reports 12.3 and 12.4), and POLVIEWS (control variable). Use gamma as the measure of association.

    Summarize your results in the table. On line 1, fill in the blank with the name of the variable you chose to measure social class. On line 2, fill in the blanks with the names of the categories of your independent variable, using as many blanks as necessary. On line 3, fill in the percentages of respondents from each social class who voted for Clinton. On line 4, fill in the percentage of liberals from each social class who voted for Clinton. On line 5, do the same for moderates, and, on line 6, do the same for conservatives.

    Lines
    1.   PRES92 by _____ by POLVIEWS
                      (Percentage Who Voted for Clinton)

    2.   ____ ____ ____ ____ Gamma

    3. % Voted for
       Clinton
       All   ____ ____ ____ ____ ____

    4. Liberals   ____ ____ ____ ____ ____

    5. Moderates   ____ ____ ____ ____ ____

    6. Conservatives ____ ____ ____ ____ ____

    Which subgroup (for example, lower-class liberals, middle-class conservatives) had the highest percentage of support for Clinton? _____ . Which had the lowest? _____ . Do people who are in the same social class but have different political ideologies vote in the same way?

(Independent Project continues)

Which was the more important factor in shaping the vote for president: social class or ideology? Explain.

2. Use the **Crosstabs** procedure to conduct a multivariate analysis of the relationship between PRES92 (dependent variable), RACE (independent variable), and POLVIEWS (control variable). Use Cramer's *V* as the measure of association.

Summarize your results in the table. On line 3, fill in the percentages of respondents from each race who voted for Clinton. On line 4, fill in the percentage of liberals from each racial group who voted for Clinton. On line 5, do the same for moderates, and, on line 6, do the same for conservatives.

Lines

1.   PRES92 by RACE by POLVIEWS
                                (Percentage Who Voted for Clinton)

2.	Whites	Blacks	Cramer's *V*
3. % Voted for Clinton All	_____	_____	_____
4. Liberals	_____	_____	_____
5. Moderates	_____	_____	_____
6. Conservatives	_____	_____	_____

Which subgroup (for example, lower-class blacks, middle-class whites) had the highest percentage of support for Clinton? _____ . Which had the lowest? _____ . Which was the more important factor in shaping the vote for president: race or ideology? Explain.

NAME _____

INSTRUCTOR _____

DATE _____

To what extent is religion a factor in how people vote? Run the **Crosstabs** procedure with PRES92 as the row (dependent) variable and RELIG and RELITEN as column (independent) variables. Get column percentages, chi square, and Cramer's *V*.

1. Summarize the results of the relationship with RELIG. On line 3, fill in the blanks with the percentage who voted for Clinton.

Lines

1.   PRES92 by RELIG

2.   Protestant   Catholic   Jew   None   Other

3. % for Clinton   _____   _____   _____ _____ _____

The column percentages _____ (do/do not) change, so there _____ (is/is not) a relationship between these variables. The significance of chi square is _____ (less than/more than) .05, so this relationship _____ (is/is not) statistically significant. The value of Cramer's *V* is _____ , so this is a _____ (weak/moderate/strong) relationship.

2. Summarize the results of the relationship with RELITEN. On line 3, fill in the blanks with the percentage who voted for Clinton.

Lines

1.   PRES92 by RELITEN

2.   Somewhat   Not Very
                  Strong   Strong   Strong   Not Religious

3. % for Clinton _____   _____   _____   _____

The column percentages _____ (do/do not) change, so there (is/is not) a relationship between these variables. The significance of chi square is _____ (less than/more than) .05, so this relationship _____ (is/is not) statistically significant. The value of Cramer's V is ____, so this is a _____ (weak/moderate/strong) relationship.

3. a. Assess the impact of RELIG and RELITEN on presidential vote. Did religion affect presidential vote? How?

   b. Compare the effect of religion with the effect of CLASS, RACE, and POLVIEWS. Which variable had the strongest effect on PRES92? Explain.

NAME _____

INSTRUCTOR _____

DATE _____

Load the GSS72.SAV data set and run the **Frequencies** procedure for VOTE68.

1. Estimating from the 1972 GSS sample, voter turnout in 1968 was about _____%. Compare this with the actual turnout reported in Table 12.1. Does the GSS overestimate voter turnout in 1968 as in 1992? Explain.

2. Choose two independent variables from Research Report 12.1 (DEGREE, INCOME, RACE, or AGE) and assess their impact on voter turnout in 1968. Run the **Crosstab** procedure with VOTE68 as the row variable and your two variables as column (independent) variables. Get column percentages, chi square, and Cramer's *V* or gamma.

3. a. Summarize results for your first independent variable. On line 1 of the summary table, fill in the blank with the name of your independent variable. On line 2, write in the names of the categories of your independent variable, using as many blanks as necessary. On line 3, fill in the blanks with the percentage of respondents who voted in 1968.

   Lines

   1.   VOTE68 by _____

   2.   _____ _____ _____ _____ _____

   3. % Who Voted   _____ _____ _____ _____ _____

   The column percentages _____(do/do not) change, so there _____ (is/is not) a relationship between these variables. The significance of chi square is _____(less than/more than) .05, so this relationship _____(is/is not) statistically significant.

   *If the independent variable is **not** numerical*: The value of Cramer's *V* is _____, so this is a _____(weak/moderate/strong) relationship.

   *If the independent variable **is** numerical*: The value of gamma is _____, so this is a _____(weak/moderate/strong)

(*Comparative Analysis continues*)

relationship. The sign of gamma indicates that this is a

_____ (positive/negative) relationship. As _____

(name of your independent variable) increases, _____

voter turnout (increases/decreases).

b. Summarize results for your second independent variable. On line 1 of the summary table, fill in the blank with the name of your independent variable. On line 2, write in the names of the categories of your independent variable, using as many blanks as necessary. On line 3, fill in the blanks with the percentage of respondents who voted in 1968.

Lines

1.   VOTE68 by _____

2.   _____ _____ _____ _____ _____

3. % Who Voted   _____ _____ _____ _____ _____

The column percentages _____(do/do not) change, so

there_____ (is/is not) a relationship between these vari-

ables. The significance of chi square is _____(less

than/more than) .05, so this relationship _____(is/is not)

statistically significant.

*If the independent variable is **not** numerical*: The value of Cramer's

V is _____ , so this is a_____ (weak/moderate/strong)

relationship.

*If the independent variable **is** numerical*: The value of gamma is

_____ , so this is a_____(weak/moderate/strong) rela-

tionship. The sign of gamma indicates that this is a

(positive/negative) relationship. As_____(name of your

independent variable) increases, _____voter turnout

(increases/decreases).

4. Summarize your results. Did voter turnout have the same correlates in 1968 as in 1992?

NAME _____

INSTRUCTOR _____

DATE _____

1. Load the GSS72.SAV data set and run the **Frequencies** procedure for PRES68. As was the case in 1992, the 1968 presidential race included three candidates. The Democratic candidate was Hubert Humphrey and Richard M. Nixon was the nominee of the Republican Party and the winner of the election. The third candidate was Governor George Wallace of Alabama, a very conservative, "right wing" politician well known for his opposition to racial integration, student protest against the Vietnam war, and other "liberal" causes. Report the percentage voting for each candidate:

    Humphrey _____

    Nixon _____

    Wallace _____

2. Choose two independent variables from those you used in Research Report 12.3 or 12.5 or Independent Project 12.3 or 12.5 (not all variables are available for 1972) and use the **Crosstabs** procedure to analyze their relationship with PRES68. Get column percentages, chi square, and Cramer's *V*.

    a. Summarize results for your first independent variable and PRES68. On line 1 of the summary table, fill in the blank with the name of your independent variable. On line 2, fill in the blanks with the names of the categories of your independent variable, using as many blanks as necessary. On line 3, fill in the blanks with the percentage of respondents in each category of the independent variable who voted for Nixon.

    Lines

    1. PRES92 by _____

    2. _____ _____ _____ _____

    3. % Voted for
        Nixon _____ _____ _____ _____

    The column percentages _____ (do/do not) change, so there _____ (is/is not) a relationship between these variables. The significance of chi square is _____ (less than/more than) .05, so this relationship _____ (is/is not) statistically significant. The value of Cramer's *V* is _____ , so this is a _____ (weak/moderate/strong) relationship.

b. Summarize results for your second independent variable and
    PRES68. On line 1 of the summary table, fill in the blank with the
    name of your independent variable. On line 2, fill in the blanks
    with the names of the categories of your independent variable,
    using as many blanks as necessary. On line 3, fill in the blanks
    with the percentage of respondents in each category of the inde-
    pendent variable who voted for Nixon.

Lines

1.   PRES92 by ＿＿＿＿＿＿

2.   ＿＿＿＿ ＿＿＿＿ ＿＿＿＿ ＿＿＿＿

3. % Voted for
   Nixon   ＿＿＿＿ ＿＿＿＿ ＿＿＿＿ ＿＿＿＿

The column percentages ＿＿＿＿＿＿(do/do not) change, so

there ＿＿＿＿＿ (is/is not) a relationship between these vari-

ables. The significance of chi square is ＿＿＿＿＿(less

than/more than) .05, so this relationship ＿＿＿＿＿(is/is not)

statistically significant. The value of Cramer's *V* is＿＿, so this is

a ＿＿＿＿＿ (weak/moderate/strong) relationship.

3. Summarize your results. Were your independent variables related to
    the party of the presidential choice (Democrat, Republican,
    Independent) in the same way in both years?

Main Points

- The 1994 GSS overestimates participation in the 1992 presidential elections, in part because 1994 respondents inflated their actual participation in the election.

- Possible correlates of voter turnout and presidential preference were investigated.

- A gender gap in presidential voting appeared in 1980 and has persisted since that time. The gap may in part be due to the greater economic vulnerability of women and their greater support for gender equality.

SPSS Commands Introduced in This Chapter

No new commands were introduced in this chapter.

Appendix A   Variable Names, Item Wordings, and Codes for All Data Sets

GSS94TAB.SAV Data Set

Please tell me if you think that it should be possible for a pregnant woman to obtain a legal abortion if . . .

ABANY   The woman wants it for any reason?
1. Yes
2. No

ABHLTH   The woman's health is seriously endangered by the pregnancy?
1. Yes
2. No

ABNOMORE   She is married and does not want any more children?
1. Yes
2. No

ABINDEX   An index computed from ABANY, ABHLTH, and ABNOMORE.
3. Strongly in favor
4. Moderately in favor
5. Moderately opposed
6. Strongly opposed

AGE   Respondent's age in years. (This variable has been recoded into three age groups of approximately equal size for the GSS94TAB.SAV data set. When selecting independent variables, it may be useful to note that the first age group corresponds roughly to "Generation X," the second to "baby boomers," and the third to the "depression generation.")
1. 18 through 33
2. 34 through 49
3. 50 and older

ATTEND   How often do you attend religious services? (This variable has been recoded from eight to four categories for the GSS94TAB.SAV data set.)
0. Never
1. Rarely
2. About Monthly
3. Weekly or more

BURGLR   During the last year, did anyone break into or somehow illegally get into your (apartment/house)?
              1. Yes
              2. No

BUSING   In general, do you favor or oppose the busing of black and white schoolchildren from one school district to another?
              1. Favor
              2. Oppose

CAPPUN   Do you favor or oppose the death penalty for persons convicted of murder?
              1. Favor
              2. Oppose

CLASS   If you were asked to use one of four names for your social class, which would you say you belong to?
              1. Lower class
              2. Working class
              3. Middle class
              4. Upper class

DEGREE   Respondent's degree. (This variable has been recoded from five to three categories for the GSS94TAB.SAV data set.)
              0. Less than high school
              1. High school
              2. At least some college

DIVORCE   Have you ever been divorced or legally separated?
              1. Yes
              2. No

EVSTRAY   Have you ever had sex with someone other than your husband or wife while you were married? (Respondents who have never been married have been eliminated.)
              1. Yes
              2. No

FAMTYPE   Household type (Recoded from HHTYPE1)
              1. Childless couple
              2. Single parent
              3. Single adult
              4. Cohabiting
              5. Nuclear family

FEAR   Is there any area right around here—that is, within a mile—where you would be afraid to walk alone at night?
              1. Yes
              2. No

FEPOL   Do you agree or disagree with this statement: most men are better suited emo-
               tionally for politics than are most women?
               1. Agree
               2. Disagree

FEWORK   Do you approve or disapprove of a married woman earning money in business or
               industry if she has a husband to support her?
               1. Approve
               2. Disapprove

GRASS   Do you think the use of marijuana should be made legal or not?
               1. Legal
               2. Not legal

GRNTAXES   How willing would you be to pay much higher taxes in order to protect the envi-
               ronment?
               1. Very willing
               2. Neither willing nor unwilling
               3. Not willing

GUNLAW   Would you favor or oppose a law which would require a person to obtain a police
               permit before he or she could buy a gun?
               1. Favor
               2. Oppose

HAPPY   Taken all together, how would you say things are these days—would you say that
               you are
               1. Very happy?
               2. Pretty happy?
               3. Not too happy?

INCOME   In which category did your total family income, from all sources, fall last year—
               before taxes, that is? (This variable has been recoded for the GSS94TAB.SAV
               data set.)
               1. Lower: $24,999 and less
               2. Middle: $25,000 to $50,000
               3. Higher: $50,000 and more

LETDIE1   Do you think a person has the right to end his or her own life if this person has
               an incurable disease?
               1. Yes
               2. No

MARITAL   Are you currently:
               1. Married?
               2. Widowed?
               3. Divorced?
               4. Separated?
               5. Never married?

NEWS   How often do you read the newspaper?
                1. Every day
                2. Less than every day

OBEYTHNK   Which of these would you say is more important in preparing children for life:
                (1) to be obedient or, (2) to think for themselves?
                1. to be obedient
                2. to think for themselves

PILLOK   Do you strongly agree, agree, disagree, or strongly disagree that methods of birth
                control should be available to teenagers between the ages of 14 and 16 if their
                parents do not approve?
                1. Strongly agree
                2. Agree
                3. Disagree
                4. Strongly Disagree

POLVIEWS   We hear a lot of talk these days about liberals and conservatives. I'm going to
                show you a seven-point scale on which the political views that people might hold
                are arranged from extremely liberal to extremely conservative. Where would you
                place yourself on this scale? (This variable has been recoded into three cate-
                gories for the GSS94TAB.SAV data set.)
                1. Liberal
                2. Moderate
                3. Conservative

POSTLIFE   Do you believe there is a life after death?
                1. Yes
                2. No

PREMARSX   There's been a lot of discussion about the way morals and attitudes about sex are
                changing in this country. If a man and a woman have sex relations before mar-
                riage, do you think it is
                1. Always wrong?
                2. Almost always wrong?
                3. Wrong only sometimes?
                4. Not wrong at all?

PRES92   Did you vote for Clinton, Bush, or Perot in the presidential election of 1992?
                (Respondents who voted for other candidates and those who did not vote have
                been omitted.)
                1. Clinton
                2. Bush
                3. Perot

PRESTIGE   Respondent's occupational prestige. (This variable has been recoded from PRESTG80 for the GSS94TAB.SAV data set.)
1. Low (scores of 17–35)
2. Moderate (scores of 36–47)
3. High (scores of 48–86)

On the average, blacks have worse jobs, income, and housing than white people. Do you think these differences are

RACDIF2   Because most blacks have less inborn ability to learn?
1. Yes
2. No

RACDIF4   Because most blacks just don't have the motivation or willpower to pull themselves out of poverty.
1. Yes
2. No

RACE   Determined by interviewer observation. "Others" have been eliminated.
1. White
2. Black

REGION   Respondent's region. (This variable has been recoded for the GSS94TAB.SAV data set.)
1. North (New England and N.Y., N.J., Pa.)
2. Midwest (Ohio, Ill., Ind., Mich., Wis., Minn., Iowa, Mo., N.Dak., S.Dak., Nebr., Kans.)
3. South (Del., Md., W.Va., Va., N.C., S.C., Ga., Fla., D.C., Ky., Tenn., Ala., Miss., Ark., Okla., Tex., La.)
4. West (Mont., Idaho, Wyo., Nev., Utah, Colo., Ariz., N.Mex, Wash., Oreg., Calif., Alaska, Hawaii)

RELIG   What is your religious preference?
1. Protestant
2. Catholic
3. Jewish
4. None
5. Other

RELITEN   Would you call yourself a —————(preference named for RELIG)? (The values "somewhat strong" and "not very strong" have been switched for this variable for the GSS94TAB.SAV data set.)
1. Strong
2. Somewhat strong
3. Not very strong
4. No religion

SATJOB   On the whole, how satisfied are you with the work you do? (This variable has been recoded for the GSS94TAB.SAV data set.)
1. Satisfied
2. Dissatisfied

SEX   Determined by interviewer observation
1. Male
2. Female

SEXHAR   Have you ever been sexually harassed at work?
              (Respondents who have never worked have been eliminated.)
              1. Yes
              2. No

SPANKING   Do you agree or disagree that it is sometimes necessary to discipline a child with
              a good, hard spanking? (This variable has been recoded for the GSS94TAB.SAV
              data set.)
              1. Agree
              2. Disagree

SRCBELT   Respondent's type of residence.   (This variable has been recoded for the
              GSS94TAB.SAV data set.)
              1. Larger city
              2. Suburbs
              3. Smaller town
              4. Rural area

TRUST   In general, would you say that most people can be trusted or that you can't be too
              careful in dealing with people?
              1. Can trust
              2. Cannot trust

VOTE92   Do you remember for sure whether or not you voted in the 1992 presidential
              election? (Respondents not eligible to vote and those that refused to answer have
              been eliminated.)
              1. Voted
              2. Did not vote

XMOVIE   Have you seen an X-rated movie in the last year?
              1. Yes
              2. No

GSS94COR.SAV

AGE   Respondent's age in years.

AGEWED   How old were you when you first married? (Scores are actual years.)

ATTEND   How often do you attend religious services?
              0. Never
              1. Less than once a year
              2. Once a year
              3. Several times a year
              4. Once a month
              5. Two to three times a month
              6. Nearly every week
              7. Every week
              8. More than once a week

CHILDS

How many children have you ever had? Please count all that were born alive at any time (including any you had from a previous marriage).
0. None
1. One
2. Two
3. Three
4. Four
5. Five
6. Six
7. Seven
8. Eight or more

CHLDIDEL

What do you think is the ideal number of children for a family to have?
0. None
1. One
2. Two
3. Three
4. Four
5. Five
6. Six
7. Seven or more
8. As many as you want

CLASS

If you were asked to use one of four names for your social class, which would you say you belong to?
1. Lower class
2. Working class
3. Middle class
4. Upper class

EDUC

Respondent's education (years of formal schooling).

HRS1

How many hours were you at work last week? (Actual hours)

INCOME91

In which of the following categories did your total family income, from all sources, fall last year before taxes?
 1. less than $1000
 2. 1000 to 2999
 3. 3000 to 3999
 4. 4000 to 4999
 5. 5000 to 5999
 6. 6000 to 6999
 7. 7000 to 7999
 8. 8000 to 9999
 9. 10000 to 12499
10. 12500 to 14999
11. 15000 to 17499
12. 17500 to 19999
13. 20000 to 22499
14. 22500 to 24999
15. 25000 to 29999
16. 30000 to 34999
17. 35000 to 39999

18. 40000 to 49999
19. 50000 to 59999
20. 60000 to 74999
21. 75000+

MAEDUC   Education of respondent's mother (years of formal schooling).

PAEDUC   Education of respondent's father (years of formal schooling).

PAPRES80   Occupational prestige score for respondent's father

PARTNRS5   How many sex partners have you had in the last five years?
0. No partners
1. 1 partner
2. 2 partners
3. 3 partners
4. 4 partners
5. 5 to 10 partners
6. 11 to 20 partners
7. 21 to 100 partners
8. More than 100 partners

POLVIEWS   We hear a lot of talk these days about liberals and conservatives. I'm going to show you a seven-point scale on which the political views that people might hold are arranged from extremely liberal to extremely conservative. Where would you place yourself on this scale?
1. Extremely liberal
2. Liberal
3. Slightly liberal
4. Moderate
5. Slightly conservative
6. Conservative
7. Extremely conservative

PRESTG80   Respondent's occupational prestige score

RACE   Determined by interviewer observation. "Others" have been eliminated.
1. White
2. Black

RELIG   What is your religious preference?
1. Protestant
2. Catholic
3. Jewish
4. None
5. Other

RELITEN   Would you call yourself a _____ (preference named for RELIG)?
(The values "somewhat strong" and "not very strong" have been switched for this variable for the GSS94COR.SAV data set.)
1. Strong
2. Somewhat strong
3. Not very strong
4. No religion

RINCOME91   In which of the following categories did your income fall last year before taxes?

1. less than $1000
2. 1000 to 2999
3. 3000 to 3999
4. 4000 to 4999
5. 5000 to 5999
6. 6000 to 6999
7. 7000 to 7999
8. 8000 to 9999
9. 10000 to 12499
10. 12500 to 14999
11. 15000 to 17499
12. 17500 to 19999
13. 20000 to 22499
14. 22500 to 24999
15. 25000 to 29999
16. 30000 to 34999
17. 35000 to 39999
18. 40000 to 49999
19. 50000 to 59999
20. 60000 to 74999
21. 75000+

SATJOB   On the whole, how satisfied are you with the work you do?

1. Very satisfied
2. Moderately satisfied
3. A little dissatisfied
4. Very dissatisfied

SEX   Determined by interviewer observation

1. Male
2. Female

SEXFREQ   About how often did you have sex during the last 12 months?

0. Not at all
1. Once or twice
2. Once a month
3. Two to three times a month
4. Weekly
5. Two to three times a week
6. Four or more times a week

SIBS   How many brothers and sisters did you have? Please count all those born alive, but no longer living, as well as those alive now. Also include stepbrothers and stepsisters, and children adopted by your parents. (Actual numbers)

SRCBELT   Respondent's residence

1. 12 largest SMSAs
2. SMSAs 13–100
3. Suburb, 12 largest SMSAs
4. Suburb, SMSAs 13–100
5. Other urban
6. Other rural

TVHOURS	On the average day, how many hours do you personally watch television. (Actual hours)

GSS72.SAV

Please tell me if you think that it should be possible for a pregnant woman to obtain a legal abortion if . . .

ABHLTH	The woman's health is seriously endangered by the pregnancy? 1. Yes 2. No
ABNOMORE	She is married and does not want any more children? 1. Yes 2. No
AGE	Respondent's age in years
AGEWED	How old were you when you first married? (Scores are actual years.)
ATTEND	How often do you attend religious services? (This variable has been recoded from eight to four categories for the GSS72.SAV data set.) 0. Never 1. Rarely 2. About monthly 3. Weekly or more
BUSING	In general, do you favor or oppose the busing of black and white schoolchildren from one school district to another? 1. Favor 2. Oppose
CAPPUN2	Are you in favor of the death penalty for persons convicted of murder? 1. Yes 2. No
CHLDIDEL	What do you think is the ideal number of children for a family to have? 0. None 1. One 2. Two 3. Three 4. Four 5. Five 6. Six 7. Seven or more 8. As many as you want
CHILDS	How many children have you ever had? Please count all that were born alive at any time (including any you had from a previous marriage). 0. None 1. One 2. Two 3. Three 4. Four

5. Five
6. Six
7. Seven
8. Eight or more

CLASS
If you were asked to use one of four names for your social class, which would you say you belong to?
1. Lower class
2. Working class
3. Middle class
4. Upper class

DEGREE
Respondent's degree. (This variable has been recoded from five to three categories for the GSS72.SAV data set.)
0. Less than high school
1. High school
2. At least some college

DIVORCE
Have you ever been divorced or legally separated?
1. Yes
2. No

EDUC
Respondent's education (years of formal schooling)

FEPRES
If your party nominated a woman for President, would you vote for her if she were qualified for the job?
1. Yes
2. No

FEWORK
Do you approve or disapprove of a married women earning money in business or industry if she has a husband to support her?
1. Approve
2. Disapprove

GUNLAW
Would you favor or oppose a law which would require a person to obtain a police permit before he or she could buy a gun?
1. Favor
2. Oppose

HAPPY
Taken all together, how would you say things are these days—would you say that you are
1. Very happy?
2. Pretty happy?
3. Not too happy?

HELPFUL
Would you say that most of the time people try to be helpful, or that they are mostly just looking out for themselves?
1. Helpful
2. Look out for self
3. Depends

HOMPOP
Household size (number of members)

INCOME72   Total family income
    1. Less than $2000
    2. 2000 to 3999
    3. 4000 to 5999
    4. 6000 to 7999
    5. 8000 to 9999
    6. 10000 to 12499
    7. 12500 to 14999
    8. 15000 to 17499
    9. 17500 to 19999
    10. 20000 to 24999
    11. 25000 to 29999
    12. 30000+

MARITAL   Are you currently:
    1. Married?
    2. Widowed?
    3. Divorced?
    4. Separated?
    5. Never married?

NEWS   How often do you read the newspaper?
    1. Everyday
    2. A few times a week
    3. Once a week
    4. Less than once a week
    5. Never

PADEG   Degree of respondent's father. (This variable has been recoded from five to three categories for the GSS72.SAV data set.)
    1. Less than high school
    2. High school
    3. At least some college

PAEDUC   Education of respondent's father (years of formal schooling).

PAPRES16   Occupational prestige score of respondent's father

PARTYID   Generally speaking, do you think of yourself as a Republican, Democrat, Independent, or what? (This variable has been recoded for the GSS72.SAV data set.)
    1. Democrat
    2. Independent
    3. Republican

PREMARSX   There's been a lot of discussion about the way morals and attitudes about sex are changing in this country. If a man and a woman have sex relations before marriage, do you think it is
    1. Always wrong?
    2. Almost always wrong?
    3. Wrong only sometimes?
    4. Not wrong at all?

PRES68   Did you vote for Humphrey, Nixon, or Wallace in the presidential election of 1968? (Respondents who voted for other candidates and those that did not vote have been omitted.)
1. Humphrey
2. Nixon
3. Wallace

PRESTIGE   Respondent's occupational prestige score

RACE   Determined by interviewer observation. "Others" have been eliminated.
1. White
2. Black

RACPRES   If your party nominated a Black for president, would you vote for him if he were qualified for the job?
1. Yes
2. No

REGION   Respondent's region. (This variable has been recoded for the GSS72.SAV data set.)
1. North (New England and N.Y, N.J, Pa.)
2. Midwest (Ohio, Ill., Ind., Mich., Wis., Minn., Iowa, Mo., N.Dak., S.Dak., Nebr., Kans.)
3. South (Del., Md., W.Va., Va., N.C., S.C., Ga., Fla., D.C., Ky., Tenn., Ala., Miss., Ark., Okla., Tex., La.)
4. West (Mont., Idaho, Wyo., Nev., Utah, Colo., Ariz., N.Mex., Wash., Oreg., Calif., Alaska, Hawaii)

RELIG   What is your religious preference?
1. Protestant
2. Catholic
3. Jewish
4. None
5. Other

SATFIN   So far as you and your family are concerned, would you say that you are pretty well satisfied with your present financial situation, more or less satisfied, or not satisfied at all?
1. Pretty well satisfied
2. More or less satisfied
3. Not at all satisfied

SATJOB   On the whole, how satisfied are you with the work you do? (This variable has been recoded for the GSS72 data set.)
1. Satisfied
2. Dissatisfied

SEX   Determined by interviewer observation
1. Male
2. Female

SIBS

How many brothers and sisters did you have? Please count all those born alive, but no longer living, as well as those alive now. Also include stepbrothers and stepsisters and children adopted by your parents. (Actual numbers)

SRCBELT

Respondent's type of residence.   (This variable has been recoded for the GSS72.SAV data set.)
1. Larger city
2. Suburbs
3. Smaller town
4. Rural area

VOTE68

Do you remember for sure whether or not you voted in the 1968 presidential election? (Respondents not eligible to vote and those that refused to answer have been eliminated.)
1. Voted
2. Did not vote

WRKSTAT

Last week, were you
1. Working full-time?
2. Working part-time?
3. Temporarily not at work?
4. Unemployed, laid off?
5. Retired?
6. At school?
7. Keeping house?
8. Other?

Appendix B SPSS Commands Used in This Book

Opening a Data File

> **File** → **Open** → **Data. . .** →
> Click the name of the data file
> Click **OK**

Ending an SPSS Session

> Click **File** → **Exit**

Graphs and Charts

Procedures are listed alphabetically.

Bar Charts

> Click **Chart** → **Bar** →
> Highlight the variable name (for example, **RELIG**) →
> Click the arrow pointing to the **Category Axis:** box →
> Click **Options. . .** →
> Make sure the **Display groups defined by missing values** option is *not* checked →
> Click **Continue** →
> Click **OK**

Line Charts

> Click **Chart** → **Line** →
> Highlight a variable name →
> Click the arrow pointing to the **Category Axis:** box →
> Click **Options. . .** →
> Make sure the **Display groups defined by missing values** option is *not* checked →
> Click **Continue** →
> Click **OK**

Multiple Line Charts

> Click **Graphs** → **Line. . .** →
> Click **Multiple** on the **Define Line Chart** dialog box → Click **Define** →
> In the **Define Multiple Line Chart** dialog box, highlight the name of the dependent variable (this variable should be numerical)→
> Click the arrow pointing to the **Category Axis:** box →
> Highlight the name of the independent variable →
> Click the arrow pointing to the **Define Lines by:** box →
> If you wish, click the radio button next to % of cases in the **Lines Represent** box →
> Click the **Options. . .** button →
> Make sure the box next to **Display groups defined by missing values** is *not* checked →
> Click **Continue** →
> Click **OK**

Saving and Printing Output

To Save the Contents of the !Output1 Window

> Click **File** → **Save SPSS Output**

To Print the Contents of the !Output1 Window

> Click **File** → **Print** → **OK**

Statistical Procedures

Procedures are listed alphabetically by procedure name.

Crosstabs with Column Percentages

Click **Statistics** → **Summarize** → **Crosstabs** →
Highlight the name of the dependent variable(s) →
Click the arrow pointing to the **Row(s):** box →
Highlight the name of the independent variable(s) →
Click the arrow pointing to the **Column(s):** box
Click **Cells** in the **Crosstabs** dialog box →
Click **Columns** in the **Percentages** box →
Click **Continue** →
Click **OK**

Crosstabs with Column Percentages, Chi Square, and Cramer's _V_

Click **Statistics** → **Summarize** → **Crosstabs** →
Highlight the dependent variable →
Click the arrow pointing to the **Row(s):** box →
Highlight the independent variable →
Click the arrow pointing to the **Column(s):** box →
Click **Cells** to get the **Cell Display** window →
In the **Percentages** box, choose **Columns** →
Click **Continue** to close this dialog box →
In the **Crosstabs** dialog box, click **Statistics** →
Select **Chi square** and **Cramer's V** →
Click **Continue** →
Click **OK**

Crosstabs with Column Percentages, Chi Square, and Gamma

Click **Statistics** → **Summarize** → **Crosstabs** →
Highlight the name of the dependent variable →
Click the arrow pointing to the **Row(s):** box →
Highlight the name of the independent variable →
Click the arrow pointing to the **Column(s):** box →
Click **Cells** →
Click **Columns** in the **Percentages** box →
Click **Continue** to close this dialog box →
In the **Crosstabs** dialog box, click **Statistics** →
Select **Chi square** and **Gamma** →
Click **Continue** →
Click **OK**

Crosstabs with a Control Variable

Click **Statistics** → **Summarize** → **Crosstabs** →
Highlight the name of the dependent variable →
Click the arrow pointing to the **Row(s):** box →
Highlight the name of the independent variable →
Click the arrow pointing to the **Column(s):** box →
Highlight the name of the control variable →
Click the arrow pointing to the box at the bottom of the window →
Click **Cells** →
Click **Columns** in the **Percentages** box →
Click **Continue** →
In the **Crosstabs** dialog box, click **Statistics** →
Select **Chi square** and **Cramer's V** or **Gamma** →
Click **Continue** →
Click **OK**

Descriptive Statistics

Click **Statistics** → **Summarize** → **Descriptives** →
Highlight the name of the variable →
Click the arrow pointing to the **Variable(s):** box →
Highlight the second variable name →
Click the arrow pointing to the **Variable(s):** box →
Continue until all variables have been moved to the **Variable(s):** box →
Click **OK**

Frequency Distributions

Click **Statistics** → **Summarize** → **Frequencies** →
Highlight the first variable name →
Click the arrow pointing to the **Variable(s):** box →
Highlight the second variable name →
Click the arrow pointing to the **Variable(s):** box →
Continue until all variables have been moved to the
Variable(s): box →
Click **OK**

Pearson's *r*

Click **Statistics** → **Correlate** → **Bivariate** →
Highlight the variable name →
Click the arrow to transfer the variable name to the **Variable(s):** box →
Highlight the next variable name →
Click the arrow to transfer the variable name to the **Variable(s):** box →
Repeat until all the variables are listed in the **Variable(s):** box →
Click **OK**

Scatterplot

Click **Graphs** → **Scatter. . .** →
Click **Simple** → **Define** →
Highlight the name of the dependent variable →
Click the arrow pointing to the **Y Axis:** box →
Highlight the name of the independent variable →
Click the arrow pointing to the **X Axis:** box →
Click **OK**

Scatterplot with Regression Line

Click **Edit** →
Click **Chart** → **Options** →
From the **Scatterplot Options** dialog box, click **Total** in the **Fit line** box →
Click **OK**

T Tests (for Independent Variables with Only Two Categories)

Click **Statistics** → **Compare Means** → **Independent Samples T Test** →
Highlight the names of each dependent variable →
Click the arrow pointing to the **Test Variable(s):** box →
Highlight the name of the independent variable →
Click the arrow pointing to the **Grouping Variable:** box →
Click the **Define Groups** button →
Click on the **Group 1** box and type **1** →
Click on the **Group 2** box and type **2** →
Click **Continue** → Click **OK**

Transforming Variables and Selecting Cases

Computing a Summary Variable

Click **Transform** → **Compute** →

Click **Target Variable** →

Type a name for the new variable →

Use existing variables and mathematical procedures to state an expression that defines the new variable in the **Numerical Expression:** box →

Click **OK**

Save the data file

Selecting Cases

Click **Data** → **Select Cases** →

The **Select Cases** dialog box appears →

Choose options, variables, values, and numerical and logical operations to establish conditions for selecting cases →

Click **Continue** →

Click **OK**

To Find Information on Variables

Utilities → **Variables**

Answers to Selected Exercises

Answers to some items in selected research reports are provided so that you can check your work and make sure that you are using SPSS correctly. In general, answers are provided for reports that use an SPSS procedure for the first time. For research reports in which students have a choice of variables, results for the first variable(s) mentioned in the text are shown.

Chapter 1

Research Report 1.1

1. (RELIG) For the 1994 GSS sample, the most common religious affiliation was _Protestant_ with _60_ % of the sample. The second most common was _Catholic_ with _25_ %. The least common religious affiliation was _Jewish_ with _2_ % of the sample. About _10_ % of the respondents have no religious affiliation ("None").

Chapter 2

Research Report 2.2

1. In 1994 the percentage of respondents who had been divorced is _23%_ .

4. If you choose DEGREE as an independent variable:

DIVORCE by DEGREE

	Less Than High School	High School	At Least Some College
Divorce = Yes	24	27	14

6. Epsilon = _13_

Chapter 3

Research Report 3.1

1. About _50_ % of the sample are married, and about _11_ % are widowed.

2. The most common place of residence for the sample is _smaller towns_, and the least common is _rural areas_.

Research Report 3.2

1. The sample has completed an average of _13.12_ years of schooling. The most educated respondents completed _20_ years, and the least educated finished _0_ years. The range of the scores was _20_.

Research Report 3.3

1. For years of education (EDUC), the highest peak (most common score) was _12_. The lowest point of the graph was at _0–3_ years of education. Most cases seemed to be grouped around _12_ years of schooling.

Chapter 4

Research Report 4.2

1. _37.6_ % of white respondents are strong in their religious faith vs. _51.5_ % of the black respondents. RELITEN is strongest for _blacks_ (blacks/whites) and there _is_ (is/is not) a relationship between these two variables. This table _does_ (does/does not) support the deprivation theory. Explain.

Research Report 4.3

1.

	Percentage (Yes)	Significance Chi Square	Strength Cramer's V
RACE			
White	82.2		
Black	81.5	.84	.01

2. For RACE: The column percentages _do not_ (do/do not) change, so there _is not_ (is/is not) a relationship between these variables. The significance of chi square is _more than_ (less than/more than) .05, so the relationship between RACE and POSTLIFE _is not_ (is/is not) statistically significant. The value of Cramer's V for RACE and POSTLIFE is _.01_, so this is a _weak_ (weak/moderate/strong) relationship.

Chapter 5

Research Report 5.4

3. For RELIG:

	ABINDEX by RELIG				
	Protestant	Catholic	Jewish	None	Other
% Strongly in Favor	39	38	100	67	62

The column percentages _do_ (do/do not) change, so there _is_ (is/is not) a relationship between these variables. The significance of chi square for this relationship is _less than_ (less than/more than) .05, so this relationship _is_ (is/is not) statistically significant. The value of Cramer's V is _.14_ , so this is a _moderate_ (weak/moderate/strong) relationship.

Chapter 6

Research Report 6.5

3.

SPANKING by DEGREE

	Less Than High School	High School	At Least Some College
% Strongly Agree	75	75	62

The column percentages _do_ (do/do not) change, so there _is_ (is/is not) a relationship between these variables. The significance of chi square is _less than_ (less than/more than) .05, so this relationship _is_ (is/is not) statistically significant. The value of gamma is _.23_ , so this is a _moderate_ (weak/moderate/strong) relationship. The sign of gamma indicates that this is a _positive_ (positive/negative) relationship. As the education increases, disapproval of spanking _increases_ (increases/decreases).

Chapter 7

Research Report 7.1

2. a. For INCOME:

	INCOME		
BURGLR	Low	Middle	High
% Yes	10	5	2

The column percentages _do_ (do/do not) change, so there _is_ (is/is not) a relationship between these variables. The significance of chi square is _less than_ (less than/more than) .05, so this relationship _is_ (is/is not) statistically significant. The value of gamma is _.48_ , so this is a _strong_ (weak/moderate/strong) relationship. The sign of gamma indicates that this is a _positive_ (positive/negative) relationship. As INCOME increases, victimization _decreases_ (increases/decreases).

Note: Be careful when interpreting the direction of relationships. Gamma indicates the direction of the relationship between the scores of the variables. In this case, BURGLR is coded so that the score for "no" *is greater than* the score for "yes." The positive gamma means that as *score* on INCOME increased, so did *score* on BURGLR. People with more income were more likely to have a score of '2' on BURGLR or *less* likely to be victims. This relationship is actually negative.

Research Report 7.2

1.

	Victims of Burglary by INCOME and SEX			
	Lower Income	Middle Income	Higher Income	Gamma
All	10%	5%	2%	.48
Males	10%	6%	3%	.36
Females	9%	4%	0%	.63

2. For the full sample, victimization by burglary decreases as income increases. Describe the effect of controlling for SEX.

   a. *For males*: The rate of victimization __decreases__ (increases/decreases) as income increases. The gamma of __.36__ indicates a __strong__ (weak/moderate/strong) relationship.

Research Report 7.4

1.

	FEAR by INCOME by SEX			
	Lower Income	Middle Income	Higher Income	Gamma
All	54%	44%	45%	.14
Males	33%	31%	23%	.15
Females	67%	58%	67%	.06

Chapter 8

Research Report 8.1

1. b. Pearson's r for EDUC and RINCOME91 is __.38__. This indicates a __strong__ (weak/moderate/strong) relationship that is __positive__ (negative/positive) in direction. The relationship __is__ (is/is not) statistically significant.

Chapter 9

Research Report 9.1

1. On years of education (EDUC), men are generally __the same as__ (higher than/lower than/the same as) women. This chart indicates that the genders __are__ (are/are not) equal in level of education.

Research Report 9.2

	Mean on EDUC	2-Tail Sig		Mean on PRESTG80	2-Tail Sig
Men	13.11		Men	42.85	
Women	13.12	.948	Women	43.23	.61

1. Men's average occupational prestige was __lower than__ women's, and the difference __is not__ significant.

Research Report 9.4

1. For the first control variable (SEX):
FEWORK by INCOME by SEX

	Low	Moderate	High	Gamma
3. All	23%	14%	11%	−.30
4. Men	27%	14%	11%	−.35
5. Women	21%	14%	11%	−.27

Chapter 10

Research Report 10.1

1. On years of education (EDUC), blacks are generally _lower than_ (higher than/lower than/the same as) whites. This chart indicates that the races _are not_ (are/are not) equal in level of education.

Research Report 10.2

	Mean on PRESTG80	2-Tail Sig
Whites	43.69	
Blacks	39.18	.000

1. Whites are _higher than_ (higher than/lower than/the same as) blacks on occupational prestige, and the difference _is_ (is/is not) statistically significant.

RESEARCH REPORT 10.5

2. a.   RACDIF2 by INCOME by SEX

	Low	Moderate	High	Gamma
3: % Prejudiced				
All	18	13	7	.31
4: Men	26	14	9	.40
5: Women	14	13	6	.24

Chapter 11

Research Report 11.1

3. a. For "married" respondents, _49_ % are childless couples, whereas _50_ % are nuclear families.

   b. The household arrangement for the great majority of the "widowed" respondents is _single adult_.

Research Report 11.2

2. a. For AGE: Name of the category of your independent variable that had the highest column percentage for each category of FAMTYPE.

	Name of Category	Percentage
Childless couple	50 and older	47%
Single parent	18 to 33	11%
Single adult	50 and older	43%
Cohabitants	18 to 33	9%
Nuclear family	34 to 49	46%

b. The significance of chi square for this relationship was __.000__ , which is __less than__ (less than/more than) .05, so this __is__ (is/is not) a significant relationship. The value of Cramer's V was __.36__ , so this is a __strong__ (weak/moderate/strong) relationship.

Research Report 11.4

1.   HAPPY by FAMTYPE by INCOME

	Childless Couple	Single Parent	Single Adult	Cohabitants	Nuclear Family	Cramer's V
ALL	41%	9%	19%	16%	34%	.19
Low	35%	10%	17%	14%	30%	.17
Middle	42%	17%	22%	6%	25%	.17
High	42%	0%	19%	38%	42%	.12

Research Report 11.6

3. For SEXFREQ and INCOME91: Pearson's r = __.13__

This is a __moderate__ (weak/moderate/strong) relationship that is __positive__ (negative/positive) in direction. The relationship __is__ (is/is not) statistically significant.

Chapter 12

Research Report 12.1

3. a. For DEGREE:

VOTE92 by DEGREE

	Less Than High School	High School	College	Gamma
% Voted	55	68	84	−.42

The column percentages __do__ (do/do not) change, so there __is__ (is/is not) a relationship between these variables. The significance of chi square is __less than__ (less than/more than) .05, so this relationship __is__ (is/is not) statistically significant. The value of gamma is __−.42__ , so this is a __strong__ (weak/moderate/strong) relationship. The sign of gamma indicates that this is a __negative__ (positive/negative) relationship. As education increases, voter turnout __increases__ (increases/decreases).

Note: Be careful when interpreting the direction of relationships. Gamma indicates the direction of the relationship between the *scores* of the variables. In this case, VOTE92 is coded so that the score for "did not vote" is *greater than* the score for "voted." The negative gamma means that as the score on DEGREE increases (as education increases), the score on VOTE92 *de*creases—which means that turnout *increases*. This relationship between education and voter turnout is actually *positive*.

Research Report 12.2

1.   VOTE92 by DEGREE by RACE
                               (Percentage Who Voted)

	Less Than High School	High School	At Least Some College	Gamma
% Who Voted:				
All	55%	68%	84%	−.42
Whites	51%	69%	85%	−.46
Blacks	70%	66%	88%	−.22

Research Report 12.5

1. FOR SEX and PRES92: _52_ % of the women voted for Clinton compared to _45_ % of the men. The significance of chi square for the relationship between SEX and PRES92 was _.003_, which is _less than_ (less than/more than) .05, so this _is_ (is/is not) a significant relationship. The value of Cramer's *V* was _.11_, so this is a _moderate_ (weak/moderate/strong) relationship.

2.   PRES92 by SEX by INCOME
                        (Percentage Who Voted for Clinton)

	Males	Females	Cramer's *V*
% Voted for Clinton:			
All	45%	52%	.11
Low Income	52%	61%	.18
Middle income	39%	48%	.11
High income	40%	46%	.07

These results _do_ (do/do not) support the idea that the gender gap is due, in part, to the greater economic vulnerability of women.

Bibliography

Babbie, Earl, & Halley, Fred. (1995). *Adventures in Social Research*. Thousand Oaks, CA: Pine Forge Press.

Bobo, Lawrence, & Kluegal, James R. (1993). "Opposition to Race-Targeting; Self-interest, Stratification, Ideology, or Racial Attitudes?" *American Sociological Review*, 58, 443–464.

Bonacich, Edna. (1976). "Advanced Capitalism and Black/White Relations in the United States: A Split Labor Market Interpretation." *American Sociological Review*, 41, 34–51.

Glock, Charles Y., Ringer, Benjamin B., & Babbie, Earl R. (1967). *To Comfort and to Challenge*. Berkeley: University of California Press.

Healey, Joseph F. (1995). *Statistics: A Tool for Social Research*. Belmont, CA: Wadsworth.

Kohn, Melvin L. (1959). "Social Class and Parental Values." *American Journal of Sociology*, 64, 337–351.

Kohn, Melvin L., & Schooler, Carmi. (1969). "Class, Occupation, and Orientation." *American Sociological Review*, 34, 659–678.

Kohn, Melvin L., & Schooler, Carmi. (1983). *Work and Personality*. Norwood, NJ: Ablex.

Kohn, Melvin L., Slimczynski, Kazimierz, & Schooler, Carmi. (1986). "Social Stratification and the Transmission of Values in the Family: A Cross-national assessment." *Sociological Forum*, 1, 73–102.

Mueller, Carol. (1991). "The Gender Gap and Women's Political Influence." In Richard D. Lambert & Alan W. Heston (Eds.), *The Annals of the American Academy of Political and Social Science*, 515, 23–37.

Niemi, Richard G., & Weisberg, Herbert F. (1993). *Controversies in Voting Behavior*. Washington, DC: Congressional Quarterly Press.

Noel, Donald. (1968). "A Theory of the Origin of Ethnic Stratification." *Social Problems*, 16, 157–172.

Sears, David. (1988). "Symbolic Racism." In Phyllis Katz and Dalmas Taylor (Eds.), *Eliminating Racism: Profiles in Controversy*. (pp. 53–84). New York: Plenum.

Sherif, Muzafer, et. al. (1961). *Intergroup Conflict and Cooperation: The Robbers Cave Experiment*. Norman OK: The University Book Exchange.

U.S. Bureau of the Census. (1993). *Statistical Abstract of the United States: 1993* (113th ed.). Washington, DC: Government Printing Office.

Index/Glossary

population—The group, usually large, to which researchers make generalizations. The GSS sample was drawn from the population of all adult Americans.

Population, 2

Positive relationship, 133

prejudice—An attitude toward other groups that combines negative feelings or emotions and negative ideas or stereotypes.

Prejudice. *See also* Racial inequality
 comparative analysis, 277
 measuring, 251–254
 modern racism, 255–260
 multivariate analysis, 271
 selecting respondents, 249, 250
 and sexism, 265–267
 and social class, 263, 264

Premarital sex
 analyzing attitudes about, 296–298
 approval of, 307, 308
 comparative analysis, 313, 314
 multivariate analysis, 309
 overview, 295

Presidential choice
 analysis of, 327, 328
 comparative analysis, 349, 350
 multivariate analysis, 329–331
 other factors, 341
 overview, 325

Presidential elections
 and gender, 333–336
 and ideology, 343, 344
 and presidential choice. *See* Presidential choice
 and religion, 345, 346
 and voter turnout. *See* Voter turnout

probabilistic causal relationships—A type of causal relationship in which the independent variable's impact on the dependent variable is somewhat uncertain. In these causal relationships, the independent variable "tends to" affect the dependent variable.

Probabilistic causal relationships, 26

R

Race
 and criminal victimization, 145, 148
 and inequality. *See* Racial inequality

 and presidential choice, 331
 and religiosity, 79, 80

Racial inequality. *See also* Prejudice
 comparative analysis, 273–275
 multiple line chart, 239–243
 statistical significance (*t* tests), 245–247

Random sampling, 2

range—The distance from the highest score on a variable to the lowest.

Range, 53

regression line—On a scatterplot, the single straight line that touches all of the data points or comes as close to doing so as possible.

Regression line, 181, 182

Relationships, direction of, 133

Religiosity
 and afterlife, 82–85
 bar charts, 45–48
 causes of, 91
 comparative analysis, 93, 94
 deprivation theory of, 77–80, 85–90
 and divorce, 25–34
 measuring, 71–74
 and presidential voting, 345
 and sex, 75, 76

representative—A quality of a random sample. A representative sample reproduces the characteristics of the population.

Representative, 2

Research, 25

row—The horizontal dimension of a bivariate table. Each row represents a separate value of the dependent variable.

Rows, 75

S

sample—A subset of a population.

Sample, 2

sampling error—The difference that can be expected between sample characteristics and population traits by random chance alone.

Sampling error, 2

scatterplot—A graph that displays the joint scores of the cases on two numerical variables.

Scatterplots, 179–183

Science, 25

Of special interest from

AMERICAN BEHAVIORAL SCIENTIST

. . . focuses, in theme-organized issues prepared under guest editors, on emerging cross-disciplinary interests, research, and problems in the social sciences.
8x / yr: Jan, Feb, March, May, June, Aug, Sept, Nov.
Yearly rates: Individual $74 / Institution $280
1152 pages / ISSN: 0002-7642

BUSINESS & SOCIETY

Sponsored by the International Association for Business and Society
Founded by Roosevelt University
Editor: Donna J. Wood, *University of Pittsburgh*

. . . the first peer-reviewed scholarly publication devoted exclusively to the field of business and society. Publishes original research, book reviews and dissertation abstracts relating to business ethics, business-government relations, corporate governance, corporate social performance, and environmental management issues.
Quarterly: March, June, Sept, Dec
Yearly rates: Individual $52 / Institution $145
480 pages / ISSN: 0007-6503

GENDER & SOCIETY

Official Publication of Sociologists for Women in Society
Editor: Beth E. Schneider,
University of California, Santa Barbara

. . . focuses on the social and structural study of gender as a basic principle of the social order and as a primary social category. Emphasizing theory and research, this publication aims to advance both the study of gender and feminist scholarship.
Bimonthly: Feb, April, June, Aug, Oct, Dec
Yearly rates: Individual $56 / Institution $195
816 pages / ISSN: 0891-2432

JOURNAL OF SPORT & SOCIAL ISSUES

The Official Journal of Northeastern University's Center for the Study of Sport in Society
Editor: Lawrence Wenner,
Sport and Fitness Management Program, University of San Francisco

. . . publishes the latest research, discussion, and analysis on contemporary sports issues such as race, media, gender, economics, drugs, recruiting, injuries, and youth sports.
Quarterly: Feb, May, Aug, Nov
Yearly rates: Individual $52 / Institution $128
448 pages / ISSN: 0193-7325

POLITICS & SOCIETY

Edited by: The Politics & Society Editorial Board

. . . an alternative, critical voice of the social sciences that raises questions about the way the world is organized politically, economically, and socially. Presents engaged as well as rational discourse and reconstructs social inquiry through scholarship addressed to fundamental questions of theory, policy, and politics.
Quarterly: March, June, Sept, Dec
Yearly rates: Individual $57 / Institution $178
576 pages / ISSN: 0032-3292

ORDER TODAY!
Sage Customer Service: 805-499-9774 ■ Sage FaxLine: 805-499-0871

SAGE PUBLICATIONS, INC. | SAGE PUBLICATIONS LTD | SAGE PUBLICATIONS INDIA PVT. LTD
2455 Teller Road | 6 Bonhill Street | M-32 Market, Greater Kailash I
Thousand Oaks, CA 91320 | London EC2A 4PU, England | New Delhi 110 048, India

 **SAGE Periodicals Press**